Mr. Justice
Brandeis

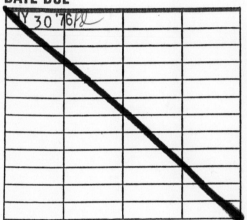

MR. JUSTICE BRANDEIS

Da Capo Press Reprints in

AMERICAN CONSTITUTIONAL AND LEGAL HISTORY

GENERAL EDITOR: LEONARD W. LEVY

Claremont Graduate School

MR. JUSTICE BRANDEIS

EDITED BY

FELIX FRANKFURTER

INTRODUCTION BY

OLIVER WENDELL HOLMES

DA CAPO PRESS • NEW YORK • 1972

Library of Congress Cataloging in Publication Data
Main entry under title:

Mr. Justice Brandeis.
    (Da Capo Press reprints in American constitutional and legal history)
    "Published on the fund established in memory of Ganson Goodyear Depew."
    CONTENTS: Introduction, by O. W. Holmes.—Mr. Justice Brandeis, by C. E.
Hughes.—The social thought of Mr. Justice Brandeis, by M. Lerner. [etc.]
    1. Brandeis, Louis Dembitz, 1856-1941. 2. Law—U.S.—Addresses, essays, lec-
tures. I. Frankfurter, Felix, 1882-1965, ed. II. Yale University. Ganson Goodyear
Depew Memorial Fund.
KF210.M55   1972   347'.73'2634 [B]   73-37766
ISBN 0-306-70430-7

This Da Capo Press edition of *Mr. Justice Brandeis* is an unabridged republication of the first edition published in New Haven, Connecticut, in 1932. It is re-
printed by special arrangement with Yale University Press and reproduced from
a copy of the original edition in the collection of the Library of the
University of Virginia

Published by Da Capo Press, Inc.
A Subsidiary of Plenum Publishing Corporation
227 West 17th Street, New York, N.Y. 10011

Mr. Justice Brandeis

Photo by *Clinedinst*

MR. JUSTICE BRANDEIS

Mr. Justice Brandeis

ESSAYS BY

CHARLES E. HUGHES
MAX LERNER
FELIX FRANKFURTER
DONALD R. RICHBERG
HENRY WOLF BIKLÉ
WALTON H. HAMILTON

EDITED BY FELIX FRANKFURTER

WITH AN

INTRODUCTION BY OLIVER WENDELL HOLMES

NEW HAVEN
YALE UNIVERSITY PRESS
LONDON : HUMPHREY MILFORD : OXFORD UNIVERSITY PRESS
1932

ACKNOWLEDGMENT

Acknowledgment is made to the following magazines for
permission to reprint these articles: the *Columbia Law Review,* the *Harvard Law Review,* the *Yale Law Journal.*

PREFACE

DESPITE its remoteness from the immediacies of the political hurly-burly and the esoteric atmosphere in which it moves, the Supreme Court, as the ultimate adjuster of contending forces, has, almost from the beginning, occupied the central place in our federal system. And certainly at any time after Marshall came to the Court, it could have been said, as the present Chief Justice said before he was Chief Justice, "we are under a Constitution, but the Constitution is what the judges say it is." Throughout the history of the Court, the public mind has grasped this truth in direct proportion to the intensity of feeling aroused by a particular political issue settled by the Supreme Court through the outward form of a lawsuit. But never so much as in our day, if one may judge by public debate and lay comment, has there been such widespread and keen awareness of the essentially political functions exercised by the Supreme Bench.

It would indeed be strange were it not so. Governments everywhere, including our own, more and more interpenetrate life. In America, the Supreme Court is the brake upon government. To the nation and the forty-eight states it may say, "Thou shalt not." Too frequently in recent years it has inclined toward kinship with Mephistopheles in being the spirit that denieth. Modern constitutional questions are not political abstractions, remote from the interests of Lincoln's common people. They are the concern of home and fireside. So, therefore, is the personnel of the highest court. Partly, doubtless, the quality which a Mr. Justice Holmes gives to our civilization has become a great tradition by which his successors may be tested. But this edifying response of the multitude to the Olympian distinction of Mr. Justice Holmes, derives from a groping realization that the judges *are* the Constitution under which we live and move and have our being.

The formal remoteness of their labors has largely conspired to consign the Justices to the limbo of impersonality. From this fate only Marshall has been adequately rescued, thanks to the toil and ardor of Senator Beveridge. The Court's prestige and American history both would be gainers by similar studies of other great judges.

The present volume has a much more modest intention. It is a collection of sketches, not a life-size portrait. The nation-wide attention to the seventy-fifth birthday of Mr. Justice Brandeis attests the popular stake in the Court. The event aroused not merely the conventional sentiments of good feeling toward a tried public servant, but voluminous discussion of the Court's work. The following essays, selected from the November contributions, attempt estimates of the labors of Mr. Justice Brandeis as they appear to diverse students of the Supreme Court—to the Chief Justice, to practitioners, to specialists in constitutional law, to critics of social institutions. Perhaps an undue austerity in these professional side-lights upon so human a personality as Louis D. Brandeis is tempered by a few intimate introductory words by an old friend and revered colleague, Mr. Justice Holmes.

F. F.

Harvard Law School
  April 2, 1932.

Contents

Introduction

JUSTICE BRANDEIS came to Boston in 1879 to become the partner of Samuel D. Warren who had been in my office and who was my dear and admired friend until his death. In that way an acquaintance began that soon was familiar and that became intimate as the years went on. Of course there were periods when, owing to the place and nature of our occupations, we met but rarely. But our meetings were renewed when possible, and since he came upon the bench of the Supreme Court they have been constant. That fact speaks louder than any words that I could write for my opinion, the result of more than half a century. Whenever he left my house I was likely to say to my wife, "There goes a really good man." I think that the world now would agree with me in adding what the years have proved "and a great judge."

Let me not omit the acknowledgment due to friendship. In the moments of discouragement that we all pass through, he always has had the happy word that lifts up one's heart. It came from knowledge, experience, courage, and the high way in which he always has taken life.

OLIVER WENDELL HOLMES

Washington, D. C.
March 30, 1932.

I

MR. JUSTICE BRANDEIS

BY

CHARLES E. HUGHES

Mr. Justice Brandeis

WHEN I first met Louis D. Brandeis—about forty years ago—he had already won distinction at the Bar and had shown the wide range of his interests by his lectures at Massachusetts Institute of Technology on the legal aspects of the problems of labor. Throughout his career he has exhibited a prodigious and uninterrupted intellectual activity which has taken him into many fields, and despite the most exacting and continuous demands, fully satisfied in every branch of his endeavor, Mr. Justice Brandeis enters upon his seventy-sixth year at the peak of mental power. As he is a vital part of the process of exposition in which the Supreme Court is engaged, it is not fitting that I should attempt a critical survey of his judicial opinions during the fifteen years that he has been upon the bench, but it is appropriate that I should join, as I do most heartily, in the testimonials which greet him on his happy anniversary.

It is expected that those selected for the highest judicial offices in State and Nation should have keen minds and analytical skill tested by long experience, and there will be no dissent from the opinion that Mr. Justice Brandeis possesses that acuteness in a very high degree. No keener blade has ever been used, but it is the knife and skill of the surgeon exploring the operations of the social organism with the purpose of cure. The combination of this analytical power, with a talent for comprehensiveness and a method of expression, which comes as near to being original as is possible under the limitations of traditional procedure, has given a rare and, I might say, a unique distinction to his judicial work. Mr. Justice Brandeis is—if I may use another figure—the master of both microscope and telescope. Nothing of importance, however minute, escapes his microscopical examination of every problem, and, through his powerful telescopic lens, his mental vision embraces distant scenes, ranging far beyond the familiar worlds of conventional thinking. The results of this comprehensive observation he brings forward in encyclopaedic reports that are not only monuments of industry but are charts intended to aid every inquirer. If a most distinguished contemporary writes for experts, it may be said that Mr. Justice Brandeis writes for students, both for those who are beginning and for those who are mature. He seeks to make his account of his researches a guide to every traveler over the same road. It is evident that, in his philosophy, the facts of life assume a greater importance than formulas and that it is his belief that the more comprehensive and accurate is our knowledge of conditions, the narrower is the field of controversy and the sharper the issue in whatever contest may remain. With his talents so persistently employed, Mr. Justice Brandeis is fortunate in the possession of an equable temperament which gives him poise and serenity in every investigation and discussion, and makes him a delightful associate.

The Supreme Court of the United States, as a national institution performing the essential service of giving an authoritative interpretation of the fundamental law, should draw its resources from the whole Nation. Demanding the proper equipment of legal training and practical experience, it is of the greatest importance that the Court should have the contributions that come from different points of view in the application of the postulates of our constitutional system. In the deliberations of the Court nothing should be left unexplored and every decision should be reached with full appraisement of all admissible contentions. Agreement thus reached is a most gratifying result. Still, it must be borne in mind that differences of opinion in the Court but reflect fundamental differences in expert opinion in the Nation, and it is through the earnest, friendly and candid conferences of sincere minds, imbued with a sense of grave responsibility for well-reasoned conclusions, and through the deliberate expression of views entertained after full consideration, that the special jurisprudence of the Supreme Court is appropriately developed.

In this enterprise of judicial coöperation, it is a high privilege to be associated with Mr. Justice Brandeis, and I join in the felicitations upon his achievements, and in the hope that he may long continue his eminent service with unabated zest and vigor.

II

The Social Thought of
Mr. Justice Brandeis

BY

Max Lerner

THE SOCIAL THOUGHT OF
MR. JUSTICE BRANDEIS

I

IN the judicial opinions of Mr. Justice Brandeis the realities of social change confront the equally powerful realities of vested interests and vested ideas. The result
is as significant a mirroring as judicial literature offers of the
essence of the American national experience. With no other
jurist are the issues that have emerged from our economic
development so clearly drawn or so sharply presented. No
other gives so immediate a sense of the heroic and, as it sometimes seems, hopeless task that the Supreme Court has wit-
tingly or otherwise assumed—the task of directing the chance
and change of the economic process. Mr. Justice Brandeis has
found himself in the thick of every battle involving important issues of statecraft. His name has therefore taken on in
the public mind implications in the realm of social policy as
well as in that of judicial opinion. The liberals have ranged
him on the side of the angels, the conservatives somewhat
lower. For a surer estimate one would wish to go beyond his
reputation to the solid fact of his written opinions, beyond
that to the body of his social thought, and finally to that in-
tegrated personal philosophy and viewpoint which never fails
to be impressive even when one disagrees with it.

But the difficulty of isolating and formulating the hard
core of Mr. Justice Brandeis' social thought can scarcely be
overestimated. He has nowhere mapped out his legal philosophy in the form of prolegomena to all future systems of
judicial decision. Nor has he, like Mr. Justice Holmes, the
gift of compressing a lifetime of thought into a single gleam-
ing sentence that lights up and integrates everything else he
has said. Mr. Justice Brandeis, it must be remembered, is
specialized to advocacy and judicial decision and not to phi-

losophizing. He is himself one of the most a-philosophical of jurists—a thinker whose thought is always directed to eventual action, a judge in the great tradition of the Anglo-American case law who proceeds from the facts of the concrete case to a particular decision, a social theorist whose "principles" are nine-tenths submerged in the form of preconceptions and crop out on the surface only as approaches to pressing issues in contemporary affairs. He has said of his own mental processes that it is only after he has found himself confronted by a specific set of facts and has thought his way through them to a conclusion, that he has found it to coincide with some well-recognized philosophical "principle."[1] As for the received classification into schools of jurisprudence, it accommodates Mr. Justice Brandeis about as badly as it does Mr. Justice Holmes, or any other non-academic and non-imitative mind. Approaching the problem of law and society from an intensely activist standpoint, Mr. Justice Brandeis has not been interested by the *Methodenstreit* of the schools. He has preferred to fight his battles on the fronts of social legislation and judicial decision rather than in the realm of method.

While this may be worth saying, it is at best only a set of half-truths. That men vary not so much in whether or not they are philosophers but in the extent to which their philosophy is articulate is a psychological commonplace. It is, in fact, one of the attractive paradoxes that emerge from a study of Mr. Justice Brandeis that with all his distaste for philosophy he is known as the judge with the most definite and coherent social philosophy, and that with all his apathy about method his greatest importance for the future may lie in the novel elements he has added to the traditional method of adjudicating legal controversy. The quest of the inarticulate major premise that Mr. Justice Holmes has inaugurated leads in the study of Mr. Justice Brandeis to consequences of some moment for legal and social theory. There is of course the ever present danger that the student will read his own preconceptions into Mr. Justice Brandeis' opinions.[2] And there is also the danger of his forgetting that the social thought of a judge cannot be estimated by the criteria that would be applied to a social theorist writing out of the plenitude of his experience and his imagination. We can scarcely expect—even if we might wish—a Supreme Court opinion to read like the *Communist Manifesto* or Sorel's *Réflexions sur la Violence*.[3] The judge cannot express an untrammeled economic or social philosophy. The facts and the issues of the specific case, the constitutional text he is seeking to apply and the precedent he must to some degree follow all link him by a sure falconry to the solid ground from which he might seek to soar too far.[4]

II

THE earliest influence in fashioning the mind of Mr. Justice Brandeis—and perhaps therefore the deepest and least eradicable—was a strain of romantic liberalism whose essence was a gallant and optimistic struggle for certain supposedly primal human rights.[5] It was a liberalism compulsive enough in its emotional force to lead his parents to emigrate to America from Bohemia after the unsuccessful revolutions of 1848.[6] These revolutions, aptly characterized by Trevelyan as "the turning-point at which modern history failed to turn," were in spirit constitutional, humanitarian, idealistic. They represented a renewal on continental soil of the equalitarian ideals of the American and French revolutions. Carried back to the United States by the emigrant groups of the mid-century they imparted a new freshness and vigor to the American tradition of civil and political liberties. Freedom and justice and democracy, which as home-grown varieties had wilted a bit in the hot climate of American experience, became when transplanted hither from Europe vigorous and even beautiful growths. They were terms that still had a genuine and simple content for these naïve newcomers. Mr. Justice Brandeis grew up thus in an atmosphere of what might be called primitive Americanism.

This Americanism took the characteristic form, in the semi-frontier Kentucky society in which the Brandeises lived, of a deeply felt individualism. The complexion of such an individualism was as varied as were the sources of the sense of release from which it sprung. To be allowed finally to do what one in Europe had always dreamed of doing and what one had regarded as the marks of a freeman, to talk or criticize or worship as one pleased, to see an immediacy of relation between economic effort and economic reward, reënforced one's sense of the dignity and sovereign importance of the individual. There were also the slaves as intense and vivid symbols to sum up for a border-state abolitionist group what it meant to lack the liberties of an individual. Mr. Justice Brandeis recalls how violent his reaction was when, during a brief sojourn in Germany as a young man, he was reprimanded by the authorities for whistling at night. The reprimand was more than a personal reproof; it was an insult to a complete and cherished way of life.

One does not become easily disengaged from a way of life thus deeply learned. The whole early career of Mr. Justice Brandeis, with its hard work and study and success, runs in the best tradition of American individualism. In fact, all the events of his first forty years had conspired to make him an idealistic yet successful liberal and civic leader, whose conspicuous ability condoned his excess of zeal, and whose mastery of the hard facts of business showed that his somewhat tiresome sermonizing was not to be taken overseriously. It is true, he showed at times a disquieting curiosity about matters into which a Boston gentleman rarely pried; as when in the eighties he began to talk with labor leaders, and to regard the labor struggle from the worker's point of view. And he showed also a somewhat unusual tendency to interpret the lawyer's function as more than mere advocacy and to set himself up now as judge and now as arbitrator. But all his offenses stayed within the limits of tolerance.

The genuinely formative years of Mr. Justice Brandeis' mind fell in the "social justice" period of American history, in the latter part of the nineties and the first decade of the twentieth century. They were years which witnessed on the one hand the rise of powerful vested interests and the expropriation of American resources by capital acting under a *laissez faire* philosophy of government, and on the other hand such movements as populism, muckraking, trust-busting and the "new freedom." The vigor of individual enterprise which had opened a continent had grown barbaric and piratical in the exploiting of it; and the pure metaphysical passion which had driven successive waves of migration to America[7] was now transferred and transformed into an intense desire for purifying the body politic. To minds educated in the dialectic of liberalism it seemed obvious that the situation could be best explained in terms of a dualism of conflicting forces. It seemed clear that the captains of industry and the masters of capital, in the exultation of success, would sweep away every landmark on the terrain of American liberty. And it seemed clear also that the only recourse for liberals lay in a militant attack on all fronts—an attack on bankers, on corporations and on politicians corruptly allied with them, a pitiless campaign of investigation and publicity.

It was amidst this planetary crash and turmoil that Mr. Justice Brandeis' world took definite shape. It was in a sense inevitable that he should have been caught up in the swirl of these forces. For it is of the essence of his mind to be receptive to the aspirations and conflicts of the world he lives in, and to desire participation in them. Possessing little of Mr. Justice Holmes's transcendence of any specific period, it is rather his genius to be immersed in his time. After the critical struggle to establish a legal practice was won, his mind, whose Hebraic sense of righteousness had been reënforced by his background of Continental liberalism, turned more and more to issues of social justice. He found in the dominant temper of this populist-muckraking period that essential continuity with his own past without which no individual enters upon a revolution in his thinking. He found room in his new philosophy for the ideals he had learned as a boy; room also for the individualism that had dominated his youth. What this period added, in his case as in the case of other liberals, was a new perception of the changes that the coming of industrial society had wrought in the conditions of American liberty and American individualism. It was clear that the old ideals could no longer be pursued in the old way. That the ideals themselves were worth while and needed no replacement formed part of those first principles which the liberals of that day did not question.

In Louis D. Brandeis, the able Boston lawyer, the forces of liberalism gained no mean ally. I say ally, because a common unquestioning soldier he could never be: stern individualist, who cared more about the integrity of his personality than about anything else, he had to fight in his own fashion. He threw into the struggle all the resources of his mind—his amazing legal acumen, his persuasiveness, his mastery of the details and refinements of corporation finance, his unwavering sense of values, his eminently precise and constructive imagination. Equipped with every weapon of information one had reckoned one's own, he was a terrifying opponent to encounter. But if he spared no one else, he was most ruthless with himself. He worked indefatigably. He sacrificed his obvious interests. He dedicated himself with a monastic fervor to what he conceived to be the service of the public. He came to be called "the People's Counsel," and if there was a touch of asperity in the way the name was applied to him by opponents, he himself took it with a high seriousness. His ideal of citizenship was Periclean, but he pursued it with a religious intensity that was medieval.

He was effective. Of that there can be no doubt. The minutes of legislative hearings and investigations, the records of lawsuits in which groups of citizens, organized as a "league" of some sort or other, applied for court action against an encroaching corporation, the newspapers that reported his speeches and activities and the journalists who commented on them, all attest to his effectiveness. There was room in that struggle for every sort of talent—for a Bryan, a La Follette, a Roosevelt, a Steffens, a Hapgood, a Wilson. But when most of the brilliant legal ability of the country was being enrolled in the service of the corporations, the talents of a first-rate legal and statistical mind were worth more than the talents of all the politicians and journalists. Mr. Brandeis found himself at home with the sort of problems that had now to be mastered. His career, winding its way from one set of financial and political intricacies to another, takes on something of the fiber of the period.

In two important respects he stands out from the group of turn-of-the-century liberals with whom his name is associated. He had a passion for detail and concreteness where most of them dealt in invective and generalities. And he had a capacity for constructive achievement in the field of social legislation and social invention. An exposure of insurance companies was accompanied by a plan for reorganizing the industry and by a new form of savings-bank insurance; an attack on the railroads gave him a chance to launch on its career the principle of scientific management; a call to arbitrate a labor dispute resulted in the "protocol" and the "preferential open shop." And he knew not only how to create and state these ideas and plans; he knew also the technique of publicity and persuasion without which in the apathy of modern life they would have been ignored. But perhaps most important of all was the will to "follow through" an idea until it was functioning, and the infinite capacity for pains which saw to the details of organization. In the stress he laid upon social invention he was closely related to the Jeremy Bentham whom Mr. Wallas interprets;[8] more closely even than was the administrative constructiveness which the Webbs were seeking to effect in London.

Yet even twenty years of unremitting effort in this direction would probably not have sufficed to rescue his name from the comparative oblivion of those who fight heroically in a hopeless cause. To say this is not to do injustice to either the seriousness or the effectiveness of Mr. Brandeis' public career before 1916. Whatever else happened, his position in the amazing history of those two decades of American life would have been distinctive and secure. Nor is this the place to enter upon an extended critique of the causes with which he was allied. From the vantage-ground of the present it seems clear that the cards were stacked against them. The forces they were fighting were too integrally part of a capitalist-industrialist society—part of the logic of its development and part of its psychological context—to be severed from it for separate destruction. None of them was either willing or ready to attack the foundations of the society itself. And to save the body while striking at the excrescences required a more subtle diagnosis of historic and economic forces and a more mature grappling with the complexities of the problem than the resources of those decades could command. If Mr. Brandeis stands out as a unique and heroic figure in the populist thought of that period, it is not for the raking fire of his cross-examinations, nor for the brave assurance of his analysis of the Money Trust;[9] not even for that stubborn command of facts and figures which made men call him the mathematician of the movement.[10] It is rather because of the stress we find him laying, even in those days, upon the necessity for the continuous application of social intelligence to social problems, and upon the inadequacy of any solution which did not have behind it the creative will of the people.

But it was Mr. Brandeis' misfortune to try to fashion a social philosophy in the midst of a crusade. The pennons wavered for a moment, fluttered anxiously, but were immediately carried forward. He was himself caught up in their contagion, and since crusades never reach their goal, he might have remained merely one of the adherents of a "fighting faith" which had had its day and given way to another. But the fervor of the crusade had reached to the White House and when, on the death of Mr. Justice Lamar in 1916, President Wilson looked about for a successor his choice fell upon the Boston lawyer who had displayed such ability and courage and who, without holding public office, had already had a crowded public life. Whatever the merit of the appointment, for us it changes the whole perspective of Mr. Justice Brandeis' work. It transformed him from a free lance into one of the ruling powers. It gave direction to his energies and meaning to the wide scattering of activities that had constituted his career. There is no need to underestimate the dramatic quality and the importance of that early career in order to see that as a result of the appointment its chief interest now lies less in its intrinsic qualities than in its having been an apprenticeship for an opportunity. We can see with some degree of clarity, with the detachment that the intervening years give, what that opportunity was and how effective was the apprenticeship. The entire focus of those two crowded decades changes, and they become preëminently a record of the education of Mr. Justice Brandeis.

Like any worth-while education it consisted both of learning and unlearning. It was comparatively easy for an energetic and responsive person amidst the social intensities of the period to unlearn the genteel tradition of restraint which tended to envelop one at Harvard[11] and the tradition of quietism in which the legal mind everywhere was wrapped.

But it was harder to unlearn what had lingered over from one's liberal-romantic background—the faith that in a democratic society there was equality of liberty and opportunity, or some immediate relation between the functioning of government and the needs of the people. From one point of view, Mr. Justice Brandeis' contacts with labor unions, corporations and bankers, with the sweated workers and the vested interests, constituted an exploration of modern industrial society unique in the education of Justices of the Supreme Court. He gained an understanding of the cleavage that lay between the "haves" and the "have-nots,"[12] and some notions of the implications of that cleavage for both. He grasped with some degree of realism the meager content of life for the vast armies of labor. He sought the answer to the riddle of how a society that gave its masses no leisure from the grinding hours of labor and no protection from exploitation in the barbaric competition for profits, that took no measures to control how much they would be paid for their work or how much they would be charged for what they bought, and that made no provisions for them when they grew too old or sick to be profitable—how such a society could expect them to form the vital and intelligent units predicated in a theory of democracy. He saw the growing institutionalization of life as it was embodied in the corporation, the trade-union and the centralization of government, and the danger that amidst it the individual might be lost. But, amazingly, his education taught him also that there was invested in the American economic system more hard work and experience than any novel scheme of control could command, and that it was dangerous to drive beyond the bounds within which initiative and skill could be continuously exerted.

So balanced and mature an education could not have been acquired in a vacuum. Whatever Mr. Justice Brandeis learned or unlearned proceeded from that direct pragmatic context of exigency and action that seems always to have been

so congenial to his mind. The fight he waged from 1896 to
1911 to keep the control of the Boston transportation system
in the hands of the city, gave him a notion of the political
intrigue through which franchises are obtained. He delved
deeper into public utility economics in the struggle that he
waged from 1903–5 for cheaper gas rates in Boston. His
fight against the New England transportation monopoly of
the New Haven railroad (1906–12) confronted him with
the problem of the relation between inflated capitalization
and railway rates, and between monopoly and service to the
community; and his appearance before the Interstate Commerce Commission in the series of railroad rate cases (1910–
13) made him think through the connection between the
management of a railroad and its expenses of operation. His
conception of the place of trade-unions in American life came
from direct experience in labor disputes. He waged a bitter
fight in 1904 against the Boston Typographical Union, in
which he discovered that unions no less than employers
might be unscrupulous and irresponsible. But, although this
caused him to think a good deal about the principles of trade-
union organization, it did not make him an antiunionist. He
had found out at least as early as 1902 what despairs lay behind the heroism of protracted strikes;[13] and he not only favored the legislative objectives of the union in obtaining
better wages and more humane working days, but he regarded them as an insurance against the irresponsibility of
employers. The year 1907 even found him at the strangely
unjuristic task of tracing the possible consequences that a
more-than-ten-hour day for women workers in an Oregon
laundry might have on their physical condition, their moral
life, or the character of the future citizenry to which they
gave birth.[14] Perhaps the most impressive item that his labor
contacts added to his education came from his experience in
arbitrating the strike of the International Ladies' Garment
Workers in 1910.[15] Here he was brought face to face with a

strange group—intelligent, idealistic, bickering, embittered, exploited in the "sweating" system, yet charged with tremendous vitality, through whom a rich and alien culture imbued with European radical ideas was being transplanted to America. His studies in connection with the Ballinger investigation of 1909, in which he had played so prominent and dramatic a rôle, presumably as counsel for Glavis but in reality as inquisitor for the public, had given him some notion of how the natural resources of the country were disposed. But here, among the Jewish garment workers in New York, he found human resources that called equally for conservation. He was successful enough, tentatively, in evolving a technique for settling their disputes with their employers, just as he had been successful in 1905–8 in evolving a technique whereby, through savings-bank insurance, the workers of Massachusetts could get protection at rates that were not excessive.[16] But the thing that troubled him was that ultimately these individuals—and all individuals—were at the mercy of those in whom economic power resided, and that this economic power went with the control of the fluid capital of the country. His experience in the life-insurance fight had shown him the degree to which the capital of the industry was concentrated in the "Big Three" companies; and in his series of *Harper's Weekly* articles in 1913–14 on the Money Trust he carried the analysis further, making it embrace the entire financial structure of the country.[17]

There was much, it is to be conjectured, that Mr. Justice Brandeis did not learn during those years of his crowded career. But considering the blind chance that fits or misfits our haphazard educations to the crucial tasks that somehow fall to us, the education of Mr. Justice Brandeis appears now as having been amazingly apposite. The social context within which, as a Justice of the Supreme Court, his thinking would have to proceed was more complex than that in which either the Constitution or the body of judicial precedent had been formed. A system of industrial organization so much more developed than that of the nineteenth century as to take on the aspects of a second industrial revolution, had created also a "great society" that was unique in its problems and temper. There were deep cleavages in social stratification and obvious injustices in distribution. Above all else, American capitalism was going through a remarkable phase of concentration. Power and control were being shifted and pyramided. The old dichotomies between political power and economic activity were rapidly becoming a matter of rhetoric rather than actuality. Here was a man who, beyond most others that might have been chosen, was qualified by his experience to understand the processes of change and the instruments of control. ·

Enough opposition was raised to Mr. Justice Brandeis' appointment to make it something of a *cause célèbre*. Among those who joined in the protest were leaders in American financial, legal and political life whose names carried great weight. The grounds advanced included infringements of legal ethics, unjudicial temperament and even chicanery and dishonesty. There was an investigation by the Senate Judiciary Committee, in which some fifteen hundred pages of testimony were taken, there were accusations and defenses and recriminations, and there was finally an acquittal in the form of a ratification of the appointment.[18] At the time and since then the protest against Mr. Justice Brandeis has been sufficiently protested against. What was its significance? Can it be dismissed as the malevolent gesture of men whose hostility Mr. Brandeis had incurred? It is clear that such a judgment would be superficial. There was much more in the struggle about the appointment than a matter of personal justice. There was a historical rationale in the utterances of the seven former Presidents of the American Bar Association, the petition of the Boston men of affairs, and the editorials in the financial papers. The protest against the appointment of

Mr. Justice Brandeis was a crucial recognition by the old order that the new order was threatening. There was a stiffening of the ranks, a closing of the gaps in the phalanx, a call for a united front. For half a century the possessing class in America had known the conditions under which they could operate and expand. The rules of the game, however advantageous they may have been, had been fixed. Surely, they could not now be revoked. A man who had formed and had expressed opinions on most of the great issues of national policy that were likely to come before the court was dangerous, especially when those opinions were original, unconventional and held with moral fervor.

The appointment was thus more than the filling of a vacancy. It represented a possible turning point in the American judicial process. For whatever Mr. Justice Brandeis might or might not be expected to do, he could not be expected to cleave to the tradition that the whole duty of a Supreme Court Justice was to maintain a decent ignorance of the world outside the Court.

III

In the fifteen years that have elapsed since the appointment of Mr. Justice Brandeis, he has become firmly intrenched in the public minds as a "liberal" jurist and one whose method of decision is "sociological." There is an essential soundness in this judgment, although both terms are shopworn to the point of vagueness and are more useful in embracing once significant similarities between jurists than in suggesting currently significant differences. Mr. Justice Brandeis has in common with other liberal jurists the fact that he has reacted against the rigor of a narrow mechanical jurisprudence which, containing within itself no principle of growth, applied old rules to new situations and ignored changing economic setups. But his unique importance is not summed up in this critical attitude but must be sought also in the positive logic of relationships between law and society that is implicit in his day-to-day opinions and dissents. In his case, as with other activists, it is the idea in action that pushes forward ideological advance.

On the Supreme Court bench it is Mr. Justice Brandeis who has made the sharpest break with the classical tradition. Whether it passed through a tory or a liberal mind, the classical tradition was concerned with the interpretation of the Constitution as an instrument of government. In the hands of Marshall and Story, Taney and Field,[19] it produced widely variant results, but it seems fair to say that the differences they revolved about were differences in political theory—the "narrow" or the "strict" construction of the Constitution, centralization or states' rights, the clash of sections. Fortifying each of these positions there was, to be sure, a social philosophy and the pressure of new or old economic forces.[20] But these remained in the rear. On the fighting line were the competing political and constitutional theories. It is Mr. Justice Brandeis' achievement to have appreciably altered the basis and the terms of the conflict. He has been the first to face squarely and consistently the problem of the relation between social change and judicial action. ·

He is thus preëminently the jurist of a transitional society, in which change is the dominant, the obtrusive fact. His thought is geared to social change. Not that Marshall and Taney lived in a static world. But the realities they and their colleagues wrestled with were the realities of constructing, consolidating and reconstructing the foundations of the American polity. Where the principles of constitutional interpretation had themselves to be outlined, they occupied the foreground despite the social changes that accompanied the beginnings of industrialism in America. But the maturity of industrialism brought an unparalleled pace of change, opened new gaps between need and aspiration, revealed in startling outlines the logic of social institutions implicit in our system of economic organization. As the task of adjusting legal thought and institutions to economic development grew more difficult, it grew also more imperative.

It is this absorption with social change that chiefly differentiates the thought of Mr. Justice Brandeis from that of Mr. Justice Holmes. While the former has his eye fixed on the mutations in the life of society, the latter delights to observe the essential identities behind them. The curious uniformity with which the human animal behaves, whatever the century, runs like the hint of a theme through the entire body of Mr. Justice Holmes's opinions. But Mr. Justice Brandeis is concerned with the more immediate consequences of changes in social institutions and the traumata they reveal in our life.[21]

To adjust the body of legal rules to a world of bewildering change requires, to start with, the fixed sense of social value and social need that accompanies a strongly functionalist way of thought. Institutions often develop their own principle of growth, not necessarily related to the need that brought them into existence, and the original need has commonly to be rediscovered and redefined. Mr. Justice Brandeis, with his Thoreau-like fervor for whittling life down to its essentials, is peculiarly qualified for such a task. Amidst the variety of conflicting practices regarding depreciation, he seeks the underlying function that a depreciation account serves;[22] in a case involving the abolition of private employment agencies he seeks to get at the functional purpose of all labor exchanges;[23] in an investigation, before he came to the bench, of the insurance business, he analyzes aptly the social function of insurance.[24]

But a jurisprudence built around social change requires even more an intimate and realistic knowledge of economic organization. Without subscribing to the economic interpretation of the social process, Mr. Justice Brandeis believes that the forces that create new tasks for law are mainly economic. This belief and the insight of economic processes that he gained from his active career in handling business relationships, give his thought its characteristic realism. Mr. Chief Justice Marshall also had a strong realistic sense, but it was of American political problems and processes; and Mr. Justice Holmes, with his mordant insight into human motives, is a consummate psychological realist. All realistic thought joins in the pursuit of the *élan* of the actual. It brushes aside form and fancy, and seeks the determining facts. Mr. Justice Brandeis' realism is chiefly economic: his thought evinces a mastery of the facts and processes of economic life hitherto unsurpassed on the Court.

It is chiefly concerned with effecting a *rapprochement* between law and the institutional life to which it is directed. Viewed typically and schematically Mr. Justice Brandeis' thought premises the process of public law as an interplay of relationships among three entities: the experience of society, out of which disputes and problems arise; some legislative body, acting alone or through administrative commissions it has created, which purports to crystallize social experience in its enactments; and the courts, which interpret the application of constitutional and common-law principles to the specific case.[25] His eye goes always beyond the superficial facts of the case to the matrix of need, maladjustment or agitation out of which it arose; it moves from the object itself to the social landscape that gives it perspective. Such a method has a tendency to shift the venue of discussion and reorient the preoccupation of the Court. Anxiety about freedom of contract gives way to an analysis of wages and the conditions of labor, due process to waste and scientific management, discussion of principle to recital of fact. This shift of emphasis was marked dramatically by the "Brandeis brief" in *Muller* v. *Oregon*[26] but it runs through the body of Mr. Justice Brandeis' decisions as well as of his advocacy.

One of the consequences of such a conception of judicial interpretation is to allow greater latitude to the enactments of state legislatures and the rulings of administrative commissions than the characteristic trend of Mr. Justice Brandeis' thinking would have seemed to require. There is no inherent apotheosis of either the legislative or the bureaucratic process to be found in his philosophy. If anything, his experience with state legislatures in the years when he was fighting insurance companies, railroad companies and trusts must have cast some doubt upon the disinterestedness of the ordinary legislator and the extent to which he represented the wishes of the "people." Nor does the broad tolerance, not unmixed with respect for the sovereignty of a morally self-sufficient group, with which Mr. Justice Holmes regards state legislative acts, occupy a central place in Mr. Justice Brandeis' thought. He is not a state-rights advocate, nor, with his distinctly humanitarian and reformist trend, does he have that skepticism about the superiority of one form of social action over another which might dictate a *laissez faire* attitude toward legislatures. In him the tendency to relax the rigor of the constitutional limitations on state legislative action as hitherto interpreted seems to proceed from another source. The recent trend of legislative action, especially in the western states affected by the populist movements, has represented the pressure of social change and social experience much more adequately than have the legal concepts handed down in the common law. Forced to choose between the two Mr. Justice Brandeis could have no hesitancy. In the test of reasonableness as applied to state legislation he has found an effective instrument ready at hand for some approximation toward a realistic jurisprudence.

The emphasis on the institutional context of a case is so characteristic an item in Mr. Justice Brandeis' method that "institutionalism" or "contextualism" might serve as readily as "realism" to describe the method. The context of a felt necessity for the particular legislative enactment is represented in a large number of his opinions—for example, the felt necessity of suppressing private employment agencies,[27] or of regulating unscrupulous steamship ticket agents,[28] or of discouraging corporate business organizations by levying a state tax upon corporations.[29] The context of the case may even involve a prolonged agitation by interested groups to secure the enactment of the law, as in the account Mr. Justice Brandeis gives in *Duplex Printing Press Co. v. Deering*[30] of the legislative history of the Clayton Act. If the experience of a state in the administration of its weights and measures laws points to the advisability of legislating against excessive weights as well as against short weights,[31] if the excesses of cutthroat competition and the normal disorder that planless competition produces in the economic order suggest the pooling of trade information by a manufacturers' association in the lumber business,[32] if a state wishing to protect its workers from the arbitrary effects of the labor injunction limits the use of the injunction in labor cases, except against acts of violence,[33] or if wishing to protect its cotton growers from exploitation by the owners of private gins it grants special privileges to gins owned by coöperatives,[34] it is the context of the case that most seriously attracts Mr. Justice Brandeis' attention, and he presents it with sympathy and with an engaging and sometimes passionate persuasiveness.[35]

The elements in the social setting of a case that Mr. Justice Brandeis inquires into in order to determine whether the legislation in question had reasonably weighed conflicting social values are invariably significant ones. Half the task of realism is to ask the right questions about which to seek adequate information. Mr. Justice Brandeis' questions revolve about the ends sought to be remedied by the legislation, the social need for it, the character and extent of the public opinion behind it, the psychological *milieu* in which it was passed, its possible consequences. "Nearly all legislation," he says, "involves a weighing of public needs as against private desires. . . . What at any particular time is the paramount public need, is necessarily largely a matter of judgment."[36] Where the judgment is not demonstrably clear he appeals to the experience in other states or countries, to the consensus of practice within relevant groups, or to the consensus of enlightened opinion.

The study of the context and the appeal to consensus, for which Mr. Justice Brandeis is to a great extent responsible, are intellectual techniques holding out such great possibilities for the judicial process that it is important to note their ultimate subservience to the social philosophy of the judge. They aid him in arriving at an opinion, but they are also almost inevitably themselves conditioned by an opinion already tentatively arrived at. For the detached political psychologist there is little difference between the pressures applied in an agricultural community in a time of low agricultural profits to obtain privileged legislation for coöperative associations, and the hysterias that in time of war result in criminal syndicalism legislation or the suppression of radical agitation. Various individuals will sympathize with one type of legislation or the other depending upon their intellectual temper; a respectable array of social experience and a consensus of judgment could with discretion be marshaled for both. Yet Mr. Justice Brandeis has consistently upheld the reasonableness of legislation in the former type of case and consistently rejected it in the latter.[37] He finds it difficult to reconcile the deviation from sound judgment involved in what he considers an encroachment of fundamental civil liberties, with any possible reasonableness in the legislation.

IV

A SIGNIFICANT social philosophy in the realm of law today must do more than eat away the lag between institutional change and legal development. That is, to be sure, of inestimable importance, especially in cases involving submerged groups such as labor whose interests have not been incorporated in the fashioning of legal rules. But it does not offer a technique for dealing with the problems emerging from the active development of business enterprise. The world that the Court operates in is a world of accomplished fact, with which one must come to the best terms possible. But it is also a world continually in the making, with many potential lines of development. To drive a wedge of direction through the flux of economic life and to turn it into socially accredited channels becomes the task of the modern state, and under our constitutional system preëminently the task of the Supreme Court.

In this sphere Mr. Justice Brandeis is easily our outstanding figure. He has stood firmly for holding business enterprise rigorously to its social responsibilities. He has kept himself sensitive to current trends in economic organization and has exercised the imagination of genuine statesmanship in envisaging their meaning for the future. He has applied on the judicial front the ideas developed in economic thought and has built up a technique of control that has appreciably added to the resources of our administrative law.

There would seem at first sight to be a contradiction between such an instrumental conception of legal function and Mr. Justice Brandeis' well-known and fervent individualism. But the contradiction is resolved when it is recalled how far his individualism is from the quietistic attitude of *laissez faire* economics. While he still borrows heavily from classical economic thought,[38] he has discarded completely the Ricardian faith in the unassisted working of the economic order. He believes in competition as being good for the competitors, good for the consumer, and good for the industrial process. But he does not fall into the nineteenth-century error of believing that with competition as motive power the economic mechanism can be left to itself. He believes instead that only through the judicious intervention of the state under the proper circumstances can it function with its necessary smoothness.

It is clear that Mr. Justice Brandeis' philosophy of control could look to no comprehensive and continuous organization of economic life in terms of state power, no system of either planning or paternalism. He is entirely in accord with what he conceives to be the normal functioning of the present economic set-up; his animus is directed only against its pathology. The huge and unwieldy corporation, the industrial monopoly, the unfair competitor, the overcapitalized public utility company, the pyramided money trust—these are the forces to be tamed. They represent unbridled economic aggrandizement and antisocial economic power. To Mr. Justice Brandeis they are not what they are to critics of capitalism—natural growths from capitalistic organization, and its characteristic products. They are rather excrescences—sinister growths in a world where no formula and no system can insure perfection.

Mr. Justice Brandeis has had to work out his theory and technique of control in the course of interpreting the application of constitutional principles to the operations under the Sherman Law and the rulings of the federal and state administrative commissions. He has had to determine what the scope and the powers of the commissions were under the laws creating them, and in passing upon the validity of their rulings he has had to crystallize in his thinking the principles to be applied in the regulation of business.

At the basis of Mr. Justice Brandeis' attitude toward the problem of regulation is his conviction that no rights are absolute.[39] In the pitting of public welfare against property rights he insists that there is no absolute right to make profits, just as there is no absolute right to do anything else within the state. The state grants qualified rights in certain property, in return for which the corporation assumes corresponding obligations of charging fair prices, engaging in no discriminations or unfair practices, and allowing a free field for all competitors. The resulting system is one of individualism, in the sense that it premises a *régime* of profits, competition and private enterprise. But it is an ethical individualism—one that emphasizes responsibilities and duties. When the conditions for vesting property rights are unsatisfactory in any situation, the courts must await legislative action by which a system of regulation can be imposed.[40]

Viewed from another angle, the rationale of Mr. Justice Brandeis' attitude toward control is furnished by his adherence to the idea of competition. Wherever monopoly has taken the place of former competitive units he wishes to restore and maintain competition; where, in a competitive situation, unfair practices threaten the competitive equilibrium he wishes to curb them and so maintain the plane of competition; where competition is impossible or undesirable due to the nature of the industry he wishes to pattern the system of control as closely as possible upon the model of a putative competition. The first of these three spheres of action for government control roughly parallels the operation of the Sherman Act, the second the Federal Trade Commission, and the last the Interstate Commerce Commission and the various state public service commissions. In all of them he projects the competitive ideal into situations where it functions with difficulty, even to the extent of introducing competition as a fiction, very much as the social contract was a fiction, to rationalize regulatory practices in the field of public utilities where in most cases it would be drastic or impossible to maintain competition.

The adherence to the competitive ideal rests, in Mr. Justice Brandeis' thought, not on an arid traditionalism but on a belief that competition best serves certain more fundamental social ideals. It keeps prices low and fair. It represents a phase of equality in that it gives the "little fellows" a chance. It advances the process of invention and fosters progress in the industrial and business arts. It keeps the business unit small enough to be manageable and creative. It prevents any concentration of economic power which might dwarf the individual and threaten liberty.[41] But while all these aims would be generally regarded as "idealistic" there is nothing of the doctrinaire in Mr. Justice Brandeis. Although he is always willing to see a "trust" smashed he is keenly aware that a problem so complex and elusive as that of the control of economic development cannot be dealt with merely by militant and repressive measures. In interpreting the "restraint of trade" provision of the Sherman Act he points out the danger of an absolutistic approach to the problem.[42] He argues forcefully that "the Sherman Law does not prohibit every lessening of competition" nor does it "demand that competition shall be pursued blindly."[43] Whether a particular agreement is illegally in restraint can be determined only by reference to its context.[44] Thus, a "call rule" on the floor of a commodity exchange does not restrain trade illegally;[45] price-fixing by the producer for the retail reselling of graphophones need not;[46] and even a manufacturers' association among hardwood lumber mills organized to pool and distribute trade information regarding prices and business policy does not.[47] On the other hand, a tying clause, linking the purchase of jute bagging to that of steel cotton ties, does under the particular circumstances restrain competition.[48]

Mr. Justice Brandeis' opinions in the cases involving interstate commerce and public utility regulation represent in consummate form a combination of realistic knowledge of business, subtle and difficult economic analysis, skilful legal reasoning and creative public policy. In the opinions bearing on the crucial question of the valuation of the rate base, he has pitted his mind against the most complex technical problem that has yet been encountered in regulation, and come away with distinguished success. The right and the wrong of the conflicting theories of valuation, while no doubt of great consequence to the nation, are less important to the present discussion than the method by which Mr. Justice Brandeis has arrived at his theories. He has passed first principles in review, inquiring into the grounds for rate regulation;[49] he has studied the intellectual history that lies behind the agitation for one rate theory or another;[50] he has assiduously sought guidance from economic thought[51] and business practice;[52] he has seen the process of valuation for what it is—not a single certitude, but a chain whose every link is a guess, an opinion or an estimate;[53] he has finally sought to measure the consequences of the adoption of one rate base or another upon economic development. We are impressed by the erudition, technical grasp and fine historical sense displayed in these amazing opinions; we cannot but admire the strategy with which, after having unsuccessfully defended historical cost against present value,[54] he retreats and takes up a new position with the theory of functional as against reproduction cost in the determination of present value.[55] But the significant fact here is not Mr. Justice Brandeis' strategy but the courage and resourcefulness with which he operates in a realm— that of economic statecraft—which must in the future increasingly absorb the energies of the Court.

In a real sense Mr. Justice Brandeis' conception of his task with respect to the control of industrial development has had as much in it of economic statesmanship as it has of judicial interpretation. In his scheme *stare decisis* has played a less important part than the effect of the decisions on industrial development and business initiative; and so far from hesitating to read his notions of public policy into the Constitution, he has deemed it his first duty to formulate a just and statesmanlike policy. To a degree there is an admixture of economic romanticism in his gallant wrestling with "these great issues of government."[56] A less vigorous mind might have flinched from them and taken refuge in a safe judicial "objectivity." A more sardonic mind might have concluded that amidst an economic welter such as ours government can at best create an illusion for us and clothe with some semblance of order what are really the workings of chance and chaos. But Mr. Justice Brandeis, with his sense of the need of man's mastering economic circumstance, is interested even as a judge in the gigantic struggle we are waging here to subjugate every natural and human resource and turn it to the uses of the nation. And it is that which makes him our most important contemporary statesman.

V

Capitalism, itself a system of economic organization, reaches out beyond its economic confines. It intrenches itself in a system of legal rules and ideas that may be called capitalist jurisprudence.[57] It creates a social system and a way of life. This way of life has written itself into the history of constitutional interpretation as it has written itself into the history of the Common Law.[58] The opinions of the Supreme Court are composed in its shadow. It furnishes a body of first principles that remain unquestioned amidst the intricacies and the fierce battles of legal discussion. It constitutes the abiding set of preconceptions that demark the limits of judicial decision.

Mr. Justice Brandeis has not completely escaped the necessity of having to do his social thinking within the context of capitalist jurisprudence. To say that is not to set down the essential meaning of his career; one does not thereby, to use a phrase of Mr. Justice Holmes, "strike at the jugular vein" of his thought. Its real meaning lies elsewhere: away from rather than reënforcing the capitalist norms. Yet to understand his relation to capitalist jurisprudence is essential to perspective, for the charge of radicalism—shadowy word—has often been leveled at Mr. Justice Brandeis. Whatever his heresies may be they are not economic radicalism. Using that term in the only sense in which it has meaning for modern economic society—adherence to proletarian theory—one may say that it is incompatible with the task of judicial interpretation in a society whose legal foundations are capitalistic. "We must never forget," Chief Justice Marshall once admonished—and here we may give his remark a meaning he never intended—"that it is *a constitution* we are expounding."[59]

Justice Brandeis' animus, as has been noted above, is directed not at the normal functioning of a capitalistic society but at its pathology. He has so much respect for private property that he wishes it more equitably distributed, so much respect for capital that he wishes it to flow freely instead of being concentrated in a Money Trust, so much respect for competition that he wishes the conditions created under which it will be possible, so much respect for profits as an incentive that he wishes it to operate unobstructed by the monstrous weight and the artificial power of corporations, so much respect for business enterprise that he wishes to make of it a responsible creative force. There is an almost idyllic freshness about the way in which he clings to the original content of economic institutions whose current form most of the rest of us accept in a somewhat jaded fashion. It is a freshness reminiscent of the manner in which the emigrant groups of '48 approached political democracy. He has thrown all his powers and all his passion into the problem of attaining freedom and justice and a fair chance for every individual to make a life within the framework of a capitalist society. To this end he uses law instrumentally, as a living organism of adjustment to a changing society, as a method for distributing power and control within that society.

Accordingly, within the framework of the present economic system Mr. Justice Brandeis' stand is for a courageous and enlightened meliorism strange and new to the traditions and convictions of the Supreme Court. He would soften the asperities of capitalism, humanize its rough competitive struggle, endow it with responsibility as well as with vigor. Mastering the field of social legislation he has made it practically his own. He has fought, off the bench and on, for hours-of-labor legislation, a minimum wage, social insurance

—all the points of contact at which the state intervenes to palliate the rigor of the economic process. He has championed the interests and defended the functions of the trade-union movement; but the support he has lent it has been far from unquestioning and uncritical enthusiasm. A trade-unionism that had no sense of responsibility, that developed a sterile bureaucracy or that used its power to advance petty interests received as little sympathy from him as a tyrannical and uncreative business aggregation.[60] He urged the merits of scientific management even against the opposition of labor.[61] He saw in it its possibilities for the cutting down of waste; and his was the broad humanism that added the cold precision of an engineer's standpoint to the social passion of the liberal.[62] Almost his principal concern has been the creation of sound conditions for the maintenance of a healthy system of business enterprise, composed of small, independent individual units, and achieving continuous advance in the industrial and management arts through the incentive of profits and the mechanics of competition. To this end he has favored the introduction of every device that made for efficiency, the dissemination of trade and market information, and the toleration of price maintenance.[63] Just as he has seen in Big Business a dangerous and irresponsible force, he has looked to a business kept at its legitimate functions and proportions to take on the attitudes and the ethics of a profession.[64]

All his efforts have been directed thus to the creation of a socialized, regulated welfare-capitalism. One may discern that to achieve this ideal he has thrown his energies into two streams of direction: he has sought to socialize and ethicize business, and he has sought to gain for labor an equality of position at a bargaining level at which it could develop creatively its own contribution to the economic process. To do this he has had to work in two camps at once. Through his opinions there has crept into the body of judicial decision, to confront the philosophy of the entrepreneur and the stock-holder, a new philosophy representing the aspirations and outlook of labor.[65] But running alongside of this there is a stream of thought in which the center of gravity of the economic system is not a militant and dominant labor group but a self-reliant body of independent business men. That these two streams meet and flow strongly together in Mr. Justice Brandeis' own thinking is indisputable. But it may be doubted whether an economic philosophy that involves the balancing and synthesizing of such diverse tendencies will have any evocative power in a world that must take sides or grow apathetic. Above partisanship himself, Mr. Justice Brandeis runs the risk of appearing partisan to both extremes. He is little short of an Antichrist to the big corporations. And to many in radical circles his refusal, on ethical grounds, to intervene in the Sacco-Vanzetti case seemed equivocal.

Such contemporary opinion may be of small importance for what must be a long-run appraisal of the validity of Mr. Justice Brandeis' economic philosophy. And any point of view that has been forged in a lifetime of active thought and is the product of mature experience must seem equivocal viewed from the anxious passions at both the left and the right. But there is a significance in such disesteem, and it lies in its indication that the object of it, in pursuing the integrity of his own thinking, may have lost touch with the new emotional trend of his time; and the emotional trend of a period often comes close to being a reflection of its deeper institutional trends. A very large body of American liberal opinion has made almost an idol of Mr. Justice Brandeis and acknowledges the leadership of his thought. But there are evidences that widening cleavages in American life may ultimately leave this body of opinion islanded and powerless.[66] The crucial premise in Mr. Justice Brandeis' economic thought—that the things he is fighting are excrescences to be lopped off, pathological diversions of energy to be brought back to their normal channels—finds less and less confirmation in the *Spätkapitalismus* stage of American economic organization. Agglomerations of capital grow more monstrous, mergers have become the order of the day, the pyramiding of economic power goes on, the individual finds himself increasingly shut out.[67] In the face of such tendencies Mr. Justice Brandeis' attempt to hold the balance scrupulously between what is legitimate in business enterprise and what is an encroachment upon the liberties of the individual seems somewhat indecisive; and his denial to capitalists of further increments of that power of which, as an interpreter of the Constitution, he could not divest them, seems a gallant but hopeless attempt to bridge two worlds.

This points to a deep strain of optimism to be found in the entire body of Mr. Justice Brandeis' social thought. Keenly sensitive to discords in the social system, his mind inevitably seeks to harmonize the jarring elements. From the enriching experience of his long career he has learned to approach every problem with a view to a constructive solution, and he falls thus easily into the constructivist's belief that no differences can defy the efforts of the human spirit to resolve them. Although he has at times pointed to the deepening cleavage between the "haves" and the "have-nots" it was essentially a note of warning that preceded a constructive and not a revolutionary program. With the contempt of a free and flexible mind for ideology and dogma he has steadily refused to see the social process in terms of the class struggle. There was no essential conflict, he felt, between capital and labor. It was at the worst a feud which could be settled by making each side see the stake it had in peace and the mutuality of benefit that lay at the basis of their relationship.[68] Although himself a hardened veteran in the wars against encroaching business interests there is nothing *kampflustig* about Mr. Justice Brandeis. He has always been willing to sue for peace on fair terms, just as he has always been ready to fight in default of them. His technique has been to act as interpreter of one side to the other, and while urging each to resist the extreme claims of the other, to base a final solution only on that genuine meeting of the minds that proceeds from a recognition of common interests. It has been essentially the technique of conciliation. In fact, it is characteristic of Mr. Justice Brandeis' thought that his conception of the economic process is a judicial one.

Or perhaps it would be truer to say it is political, as the Greeks conceived the nature and the interests of the *polis*. Amidst the chaos of economic conflict and the pull of contending loyalties Mr. Justice Brandeis' final concern has been the quality and vitality of the state. Not the state as force has engaged his allegiance and his imagination, nor the state as abstract idea, nor even the state as justice. It is rather the state as summarizing and fostering the creative possibilities resident in every individual.

It is in the living context of this faith that the political ideals which have become stereotypes with most of us still keep for Mr. Justice Brandeis their original meaning and warmth. Much of his political thinking is polarized about democracy and freedom. But in the case of both concepts the original spirit is reinterpreted in terms of our changed society. His democracy is an apotheosis of the common man, but only of the common man viewed as a bundle of potentialities. And it is the sum of the conditions that enables him to develop these potentialities that constitutes Mr. Justice Brandeis' conception of freedom. These conditions are in our society mainly economic, just as the forces that threaten and dwarf our freedom are the outcome of our recent economic development.[69] Neither is his conception of democracy the traditional one—a principle set apart in government; it is part of every activity in the state, just as freedom is part of every activity. The greatest field for democracy today lies for him in the person-to-person working out of those daily economic relationships that we call "industrial democracy." It is in such workshops that the truly political attitudes are fashioned that go into the making of the state.

VI

WHAT ties this bundle of ideas together? More than anything else, Mr. Justice Brandeis' belief in the basic importance of experience. The experience of individuals is, for him, the great source out of which society draws its strength and its growth. Social institutions are the product and distillation of experience; laws are its expression; the judicial function builds from it. It is this absorption with the theme of experience that stamps the body of Mr. Justice Brandeis' judicial opinions as pragmatic jurisprudence.

Pragmatism is not new in law. In one sense, as hardheaded militant preferment of fact to theory, as a steadfast clinging to accumulated experience, it informs the whole history of the Common Law. By its very nature a system of case law is unsystematic, antiabsolutist, capable of growth.[70] That same use of fictions which marks the reluctance of its changes to new conditions marks also the fact of them. But what gives Mr. Justice Brandeis' pragmatism its character as innovation is the fact that the experience on which it bases itself is the changing experience of the present, not the accumulated experience of the past. A tory jurisprudence has always the advantage of being evidently buttressed by past realities; a liberal jurist, since he is advancing "new ideas," must always face the charge that he is making the situation conform to his idea of it. The body of pragmatic jurisprudence which, under Mr. Justice Brandeis' leadership, is forming in America has given a new prestige to the scanning of the contemporary horizon for light on ancient legal principles.

The pragmatism of Mr. Justice Brandeis is in essence experimental.[71] It sees two experimental processes going on at the same time: the attempt of society to work out its problems, and the attempt of the courts to find the right rule of law. The experimental process going on in society is to Mr. Justice Brandeis generally a blind one and often ignorant; the formulations that it presents at any given time are tentative and imperfect. But they embrace the energies and aspirations of men, and a "living law" cannot ignore them.[72] The law is itself therefore in experimental flux, changing with the changing configurations that society presents. Of the "search by the court of last resort for the true rule," Mr. Justice Brandeis has said—"The process of inclusion and exclusion, so often applied in developing a rule, cannot end with its first enunciation. The rule as announced must be deemed tentative. For the many and varying facts to which it will be applied cannot be foreseen. Modification implies growth. It is the life of the law."[73]

In this philosophy of experiment and experience the individual is the unit. Mr. Justice Brandeis believes, as Emerson did, in the sovereign reality of individual experience. In common with more recent psychological thought he believes that one can learn nothing except as it passes through one's own experience; every attempt to impose artificial mechanisms results in failure.[74] Whatever social programs or techniques fall outside the ambit of the individual mind are therefore sterile; the unit of organization should never be made so large that the individual experience cannot compass it. Mr. Justice Brandeis applies this principle to government, and emerges with a belief in decentralization. When he applies it to business organization it leads him to his well-known position that an overgrown corporate unit is wasteful and unwieldy, and that the men at the top of it are incapable of having that direct mastery and comprehension of its affairs that makes business enterprise a creative activity. A group of small units, each psychologically autonomous and self-contained, represents for Mr. Justice Brandeis the most satisfactory organization of any sphere of action.

Although Mr. Justice Brandeis' individualism is reminiscent, in its fire and conviction, of the fine nineteenth-century libertarianism of John Stuart Mill, it is far from being imitative of it. Where the English liberals feared the tyranny of political power, Mr. Justice Brandeis is solicitous for the liberty of the individual when confronted with the huge engines of economic power and large aggregations of capital. Where they wished to protect the individual from the state, Mr. Justice Brandeis invokes the state to protect him from menacing forces within it. "It was urged," he says in his opinion in *Truax* v. *Corrigan*, "that the real motive in seeking the injunction was not ordinarily to prevent property from being injured nor to protect its owner in its use, but to endow property with active militant power which would make it dominant over men."[75] It is against this dominance of things over men that the whole force of Mr. Justice Brandeis' humanism is directed. Beyond the intent that this humanism embraces of protecting the individual from being hurt is its fear that he will be lost; that in a society in which things in themselves are invested with active power the initiative and creativeness of men will find no room for expression.

There is throughout Mr. Justice Brandeis' thinking an unmistakable ethical note. It keeps him, on the one hand, from a rule-of-thumb method of judicial decision; he does not decide cases atomistically but by reference to a deeply held code of valuations. On the other hand it keeps him from the doctrinaire mistake of dealing with concepts as undifferentiated counters. To him the autonomy of the individual is eminently desirable; but economic individualism as the nineteenth century conceived it, since it brings disastrous consequences in the modern situation, is a thing to be fought. It is not to be confused with ethical and psychological individualism, which involves responsibilities as well as liberties. In this spirit Mr. Justice Brandeis refuses also to accept the validity of the issue between individualism and collectivism. Here again an ethical differentiation is necessary. The collective action involved in control of economic development is quite different in value from that involved in government owner-ship. Some collectivities are desirable, like trade-unions and coöperatives; others, like large corporations, are undesirable. But Mr. Justice Brandeis carries his differentiation even fur-ther. Corporations and trade-unions may both be, in the spe-cific instance, good or bad. What determines that is not an *a priori* ethical theory but an ethical judgment of their moti-vation and their consequences.

Amidst the difficult and technical legal reasoning in his opinions this ethical fervor might appear a gratuitous and harmless addition. But actually his moral earnestness does not merely run parallel to his legal reasoning. It interpene-trates it. It determines its course. It saves his amazing legal competence from becoming virtuosity.

VII

BEHIND the uniform array of United States Reports reposing on the shelves of the law libraries a battle is being fought and constitutional history made. The dramatic quality of Mr. Justice Brandeis' career of advocacy has followed him to the bench, and as one of a militant liberal minority on the Court he has focused the attention of the nation. He has had to in-troduce his social philosophy into a *milieu* for the most part alien to its spirit and formulations, among justices whom the intellectual traditions of their class and period had educated to a conception of their tasks radically different from his own. Dealing with cases involving the gravest problems the Court has had to face since the initial period of constitutional inter-pretation, and in an atmosphere in which every legal doctrine has been charged with the emotional tensions of social strug-gles outside the Court, he has had to devote himself to a laborious exposition of the fundamental economic facts that determine the issues. He has had finally to contend with a conception of legal precedent that regarded the body of past decisions as something very like the *traditio divina* of the canon law.

In the face of a task of such proportions Mr. Justice Brandeis has been remarkably successful. He has not altogether kept the Supreme Court from appearing to liberal opinion as something of a Heartbreak House. But he has drawn the issues clearly, taken a positive and constructive stand, and polarized every liberal tendency in the Court.[76] A more radical philosophy, a less statesmanlike attitude than his might have failed utterly. But Mr. Justice Brandeis' intellectual creed, although always clear-cut and decisive, contains that admirable balancing of tradition and innovation which represents the greatest assurance of eventual success. There has been no intent in it to break with the essential Supreme Court traditions. Mr. Justice Brandeis' doctrine of *stare decisis* is mature as well as flexible.[77] He has adhered to the American tradition of individualism, redefining it to suit the realities of the age. In his emphasis on democracy and freedom he has insisted that as a nation we bid fair to alienate ourselves from the psychological drives that have conditioned our history. The pragmatic cast of his thought, its ethical strain, have set up responses in the American mind. His method—factual, experimental, inductive—strives only to assimilate law to those other procedures that already have those characteristics. He has advocated not the creation of new institutions but the instrumentalism that will use law to bring out the best implications of existing institutions.

It would be strange indeed if twentieth-century America which has in almost every field of thought and art produced its characteristic expression should fail to do so in jurisprudence. Mr. Justice Brandeis has admirably evoked and summed up contemporary tendencies in legal thought. It seems likely that the future of judicial decision lies with these tendencies rather than with those that have opposed them. But if that should prove true will Mr. Justice Brandeis' work, in the phrase Fitz James Stephen used of Bentham, "be buried in the ruins it has made"? To the extent that his thought merely merges with contemporary trends, that is likely. But there is permanence and distinctiveness in Mr. Justice Brandeis' conception of the "living law." His realistic method of shifting the battle from the barren ground of precedent and logic to the higher ground of social function and social situation must prove an enduring contribution to the process of constitutional interpretation. Even the *epigoni* when they come will find it a technique which they can use.

III

Mr. Justice Brandeis and the Constitution

by

Felix Frankfurter

MR. JUSTICE BRANDEIS AND THE CONSTITUTION

I

ADEFINITIVE history of great political events may challenge the fecundity of historians, but of necessity escapes them. Even an adequate history of the Supreme Court awaits writing, to say which is no failure of gratitude to Mr. Charles Warren, who did not purport to paint a full canvas. He attempted only an essay on "The Supreme Court in United States History." To write the history of the Court presupposes an adequate social history of the United States, which, as yet, we lack. Much brave scholarship is now enlisted to give a critical understanding of our past. And the illuminating chapters of the Beards and of Parrington, together with the *History of American Life,* edited by Professors Schlesinger and Fox, bring nearer the day of a comprehensive history of our civilization.

Moreover, the work of the Supreme Court is the history of relatively few personalities. However much they may have represented or resisted their *Zeitgeist,* symbolized forces outside their own individualities, they were also individuals. The fact that they were "*there*"[1] and that others were not, surely made decisive differences. To understand what manner of men they were is crucial to an understanding of the Court. Yet how much real insight have we about the seventy-five men who constitute the Supreme Court's roll of judges? How much is known about the inner forces that directed their action and stamped the impress of their unique influence upon the Court? Only of Marshall have we an adequate biography;[2] Story's revealing correspondence takes us behind his scholarly exterior;[3] very recently not a little light has been shed on the circumstances and associations that helped to mold Field's outlook.[4] About most of the Justices we have only mortuary estimates.

However little we may know about the personal and social influences in which the Court's history is enmeshed, we know enough to know that the essential history of the United States is mirrored in the controversies before the Court. The thrust of the American empire against the hostility to extension, the eternal conflict between creditor and debtor classes and between rich and poor, the push toward economic concentration and the resistance of individual enterprise, the struggles between *étatisme* and libertarianism, between racial homogeneity and diversity of strains, the conflict between the attachments of localism and the march of centralization —all the contending forces in our society, throughout our national life, lie buried within the interstices of the two hundred and eighty-three volumes of United States Reports, ready to be quickened into life by the artist's magic touch.

Of spontaneous generation there is little in history. Epochal changes germinate slowly, and dates in history are deluding. They mark fruition rather than beginning. Yet "every schoolboy knows," though without the omniscience which Macaulay attributed to him, that the Great War ushered in a new era. While the forces which burst upon the world in a cataclysmic war had long been burrowing underground, the *débâcle* of three mighty empires, the Russian Revolution and its violent break with the past, the intensification of technological processes induced by the War, loosed economic and social forces far more upsetting to the preëxisting equilibrium than the changes wrought by the French Revolution and the Napoleonic Wars. All these conflicts and confusions of recent history also are registered in the recent history of the Supreme Court. Mr. Justice Brandeis came to the Supreme Court at the threshold of this new epoch.[5]

II

TIME is an almost indispensable condition for weaving the impress of distinction upon the work of the Court.[6] Mr. Justice Brandeis has now entered upon his sixteenth term and written four hundred and fifteen opinions. These reveal an organic constitutional philosophy, which expresses his response to the deepest issues of society. Other Justices have brought to the Court the matured outlook of a lifetime's brooding. But probably no other man has come to the Court with his mind dyed, as it were, in the very issues which became his chief judicial concern. Indeed, his work as Justice may accurately be described as a continuation of devotion to the solution of those social and economic problems of American society with which he was preoccupied for nearly a generation before his judicial career. Some years before going on the Court he had practically withdrawn from private practice and given unique meaning to what Senator Root has called the "public profession" of the law. Whenever some particularly pressing or difficult issue absorbed his interest and his energy, his passion for law and his mastery of its processes were engaged on behalf of the community; the community which he served was increasingly as wide as the nation. And he gave himself to public affairs as a private citizen. He is one of the very few men who became a Justice without having held prior judicial or political office,[7] except for his service as special counsel for the Interstate Commerce Commission in the proceedings for general rate increases in 1913–14.[8] Even this inquiry he conducted not as a partisan but in a judicial spirit, to see "that all sides and angles of the case are presented of record, without advocating any particular theory for its disposition."[9]

Thus for years Mr. Justice Brandeis had been immersed in the intricacies which modern industry and finance have created for society and in the conflicts engendered by them.

Hardly another lawyer had amassed experience over so wide a range and with so firm a grip on the details that matter. The intricacies of large affairs, railroading, finance, insurance, the public utilities, and the conservation of our natural resources, had yielded to him their meaning. In all these fields the impact of the concrete instance started his inquiries, but it is of the very nature of his mind to explore a subject with which he is grappling until he sees it in all its social bearing.[10]

But his approach to these problems was always that of the lawyer-statesman, seeking to tame isolated instances to the largest possible general rule and to make thereby the difficult reconciliation between order and justice. At a time when our constitutional law was becoming dangerously unresponsive to drastic social changes, when sterile *clichés* instead of facts were deciding cases, he insisted, as the great men of law have always insisted, that law must be sensitive to life. And he preached the doctrine by works more than by faith.[11] By a series of arguments and briefs he created a new technique in the presentation of constitutional questions. Until his famous brief in *Muller* v. *Oregon*,[12] social legislation was supported before the courts largely *in vacuo*—as an abstract dialectic between "liberty" and "police power," unrelated to a world of trusts and unions, of large-scale industry and all its implications. In the *Oregon* case, the facts of modern industry which provoke regulatory legislation were, for the first time, adequately marshaled before the Court. It marks an epoch in the disposition of cases presenting the most important present-day constitutional issues.[13]

III

NEVER was there an easier transition from forum to bench than when Mr. Brandeis became Mr. Justice Brandeis. Since the significant cases before the Supreme Court always involve large public issues and are not just cases between two litigants, the general outlook of the Justices largely determines their views and votes in doubtful cases. Thus the divisions on the Court run not at all along party lines. They reflect not past political attachments, but the philosophy of the judges about government and our Government, their conception of the Constitution and of their own function as its interpreter.

Rich experience at the bar confirmed the teachings which Mr. Brandeis had received from James Bradley Thayer, the great master of constitutional law, that the Constitution had ample resources within itself to meet the changing needs of successive generations. The Constitution provided for the future partly by not forecasting it and partly by the generality of its language. The ambiguities and lacunae of the document left ample scope for the unfolding of life. If the Court, aided by the bar, has access to the facts and heeds them, the Constitution, as he had shown, is flexible enough to respond to the demands of modern society. The work of Mr. Justice Brandeis is in the tradition of Marshall, for, underlying his opinions, is the realization "that it is a *constitution* we are expounding."[14] In essence, the Constitution is not a literary composition but a way of ordering society, adequate for imaginative statesmanship, if judges have imagination for statesmanship.

But even if imprisonment at hard labor elsewhere than in a penitentiary had, in the past, been deemed an infamous punishment, it would not follow that confinement, or rather service, at a workhouse like Occoquan [the workhouse of the District of Columbia], under the conditions now prevailing should be deemed so. . . . The Constitution contains no reference to hard labor. The prohibition contained in the Fifth Amendment [against prosecution except by indictment] refers to infamous crimes—a term obviously inviting interpretation in harmony with conditions and opinion prevailing from time to time. And today commitment to Occoquan for a short term for nonsupport of minor children is certainly not an infamous punishment.[15]

"We must never forget," said Mr. Chief Justice Marshall in Mc-

Culloch v. *Maryland,* 4 Wheat. 316, 407, "that it is a constitution we are expounding." Since then, this Court has repeatedly sustained the exercise of power by Congress, under various clauses of that instrument, over objects of which the Fathers could not have dreamed. See *Pensacola Telegraph Co.* v. *Western Union Telegraph Co.,* 96 U.S. 1, 9; *Northern Pacific Ry. Co.* v. *North Dakota,* 250 U.S. 135; *Dakota Central Telephone Co.* v. *South Dakota,* 250 U.S. 163; *Brooks* v. *United States,* 267 U.S. 432. We have likewise held that general limitations on the powers of Government, like those embodied in the due process clauses of the Fifth and Fourteenth Amendments, do not forbid the United States or the States from meeting modern conditions by regulations which "a century ago, or even half a century ago, probably would have been rejected as arbitrary and oppressive." *Village of Euclid* v. *Ambler Realty Co.,* 272 U.S. 365, 387; *Buck* v. *Bell,* 274 U.S. 200. Clauses guaranteeing to the individual protection against specific abuses of power, must have a similar capacity of adaptation to a changing world.[16]

This general point of view has led Mr. Justice Brandeis to give free play to the States and the Nation within their respective spheres.

For him, the Constitution affords the country, whether at war or at peace, the powers necessary to the life of a great nation. It is amply equipped for the conduct of war. It has the widest discretion in raising the fighting services; to strengthen these, it may also mobilize the social and moral forces of the nation. Whether to wage war or to enforce its revenue laws, the United States, like other nations, has all the rights on the high seas recognized by international law.

Congress has the exclusive power to legislate concerning the Army and the Navy of the United States, and to determine, among other things, the conditions of enlistment. It has likewise exclusive power to declare war, to determine to what extent citizens shall aid in its prosecution and how effective aid may best be secured. Congress, which has power to raise an army and naval forces by conscription when public safety demands, may, to avert a clear and present danger, prohibit interference by persuasion with the process of either compulsory or voluntary enlistment. As an incident of its power to declare war it may, when the public safety demands, require from every citizen full support, and may, to avert a clear and present danger, prohibit interference by persuasion with the giving of such support. But Congress might conclude that the most effective Army or Navy would be one composed wholly of men who had enlisted with full appreciation of the limitations and obligations which the service imposes, and in the face of efforts to discourage their doing so. It might conclude that the most effective Army would be one composed exclusively of men who are firmly convinced that war is sometimes necessary if honor is to be preserved, and also that the particular war in which they are engaged is a just one. Congress, legislating for a people justly proud of liberties theretofore enjoyed and suspicious or resentful of any interference with them, might conclude that even in times of grave danger, the most effective means of securing support from the great body of citizens is to accord to all full freedom to criticise the acts and administration of their country, although such freedom may be used by a few to urge upon their fellow-citizens not to aid the Government in carrying on a war, which reason or faith tells them is wrong and will, therefore, bring misery upon their country.[17]

Plaintiff's argument is equivalent to saying that the war power of Congress to prohibit the manufacture and sale of intoxicating liquors does not extend to the adoption of such means to this end as in its judgment are necessary to the effective administration of the law. The contention appears to be, that since the power to prohibit the manufacture and sale of intoxicating liquors is not expressly granted to Congress, but is a power implied under §8 of Article 1 of the Constitution, which authorizes Congress "to make all laws which shall be necessary and proper for carrying into execution" powers expressly enumerated, the power to prohibit non-intoxicants would be merely an incident of the power to prohibit intoxicants; and that it cannot be held to exist, because one implied power may not be grafted upon another implied power. This argument is a mere matter of words. The police power of a State over the liquor traffic is not limited to the power to prohibit the sale of intoxicating liquors supported by a separate implied power to prohibit kindred nonintoxicating liquors so far as necessary to make the prohibition of intoxicants effective; it is a single broad power to make such laws, by way of prohibition, as may be required to effectively suppress the traffic in intoxicating liquors. Likewise the implied war power over intoxicating liquors extends to the enactment of laws which will not merely prohibit the sale of intoxicating liquors but will effectually prevent their sale.[18]

There is no limitation upon the right of the sovereign to seize without a warrant vessels registered under its laws, similar to that imposed by the common law and the Constitution upon the arrest of persons and upon the seizure of "papers and effects." See *Carroll* v. *United States*, 267 U.S. 132, 151–153. Smuggling is commonly attended by violation of the navigation laws. From the beginning of our Government officers of revenue cutters have, for the purpose of enforcing the customs laws, been expressly authorized to board and search inbound vessels on the high seas within twelve miles of our coast. It is not to be lightly assumed that Congress intended to deny to revenue cutters so engaged authority to seize American vessels found to be violating our navigation laws. Nor is it lightly to be assumed that Congress intended to deny to officers of revenue cutters engaged in enforcing other laws of the United States beyond the twelve-mile limit, the authority to seize American vessels found to be violating our navigation laws beyond those limits.[19]

Taxation has always been the most sensitive nerve of government. The enormous increase in the cost of society and the extent to which wealth is represented by intangibles, are putting public finance to its severest tests. To balance budgets, to pay for the cost of progressively civilized social standards, to safeguard the future and to divide these burdens with substantial fairness to the different interests in the community, strains to the utmost the ingenuity of statesmen. They must constantly explore new sources of revenue and find means to prevent the circumvention of their discovery. Subject as they are, in English-speaking countries, to popular control, they must be allowed the widest latitude of power. No finicky limitation upon their discretion nor jejune formula of equality should circumscribe the necessarily empirical process of tapping new revenue or stopping new devices for its evasion. To these needs Mr. Justice Brandeis has been imaginatively alive. He has consistently refused to accentuate the fiscal difficulties of government by injecting into the Constitution his own notions of fiscal policy. In the "vague contours of the Fifth Amendment"[20] he reads no restriction upon historic methods of taxation. Nor has he found in the Constitution compulsion to grant additional immunity or benefit to taxpayers merely because they already hold tax-exempt securities.

It [the Court] holds the Act void because the action of the law-making body is, in its opinion, unreasonable. Tested by the standard of reasonableness commonly adopted by man—use and wont—that action appears to be reasonable. Tested by a still higher standard to which all Americans must bow—long continued practice of Congress repeatedly sanctioned by this Court after full argument—its validity would have seemed unquestionable, but for views recently expressed. No other standard has been suggested.

For more than half a century, it has been settled that a law of Congress imposing a tax may be retroactive in its operation. . . . Each of the fifteen income tax acts adopted from time to time during the last sixty-seven years has been retroactive, in that it applied to income earned, prior to the passage of the act, during the calendar year. . . .

The Act with which we are here concerned had, however, a special justification for retroactive features. The gift tax was imposed largely to prevent evasion of the estate tax by gifts *inter vivos*, and evasion of the income tax by the splitting up of fortunes and the consequent diminution of surtaxes. If, as is thought by the Court, Congress intended the gift tax to apply to all gifts during the calendar year, its purpose may well have been to prevent evasion of the gift tax itself, by the making of gifts after its introduction and prior to its passage. Is Congress powerless to prevent such evasion by the vigilant and ingenious? This Court has often recognized that a measure may be valid as a necessary adjunct to a matter that lies within legislative power, even though, standing alone, its constitutionality might have been subject to doubt. *Purity Extract Co.* v. *Lynch,* 226 U.S. 192; *Ruppert* v. *Caffey,* 251 U.S. 264, 289; *Everard's Breweries* v. *Day,* 265 U.S. 545, 560. If the legislature may prohibit the sale of confessedly innocent articles in order to insure the effective prohibition of others, I see no reason why it may not spread a tax over a period in advance of its enactment sufficiently long to insure that the tax will not be evaded by anticipating the passage of the act. Compare *United States* v. *Doremus,* 249 U.S. 86, 94. In taxation, as well as in other matters, "the law allows a penumbra to be embraced that goes beyond the outline of its object in order that the object may be secured." See Mr. Justice Holmes, in *Schlesinger* v. *Wisconsin,* 270 U.S. 230, 241. Under the rule now applied, even a measure framed to prevent evasion of a tax from a date when it is practically certain that the act will become law, is deemed unreasonable and arbitrary.

The problem of preventing loss of revenue by transactions intervening between the date when legislation is introduced and its final enactment, is not a new one; nor is it one peculiar to the gift tax. Other nations have met it by a method similar to that which the Court holds to be denied to Congress. England long ago adopted the practice of making customs and excise duties retroactive to the beginning of the fiscal year or to the date when the government's resolutions were agreed to by the House of Commons sitting as a Committee of Ways and Means. A similar practice prevails in Ireland, in all the self-governing Dominions, and to some extent in France and Italy. In the United States, retroactive operation of the tariff has been repeatedly recommended by the Tariff Commission and by the Secretary of Commerce. Legislation to that end was reported by the Committee on Ways and Means of the House of Representatives. No suggestion seems to have been made that such legislation would by its retroactive feature violate the due process clause.[21]

The only factual basis for complaint by the Company is that, although a holder of tax-exempt bonds, it is, in respect to this particular tax, no better off than it would have been had it held only taxable bonds. Or, to put it in another way, the objection is not that the plaintiff is taxed on what is exempt, but that others, who do not hold tax-exempt securities, are not taxed more. But neither the Constitution, nor any Act of Congress, nor any contract of the United States, provides that, in respect to this tax, a holder of tax-exempt bonds, shall be better off than if he held only taxable securities. Nowhere can the requirement be found that those who do not hold tax-exempt securities shall, in respect to every tax, be subjected to a heavier burden than the owners of tax-exempt bonds. . . .

To hold that Congress may not legislate so that the tax upon an insurance company shall be the same whether it holds tax-exempt bonds or does not, would, in effect, be to read into the Constitution a provision that Congress must adapt its legislation so as to give to state securities, not merely tax exemption, but additional privileges; and to read into the contract of the United States with its own bondholders a promise that it will, so long as the bonds are outstanding, so frame its system of taxation that its tax-exempt bonds shall, in respect to all taxes imposed, entitle the holder to greater privileges than are enjoyed by holders of taxable bonds. But no rule is better settled than that provisions for tax exemption, constitutional or contractual, are to be strictly construed.[22]

IV

FOR the States, within their ambit, Mr. Justice Brandeis also finds ample scope in the Constitution. He feels profoundly the complexities of their problems. Adequate opportunity for experimentation should not, he believes, be denied to them by a static conception of the Constitution. Here, again, the general intimations of fairness and reason in the due process clause were not intended to shut off remedies, however tentative, for the moral and economic waste, the friction of classes, urban congestion, the relaxation of individual responsibility, the subtler forms of corruption, and the abuses of power which have followed in the wake of a highly developed *laissez faire* industrialism.

The problem which confronted the people of Washington was far more comprehensive and fundamental than that of protecting workers applying to the private agencies. It was the chronic problem of unemployment—perhaps the gravest and most difficult problem of modern industry—the problem which, owing to business depression, was the most acute in America during the years 1913–15. In the State of Washington the suffering from unemployment was accentuated by the lack of staple industries operating continuously throughout the year and by unusual fluctuations in the demand for labor with consequent reduction of wages and increase of social unrest. Students of the larger problem of unemployment appear to agree that establishment of an adequate system of employment offices or labor exchanges is an indispensable first step toward its solution. There is reason to believe that the people of Washington not only considered the collection by the private employment offices of fees from employees a social injustice; but that they considered the elimination of the practice a necessary preliminary to the establishment of a constructive policy for dealing with the subject of unemployment.

It is facts and considerations like these which may have led the people of Washington to prohibit the collection by employment agencies of fees from applicants for work. And weight should be given to the fact that the statute has been held constitutional by the Supreme Court of Washington and by the Federal District Court (three judges sitting)—courts presumably familiar with the local conditions and needs.[28]

The Kohler Act prohibits, under certain conditions, the mining of anthracite coal within the limits of a city in such a manner or to such an extent "as to cause the . . . subsidence of any dwelling or other structure used as a human habitation, or any factory, store, or other industrial or mercantile establishment in which human labor is employed." Coal in place is land; and the right of the owner to use his land is not absolute. He may not so use it as to create a public nuisance; and uses, once harmless, may, owing to changed conditions, seriously threaten the public welfare. Whenever they do, the legislature has power to prohibit such uses without paying compensation; and the power to prohibit extends alike to the manner, the character and the purpose of the use. Are we justified in declaring that the Legislature of Pennsylvania has, in restricting the right to mine anthracite, exercised this power so arbitrarily as to violate the Fourteenth Amendment? . . .

It is said that one fact for consideration in determining whether the limits of the police power have been exceeded is the extent of the resulting diminution in value; and that here the restriction destroys existing rights of property and contract. But values are relative. If we are to consider the value of the coal kept in place by the restriction, we should compare it with the value of all other parts of the land. That is, with the value not of the coal alone, but with the value of the whole property. The rights of an owner as against the public are not increased by dividing the interests in his property into surface and subsoil. The sum of the rights in the parts can not be greater than the rights in the whole. The estate of an owner in land is grandiloquently described as extending *ab orco usque ad coelum.* But I suppose no one would contend that by selling his interest above one hundred feet from the surface he could prevent the State from limiting, by the police power, the height of structures in a city. And why should a sale of underground rights bar the State's power? For aught that appears the value of the coal kept in place by the restriction may be negligible as compared with the value of the whole property, or even as compared with that part of it which is represented by the coal remaining in place and which may be extracted despite the statute. . . .

A prohibition of mining which causes subsidence of such structures and facilities is obviously enacted for a public purpose; and it seems, likewise, clear that mere notice of intention to mine would not in this connection secure the public safety. Yet it is said that these provisions of the act cannot be sustained as an exercise of the police power where the right to mine such coal has been reserved. The conclusion seems to rest upon the assumption that in order to justify such exercise of the police power there must be "an average reciprocity of advantage" as between the owner of the property restricted and the rest of the community; and that here such reciprocity is absent. Reciprocity of advantage is an important consideration, and may even be an essential, where the State's power is exercised for the purpose of conferring benefits upon the property of a neighborhood, as in drainage projects, *Wurts* v. *Hoagland,* 114 U.S. 606; *Fallbrook Irrigation District* v. *Bradley,* 164 U.S. 112; or upon adjoining owners, as by party wall provisions, *Jackman* v. *Rosenbaum Co., ante,* 22. But where the police power is exercised, not to confer benefits upon property owners, but to protect the public from detriment and danger, there is, in my opinion, no room for considering reciprocity of advantage. There was no reciprocal advantage to the owner prohibited from using his oil tanks in 248 U.S. 498; his brickyard, in 239 U.S. 394; his livery stable, in 237 U.S. 171; his billiard hall, in 225 U.S. 623; his oleomargarine factory, in 127 U.S. 678; his brewery, in 123 U.S. 623; unless it be the advantage of living and doing business in a civilized community. That reciprocal advantage is given by the act to the coal operators.[24]

With the wisdom of the legislation we have, of course, no concern. But, under the due process clause as construed, we must determine whether the prohibition of excess weights can reasonably be deemed necessary; whether the prohibition can reasonably be deemed an appropriate means of preventing short weights and incidental unfair practices; and whether compliance with the limitation prescribed can reasonably be deemed practicable. The determination of these questions involves an enquiry into facts. Unless we know the facts on which the legislators may have acted, we cannot properly decide whether they were (or whether their measures are) unreasonable, arbitrary or capricious. Knowledge is essential to understanding; and understanding should precede judging. Sometimes, if we would guide by the light of reason, we must let our minds be bold. But, in this case, we have merely to acquaint ourselves with the art of breadmaking and the usages of the trade; with the devices by which buyers of bread are imposed upon and honest bakers or dealers are subjected by their dishonest fellows to unfair competition; with the problems which have confronted public officials charged with the enforcement of the laws prohibiting short weights, and with their experience in administering those laws.

Why did legislators, bent only on preventing short weights, prohibit, also, excessive weights? It was not from caprice or love of symmetry. It was because experience had taught consumers, honest dealers and public officials charged with the duty of enforcing laws concerning weights and measures that, if short weights were to be prevented, the prohibition of excessive weights was an administrative necessity. . . .

Much evidence referred to by me is not in the record. Nor could it have been included. It is the history of the experience gained under similar legislation, and the result of scientific experiments made, since the entry of the judgment below. Of such events in our history, whether occurring before or after the enactment of the statute or of the entry of the judgment, the Court should acquire knowledge, and must, in my opinion, take judicial notice, whenever required to perform the delicate judicial task here involved. Compare *Muller* v. *Oregon*, 208 U.S. 412, 419, 420; *Dorchy* v. *Kansas*, *ante* [264 U.S.], 286. The evidence contained in the record in this case is, however, ample to sustain the validity of the statute. There is in the record some evidence in conflict with it. The legislature and the lower courts have, doubtless, considered that. But with this conflicting evidence we have no concern. It is not our province to weigh evidence. Put at its highest, our function is to determine, in the light of all facts which may enrich our knowledge and enlarge our understanding, whether the measure, enacted in the exercise of an unquestioned police power and of a character inherently unobjectionable, transcends the bounds of reason. That is, whether the provision as applied is so clearly arbitrary or capricious that legislators acting reasonably could not have believed it to be necessary or appropriate for the public welfare.

To decide, as a fact, that the prohibition of excess weights "is not necessary for the protection of the purchasers against imposition and fraud by short weights"; that it "is not calculated to effectuate that purpose"; and that it "subjects bakers and sellers of bread" to heavy burdens, is, in my opinion, an exercise of the powers of a super-legislature—not the performance of the constitutional function of judicial review.[25]

So far as concerns the Federal Constitution, the validity of the tax may be rested, also, on other grounds. A State may defray the cost of constructing a highway, in whole or in part, by means of a special assessment upon property specially benefited thereby. But it is not obliged to do so. Road building is a public purpose which may be effected by general taxation. The cost may be defrayed out of state funds; or a tax district may be created to meet the authorized outlay. The preliminary enquiry whether it is desirable to construct the road, is one in which all landowners within the district are interested. The Fourteenth Amendment does not require that taxes laid for this purpose shall be according to the benefits to be received by the person or thing taxed. Compare *Kelly* v. *Pittsburgh*, 104 U.S. 78. The cost of making the investigation may be met by a fixed charge per acre, as in *Houck* v. *Little River Drainage District*, 239 U.S. 254, and *Miller & Lux* v. *Sacramento & San Joaquin Drainage District*, 256 U.S. 129, or by distributing the cost over all the land in the district in proportion to its value as assessed for county and state taxation, or otherwise. The fact that the money to be raised by this tax will be applied toward defraying the expenses of an abandoned road project, and not to the cost of a road wholly or partly completed, is obviously immaterial. *Houck* v. *Little River Drainage District, supra*, p. 265.[26]

Practically every change in the law governing the relation of employer and employee must abridge, in some respect, the liberty or property of one of the parties—if liberty and property be measured by the standard of the law theretofore prevailing. If such changes are made by acts of the legislature, we call the modification an exercise of the police power. And, although the change may involve interference with existing liberty or property of individuals, the statute will not be declared a violation of the due process clause, unless the court finds that the interference is arbitrary or unreasonable or that, considered as a means, the measure has no real or substantial relation of cause to a permissible end. Nor will such changes in the law governing contests between employer and employee be held to be violative of the equal protection clause, merely because the liberty or property of individuals in other relations to each other (for instance, as competitors in trade or as vendor and purchaser) would not, under similar circumstances, be subject to like abridgement. Few laws are of universal application. It is of the nature of our law that it has dealt not with man in general, but with him in relationships. That a peculiar relationship of individuals may furnish legal basis for the classification which satisfies the requirement of the Fourteenth Amendment is clear. That the relation of employer and employee affords a constitutional basis for legislation applicable only to persons standing in that relation has been repeatedly held by this court. The questions submitted are whether this statutory prohibition of the remedy by injunction is in itself arbitrary and so unreasonable as to deprive the employer of liberty or property without due process of law;—and whether limitation of this prohibition to controversies involving employment denies him equal protection of the laws.

Whether a law enacted in the exercise of the police power is justly subject to the charge of being unreasonable or arbitrary, can ordinarily be determined only by a consideration of the contemporary conditions, social, industrial and political, of the community to be affected thereby. Resort to such facts is necessary, among other things, in order to appreciate the evils sought to be remedied and the possible effects of the remedy proposed. Nearly all legislation involves a weighing of public needs as against private desires; and likewise a weighing of relative social values. Since government is not an exact science, prevailing public opinion concerning the evils and the remedy is among the important facts deserving consideration; particularly, when the public conviction is both deep-seated and widespread and has been reached after deliberation. What, at any particular time, is the paramount public need is, necessarily, largely a matter of judgment. Hence, in passing upon the validity of a law challenged as being unreasonable, aid may be derived from the experience of other countries and of the several States of our Union in which the common law and its conceptions of liberty and of property prevail. The history of the rules governing contests between employer and employed in the several English-speaking countries illustrates both the susceptibility of such rules to change and the variety of contemporary opinion as to what rules will best serve the public interest. The divergence of opinion in this difficult field of governmental action should admonish us not to declare a rule arbitrary and unreasonable merely because we are convinced that it is fraught with danger to the public weal, and thus to close the door to experiment within the law.[27]

Particularly, the States should not be hampered in dealing with evils at their points of pressure. Legislation is essentially *ad hoc*. To expect uniformity in law where there is diversity in fact is to bar effective legislation. An extremely complicated society inevitably entails special treatment for distinctive social phenomena. If legislation is to deal with realities, it must address itself to important variations in the needs, opportunities and coercive power of the different elements in the State. The States must be left wide latitude in devising ways and means for paying the bills of society and in using taxation as an instrument of social policy. Taxation is never palatable. Its essential fairness must not be tested by pedantic arguments derived from hollow abstractions. Even more dangers than have been revealed by the due process clause may lurk in the requirement of "the equal protection of the laws," if that provision of the Fourteenth Amendment is to be applied with "delusive exactness."[28] That tendency, often revealed during the post-war period, Mr. Justice Brandeis has steadily resisted.

It is settled that mere inequalities or exemptions in state taxation are not forbidden by the equal protection clause of the Fourteenth Amendment; that the power of the State to make any reasonable classification of property, occupations, persons or corporations for purposes of taxation is not abridged thereby; and that the Amendment forbids merely inequality which is the result of clearly arbitrary action and, particularly, of action attributable to hostile discrimination against particular persons or classes. *Beers* v. *Glynn*, 211 U.S. 477, 485; *Merchants' Bank* v. *Pennsylvania*, 167 U.S. 461, 463, 464; *Bell's Gap R.R. Co.* v. *Pennsylvania*, 134 U.S. 232, 237. The question presented for our decision is whether the action of Virginia in subjecting its domestic corporations which transact business within the State to a tax on all their income, wherever earned, while exempting from the tax those domestic corporations which transact no business within the State, is so clearly arbitrary or invidious, as to fall within the constitutional prohibition. . . .

It is a matter of common knowledge that some States have, in the past, made the granting of charters to non-residents for companies, which purpose transacting business wholly without the State of incorporation, an important source of revenue. The action of those States has materially affected the legislation of other States. Sometimes it has led to active competition for the large revenues believed to be available from this source. More often, it has led to protective measures. The legislature of Virginia may have believed that its own citizens interested in corporations whose business was transacted wholly in other States or countries, might be tempted to incorporate under more favorable laws of other States, but that such temptation would prove ineffective where the companies transacted a part of their business within the State of Virginia and enjoyed compensating advantages. If the legislature of Virginia enacted the laws of 1916 here in question because it held that view, we surely cannot say that its action was unreasonable or arbitrary. And with the wisdom of its action we have no concern.[29]

Nor is a State obliged to protect all property rights by injunction merely because it protects some, even if the attending circumstances are in some respects similar. The restraining power of equity might conceivably be applied to every intended violation of a legal right. On grounds of expediency its application is commonly denied in cases where there is a remedy at law which is deemed legally adequate. But an injunction has been denied on grounds of expediency in many cases where the remedy at law is confessedly not adequate. This occurs whenever a dominant public interest is deemed to require that the preventive remedy, otherwise available for the protection of private rights, be refused and the injured party left to such remedy as courts of law may afford. Thus, courts ordinarily refuse, perhaps in the interest of free speech, to restrain actionable libels. *Boston Diatite Co.* v. *Florence Manufacturing Co.*, 114 Mass. 69; *Prudential Assurance Co.* v. *Knott*, L. R. 10 Ch. App. 142. In the interest of personal liberty they ordinarily refuse to enforce specifically, by mandatory injunction or otherwise, obligations involving personal service. *Arthur* v. *Oakes*, 63 Fed. 310, 318; *Davis* v. *Foreman*, [1894] 3 Ch. 654, 657; *Gossard* v. *Crosby*, 132 Ia. 155, 163, 164. In the desire to preserve the separation of governmental powers they have declined to protect by injunction mere political rights, *Giles* v. *Harris*, 189 U.S. 475; and have refused to interfere with the operations of the police department. *Davis* v. *American Society for the Prevention of Cruelty to Animals*, 75 N.Y. 362; *Delaney* v. *Flood*, 183 N.Y. 323; compare *Bisbee* v. *Arizona Insurance Agency*, 14 Ariz. 313. Instances are numerous where protection to property by way of injunction has been refused solely on the ground that serious public inconvenience would result from restraining the act complained of. Such, for example, was the case where a neighboring land owner sought to restrain a smelter from polluting the air, but that relief, if granted, would have necessitated shutting down the plant and this would have destroyed the business and impaired the means of livelihood of a large community. There are also numerous instances where the circumstances would, according to general equity practice, have justified the issue of an injunction, but it was refused solely because the right sought to be enforced was created by statute, and the courts, applying a familiar rule, held that the remedy provided by the statute was exclusive.[30]

In Kentucky local reasons exist for treating long term mortgage loans somewhat differently from those for a short term. There is among those loans which are secured by mortgages of real or personal property, and hence require registration, commonly a marked difference in the character of the short term and the long term loans.

Probably 90 or 95 per cent of the short term loans are evidenced by promissory notes payable to the lender. The larger part are for amounts less than $300, many of them maturing within a few months and providing for the payment of interest in advance. Another large part consists of loans secured by mortgage upon the residence of the borrower and made for domestic purposes. On the other hand, the long term loans are commonly evidenced by coupon bonds; are issued for large amounts; and represent borrowings for business purposes. The rate of interest on short term mortgage loans is generally higher than that on long term loans of equal safety, in part for the following reason. Because the short term loans are usually evidenced by promissory notes payable to the lender, the registration of the mortgage discloses the identity of the holder of the notes; and he is commonly subjected to the tax of 40 cents per $100 imposed by law upon all mortgage loans. Because the long term loans are commonly represented by negotiable coupon bonds and are secured by a deed of trust, registration does not disclose to the assessors who the holders of the securities are, and they frequently escape taxation thereon. Laying the mortgage recording tax only upon the long term loans tends in some measure to reduce the disadvantage under which the short term borrower labors.

At what point the line should be drawn between short term and long term loans is, of course, a matter on which even men conversant with all the facts may reasonably differ. There was much difference of opinion concerning this in the Kentucky Legislature. The bill, as recommended by the Tax Commission, and as introduced in the House, exempted from the tax here in question only such mortgages as secured indebtedness maturing within three years; and it imposed a tax of 25 cents for $100. In the House, the bill was amended so as to exempt loans maturing in less than five years. In the Senate, the House bill was amended so as to reduce the period to three years. The House refused to concur in the Senate amendment. The Senate receded; and thereupon the bill was passed granting the exemption of loans maturing within five years, but with the rate reduced to 20 cents. Thus, we know that in making this particular classification there was in fact an exercise of legislative judgment and discretion. Surely the particular classification was not such "as to preclude [in law] the assumption that it was made in the exercise of legislative judgment and discretion." See *Stebbins* v. *Riley*, 268 U.S. 137, 143. Whether the exercise was a wise one is not our concern.[31]

Even though the corporation has become a common form of doing business, differences between corporate and individual enterprise persist. The differences are sufficiently significant legitimately to be reflected in the taxing systems of States. Again, the coöperative movement has far-reaching social implications, and the State ought to be allowed to promote it by differentiating, in a variety of ways, between coöperative and ordinary profit-seeking enterprise, even though coöperatives be formally incorporated.

It has been the consistent policy of Pennsylvania since 1840 to subject businesses conducted by corporations to heavier taxation than like businesses conducted by individuals. It has likewise been the consistent policy of the State since 1864 to subject some kinds of businesses conducted by corporations to heavier taxation than other businesses conducted by corporations. Pursuant to this policy, the legislature of Pennsylvania laid, in 1889, upon public service corporations furnishing transportation for hire, a gross receipts tax of eight mills on each dollar of gross receipts earned wholly within the State. Act of June 1, 1889, P. L. 1889, pp. 420, 431 (Pa. Stat. 1920, §20,388). That statute has remained unchanged so far as affects the question here involved. It applies equally to every corporation engaged in the same kind of business, and makes no discrimination between foreign and domestic corporations. But neither this specific tax, nor any equivalent tax, is laid upon individuals or partnerships engaged in the same business. Nor is this tax or an equivalent laid upon corporations which supply certain other public services. . . .

The equality clause does not forbid a State to classify for purposes of taxation. Discrimination through classification is said to violate that clause only where it is such as "to preclude the assumption that it was made in the exercise of legislative judgment and discretion." *Stebbins* v. *Riley*, 268 U.S. 137, 143. In other words, the equality clause requires merely that the classification shall be reasonable. We call that action reasonable which an informed, intelligent, just-minded, civilized man could rationally favor. In passing upon legislation assailed under the equality clause we have declared that the classification must rest upon a difference which is real, as distinguished from one which is seeming, specious, or fanciful, so that all actually situated similarly will be treated alike; that the object of the classification must be the accomplishment of a purpose or the promotion of a policy, which is within the permissible functions of the State; and that the difference must bear a relation to the object of the legislation which is substantial, as distinguished from one which is speculative, remote or negligible. Subject to this limitation of reasonableness, the equality clause has left unimpaired, both in range and in flexibility, the State's power to classify for purposes of taxation. Can it be said that the classification here in question is unreasonable?

The difference between a business carried on in corporate form and the same business carried on by natural persons is, of course, a real and important one. . . .

In Pennsylvania the practice of imposing heavier burdens upon corporations dates from a time when there, as elsewhere in America, the fear of growing corporate power was common. The present heavier imposition may be a survival of an early effort to discourage the resort to that form of organization. The apprehension is now less common. But there are still intelligent, informed, just-minded and civilized persons who believe that the rapidly growing aggregation of capital through corporations constitutes an insidious menace to the liberty of the citizen; that it tends to increase the subjection of labor to capital; that, because of the guidance and control necessarily exercised by great corporations upon those engaged in business, individual initiative is being impaired and creative power will be lessened;

that the absorption of capital by corporations, and their perpetual life, may bring evils similar to those which attended mortmain; that the evils incident to the accelerating absorption of business by corporations outweigh the benefits thereby secured; and that the process of absorption should be retarded. The Court may think such views unsound. But, obviously, the requirement that a classification must be reasonable does not imply that the policy embodied in the classification made by the legislature of a State shall seem to this Court a wise one. It is sufficient for us that there is nothing in the Federal Constitution which prohibits a State from imposing a heavier tax burden upon corporations organized for the purpose of engaging exclusively in intrastate commerce; and that there is nothing inherently objectionable in the instrument which Pennsylvania selected for imposing the heavier burden—the gross receipts tax.[32]

The attack upon the statute is rested mainly upon the contention that by requiring issuance of a license to so-called co-operative corporations organized under the law of 1919, the statute as amended in 1925 creates an arbitrary classification. The classification is said to be arbitrary, because the differences between such concerns and commercial corporations or individuals engaged in the same business are in this connection not material. The contention rests, I think, upon misapprehensions of fact. The differences are vital; and the classification is a reasonable one. . . .

The claim rests wholly on the fact that individuals and ordinary corporations must show inadequacy of existing facilities, while co-operatives organized under the Act of 1919 may secure a license without making such a showing, if the application is supported by a petition of one hundred persons who are citizens and taxpayers in the community. It is settled that to provide specifically for peculiar needs of farmers or producers is a reasonable basis of classification, *American Sugar Refining Co. v. Louisiana*, 179 U.S. 89; *Liberty Warehouse Co. v. Tobacco Growers*, 276 U.S. 71. And it is conceded that the classification made by the Act of 1925 would be reasonable if it had been limited to co-operatives organized under Chapter 22 of the Laws of 1917. Thus the contention that the classification is arbitrary is directed only to co-operatives organized under the law of 1919. It rests upon two erroneous assumptions: (1) That co-operatives organized under the law of 1919 are substantially unlike those organized under Chapter 22 of the Laws of 1917; and (2) that there are between co-operative corporations under the law of 1919 and commercial corporations no substantial differences having reasonable relation to the subject dealt with by the gin legislation.

The assertion is that co-operatives organized under the law of 1919, being stock companies, do business with the general public for the sole purpose of making money, as do individual or other corporate competitors; whereas co-operatives organized under the law of 1917 are "for mutual help, without capital stock, not conducted for profit, and restricted to the business of their own members." The fact is that these two types of co-operative corporations—the stock and the nonstock—differ from one another only in a few details, which are without significance in this connection; that both are instrumentalities commonly employed to promote and effect co-operation among farmers; that the two serve the same purpose; and that both differ vitally from commercial corporations. The farmers seek through both to secure a more efficient system of production and distribution and a more equitable allocation of benefits. But this is not their only purpose. Besides promoting the financial advantage of the participating farmers, they seek through co-operation to socialize their interests—to require an equitable assumption of responsibilities, while assuring an equitable distribution of benefits. Their aim is economic democracy on lines of liberty, equality, and fraternity. To accomplish these objectives, both types of co-operative corporations provide for excluding capitalist control. As means to this end, both provide for restriction of voting privileges, for curtailment of return on capital and for distribution of gains or savings through patronage dividends or equivalent devices.

In order to ensure economic democracy, the Oklahoma Act of 1919 prevents any person from becoming a shareholder without the consent of the board of directors. It limits the amount of stock which one person may hold to $500. And it limits the voting power of a shareholder to one vote. Thus, in the Durant Company, the holder of a single share of the par value of $10 has as much voting power as the holder of 50 shares. The Act further discourages entrance of mere capitalists into the co-operative by provisions which permit five per cent of the profits to be set aside for educational purposes; which require ten per cent of the profits to be set aside as a reserve fund, until such fund shall equal at least fifty per cent of the capital stock; which limit the annual dividends on stock to eight per cent; and which require that the rest of the year's profits be distributed as patronage dividends to members, except so far as the directors may apportion them to non-members.

The provisions for the exclusion of capitalist control of the nonstock type of co-operative organized under the Oklahoma Act of 1917 do not differ materially in character from those in the 1919 Act. The nonstock co-operative also may reject applicants for membership; and no member may have more than one vote. This type of co-operative is called a non-profit organization; but the term is merely one of art, indicating the manner in which the financial advantage is distributed. This type also is organized and conducted for the financial benefit of its members and requires capital with which to conduct its business. In the stock type the capital is obtained by the issue of capital stock, and members are not subjected to personal liability for the corporation's business obligations. In the nonstock type the capital is obtained partly from membership fees, partly through dues or assessments and partly through loans from members or others. And for fixed capital it substitutes in part personal liability of members for the corporation's obligations. In the stock type there are *eo nomine* dividends on capital and patronage dividends. In the nonstock type the financial benefit is distributed by way of interest on loans and refunds of fees, dues and assessments. And all funds acquired through the co-operative's operations, which are in excess of the amount desirable for a "working fund," are to be distributed as refunds of fees, dues and assessments. Both acts allow business to be done for non-members; and though the nonstock association may, it is not required, to impose obligations on the non-member for the liability of the association. Thus, for the purposes here relevant, there is no essential difference between the two types of co-operatives. . . .

That in Oklahoma a law authorizing incorporation on the stock plan was essential to the development of co-operation among farmers has been demonstrated by the history of the movement in that State. Prior to 1917 there was no statute which specifically authorized the incorporation of co-operatives. In that year the nonstock law above referred to was enacted. Two years passed and only three co-operatives availed themselves of the provisions of that Act. Then persons familiar with the farmers' problems in Oklahoma secured the passage of the law of 1919, providing for the incorporation of co-operatives with capital stock. Within the next five years 202 co-operatives were formed under it; and since then 139 more. In the twelve years since 1917 only 60 nonstock co-operatives have been organized; most of them since 1923, when through an amendatory statute, this type was made to offer special advantages for co-operative marketing. Thus over 82 per cent of all co-operatives in Oklahoma are organized under the 1919 stock act. One hundred and one Oklahoma co-operative cotton gins have been organized under the 1919 stock law; not a single one under the 1917 nonstock law. To deny the co-operative character of the 1919 Act is to deny the co-operative character not only of the gins in Oklahoma which farmers have organized and operated for their mutual benefit, but also that of most other co-operatives within the State, which have been organized under its statutes in harmony with legislation of Congress and pursuant to instructions from the United States Department of Agriculture. A denial of co-operative character to the stock co-operatives is inconsistent also with the history of the movement in other States and countries. For the stock type of co-operative is not only the older form, but is the type more widely used among English speaking peoples.[33]

The veto power of the Supreme Court over the social-economic legislation of the States, when exercised by a narrow conception of the due process and equal protection of the law clauses, presents undue centralization in its most destructive and least responsible form. The most destructive, because it stops experiment at its source, preventing an increase of social knowledge by the only scientific method available, the test of trial and error. The least responsible, because it so often turns on the fortuitous circumstances which determine a majority decision, and shelters the fallible judgment of individual Justices, in matters of fact and opinion not peculiarly within the special competence of judges, behind the impersonal authority of the Constitution. The inclination of a single Justice, the buoyancy of his hopes or the intensity of his fears, may determine the opportunity of a much-needed social experiment to survive, or may frustrate for a long time intelligent attempts to deal with a social evil. Against these dangers the only safeguards are judges thoroughly awake to the problems of their day and open-minded to the facts which may justify legislation. His wide experience, his appetite for fact, his instinct for the concrete and his distrust of generalities, equip Mr. Justice Brandeis with unique gifts for the discharge of the Court's most difficult and delicate tasks.

V

No aspect of state intervention in the conduct of private enterprise forms a more settled policy of American public law than the regulation of the social services furnished by "public utilities." Comprehensive utility control initiated a quarter of a century ago by the elder La Follette in Wisconsin,[34] and Governor Hughes in New York,[35] is now part of the governmental machinery of every state. Its rationale is public protection through administrative regulation capable of matching in power and technical resources the power and resources of the utilities. The judicial control of this regulatory system has given rise to the severest conflicts in our time between courts and popular opinion, between the Supreme Court and the States.

The heart of the difficulty has been the Court's attitude, during the period of post-war inflation, regarding the profits to which utility investors are constitutionally entitled and the rates which may be exacted from the consuming public. Economic questions were transmuted into unreal legal conceptions, for the ascertainment of the rate base and the determination of utility rates are essentially economic problems. It took nearly a generation to settle the share which the Court now exercises in these economic adjustments.[36] But the intrinsic nature of the problem was not changed by the change in forum, from legislature to commission, from commission to court. And the source of the Court's authority in this domain of litigation still remains the general admonitions of fair dealing of the due process clauses. However verbally screened, determinations by the Court in valuation cases are not adjudications governed by technical legal principles. They are exercises of judgment on economic facts and opinion. Through the generality of language in *Smyth* v. *Ames*,[37] an empiric device for preventing swollen returns on fictitious values during a period of falling prices, was in course of time, during a period of rising prices, in a series of cases beginning in 1923, turned into a most luxuriant means for creating fictitious values. For this economic legerdemain constitutional sanction was sought, and in part, for a time at least, largely gained.

Leadership against that tendency fell to Mr. Justice Brandeis. His series of massive opinions, drawn from his intimate railroad experiences and reinforced by elaborate research, constitutes a treatise on the major issues of railroad economics. The late Allyn A. Young, most sagacious of economists, characterized the dissent of Mr. Justice Brandeis in *Southwestern Bell Tel. Co.* v. *Public Serv. Comm.*[38] as the ablest critique of the economics of utility valuation. To detach part from a closely knit exposition in which each step is buttressed by proof is to mutilate. But even a torso conveys intimations of an artistic whole.

The so-called rule of *Smyth* v. *Ames* is, in my opinion, legally and economically unsound. The thing devoted by the investor to the public use is not specific property, tangible and intangible, but capital embarked in the enterprise. Upon the capital so invested the Federal Constitution guarantees to the utility the opportunity to earn a fair return. . . .

The investor agrees, by embarking capital in a utility, that its charges to the public shall be reasonable. His company is the substitute for the State in the performance of the public service; thus becoming a public servant. The compensation which the Constitution guarantees an opportunity to earn is the reasonable cost of conducting the business. Cost includes not only operating expenses, but also capital charges. Capital charges cover the allowance, by way of interest, for the use of the capital, whatever the nature of the security issued therefor; the allowance for risk incurred; and enough more to attract capital. The reasonable rate to be prescribed by a commission may allow an efficiently managed utility much more. But a rate is constitutionally compensatory, if it allows to the utility the opportunity to earn the cost of the service as thus defined.

To decide whether a proposed rate is confiscatory, the tribunal must determine both what sum would be earned under it, and whether that sum would be a fair return. The decision involves ordinarily the making of four subsidiary ones:

1. What the gross earnings from operating the utility under the rate in controversy would be. (A prediction.)

2. What the operating expenses and charges, while so operating, would be. (A prediction.)

3. The rate-base, that is, what the amount is on which a return should be earned. (Under *Smyth* v. *Ames*, an opinion, largely.)

4. What rate of return should be deemed fair. (An opinion, largely.)

A decision that a rate is confiscatory (or compensatory) is thus the resultant of four subsidiary determinations. Each of the four involves forming a judgment, as distinguished from ascertaining facts. And as to each factor, there is usually room for difference in judgment. But the first two factors do not ordinarily present serious difficulties. The doubts and uncertainties incident to prophecy, which affect them, can, often, be resolved by a test period; and meanwhile protection may be afforded by giving a bond. *Knoxville* v. *Knoxville Water Co.*, 212 U.S. 1, 18, 19; *St. Louis, Iron Mountain & Southern Ry. Co.* v. *McKnight*, 244 U.S. 368. The doubts and uncertainties incident to the last two factors can be eliminated, or lessened, only by redefining the rate base, called value, and the measure of fairness in return, now applied under the rule of *Smyth* v. *Ames*. The experience of the twenty-five years since that case was decided has demonstrated that the rule there enunciated is delusive. In the attempt to apply it insuperable obstacles have been encountered. It has failed to afford adequate protection either to capital or to the public. It leaves open the door to grave injustice. To give to capital embarked in public utilities the protection guaranteed by the Constitution, and to secure for the public reasonable rates, it is essential that the rate base be definite, stable, and readily ascertainable; and that the percentage to be earned on the rate base be measured by the cost, or charge, of the capital employed in the enterprise. It is consistent with the Federal Constitution for this Court now to lay down a rule which will establish such a rate base and such a measure of the rate of return deemed fair. In my opinion, it should do so. . . .

The expense and loss now incident to recurrent rate controversies is also very large. The most serious vice of the present rule for fixing the rate base is not the existing uncertainty; but that the method does not lead to certainty. Under it, the value for rate-making purposes must ever be an unstable factor. Instability is a standing menace of renewed controversy. The direct expense to the utility of maintaining an army of experts and of counsel is appalling. The indirect cost is far greater. The attention of officials high and low is, necessarily, diverted from the constructive tasks of efficient operation and of development. The public relations of the utility to the community are apt to become more and more strained. And a victory for the utility, may in the end, prove more disastrous than defeat would have been. The community defeated, but unconvinced, remembers; and may refuse aid when the company has occasion later to require its consent or coöperation in the conduct and development of its enterprise. Controversy with utilities is obviously injurious also to the public interest. The prime needs of the community are that facilities be ample and that rates be as low and as stable as possible. The community can get cheap service from private companies, only through cheap capital. It can get efficient service, only if managers of the utility are free to devote themselves to problems of operation and of development. It can get ample service through private companies, only if investors may be assured of receiving continuously a fair return upon the investment.

What is now termed the prudent investment is, in essence, the same thing as that which the Court has always sought to protect in using the term present value. Twenty-five years ago, when *Smyth* v. *Ames* was decided, it was impossible to ascertain with accuracy, in respect to most of the utilities, in most of the States in which rate controversies arose, what it cost in money to establish the utility; or what the money cost with which the utility was established; or what income had been earned by it; or how the income had been expended. It was, therefore, not feasible, then, to adopt, as the rate base, the amount properly invested or, as the rate of fair return, the amount of the capital charge. Now the situation is fundamentally different. These amounts are, now, readily ascertainable in respect to a large, and rapidly increasing, proportion of the utilities. The change in this respect is due to the enlargement, meanwhile, of the powers and functions of state utility commissions. The issue of securities is now, and for many years has been, under the control of commissions, in the leading States. Hence the amount of capital raised (since the conferring of these powers) and its cost are definitely known, through current supervision and prescribed accounts, supplemented by inspection of the commission's engineering force. Like knowledge concerning the investment of that part of the capital raised and expended before these broad functions were exercised by the utility commissions has been secured, in many cases, through investigations undertaken later, in connection with the issue of new securities or the regulation of rates. The amount and disposition of current earnings of all the companies are also known. It is, therefore, feasible now to adopt as the measure of a compensatory rate—the annual cost, or charge, of the capital prudently invested in the utility. And, hence, it should be done.[39]

Exact analysis and a comprehending view of large affairs mark the opinions by Mr. Justice Brandeis which deal with business. In utility cases, he illuminates the known factors, and, in view of the obscurity which still envelops the economic process, is unwilling to substitute judicial judgment for administrative judgment. And he reveals the opportunities of legal science for social invention in the solution of subtle problems like those of depreciation.

No question of law is presented by this assignment of error. The company's objection is not to the particular method selected, but that, in applying it, the master included as depreciation what is called theoretical inadequacy and obsolescence. Whether he did is a question of fact. The city denies that the reduction in value made by the master on account of accrued depreciation includes any sum representing expected loss through future abandonment of the stations. It is clear that, if any deduction was made on account of the probable abandonment of the stations, the obsolescence thus provided for was not theoretical. The new process had been introduced two years before the date as of which the valuation was made. On the facts then known, it was expected that the stations would have to be abandoned in the near future. Because it was to be expected (and was not theoretical) the company contended that to offset it more of the year's savings should have been charged against the income of that year. I cannot say that the master and the court erred in their findings of fact as to the amount of accrued depreciation.

This litigation has already extended over eleven years. The record discloses that the cases were presented below by competent counsel with the aid of competent experts, and that they received careful consideration by an able master and an able trial judge. Counsel, master and court have throughout endeavored to apply the rule of *Smyth* v. *Ames*, 169 U.S. 466. It is not shown that the rule has, in any respect, been departed from. This Court harbors a doubt whether, in applying it, some injustice may not have been done to the company. Is it probable that a nearer approach to justice, as between the parties, will be attained by a continuation of the effort to apply the same rule? To me it seems that the doubt is inherent in the rule itself. It can be overcome only by substituting some other rule for that found to be unworkable. Such other lies near at hand; and it is consistent with the Constitution.

It was settled by *Knoxville* v. *Knoxville Water Co.*, 212 U.S. 1, that every public utility must, at its peril, provide an adequate amount to cover depreciation. A depreciation charge resembles a life insurance premium. The depreciation reserve, to which it is credited, supplies insurance for the plant against its inevitable decadence, as the life insurance reserve supplies the fund to meet the agreed value of the lost human life. To determine what the amount of the annual life insurance premium should be is a much simpler task than to determine the proper depreciation charge. For life insurance is a co-operative undertaking. The premium to be fixed is not that required by the probable duration of the life of a single insured individual, but that required by the average expectancy of life of men or women of the given age. Moreover, for human lives, mortality tables have been constructed which embody the results of large experience and long study. By their use the required premium may be fixed with an approximation to accuracy. But, despite the relative simplicity of the problem, it was found that the variables leave so wide a margin for error that premiums fixed in accordance with mortality tables work serious injustice either to the insurer or to the insured. Although the purpose was to charge only the appropriate premium, the transaction resulted sometimes in bankruptcy of the insurer; sometimes in his securing profits which seemed extortionate; and, rarely, in his receiving only the intended fair compensation for the service rendered. Because every attempt to approximate more nearly the amount of required premium proved futile, justice was sought by another route. Ultimately, strictly mutual insurance was adopted. Under it, the premium charged is made clearly ample; and the part thereof which proves not to have been needed enures in some form to the benefit of him who paid it. Compare *Penn Mutual Life Insurance Co.* v. *Lederer*, 252 U.S. 523, 524, 525.

Legal science can solve the problem of the just depreciation charge for public utilities in a similar manner. Under the rule which fixes the rate base at the amount prudently invested, the inevitable errors incident to fixing the year's depreciation charge do not result in injustice either to the utility or to the community. If, when plant must be replaced, the amount set aside for depreciation proves to have been inadequate, and investment of new capital is required, the utility is permitted to earn the annual cost of the new capital. If, on the other hand, the amount set aside for depreciation proves to have been excessive, the income from the surplus reserve operates as a credit to reduce the current capital charge which the rates must earn. If a new device is adopted which involves additional investment (to buy a new plant or a patent right) the company's investment, on which the return must be paid, is increased by that amount. If the new device does not involve new investment, but the innovation involves increased current payments (like royalties for use of a process) the additional disbursement is borne by the community as an operating expense. The cost of a scrapped plant is carried as part of the investment on which a return must be paid unless and until it has been retired, that is fully paid for, out of the depreciation reserve. Thus, justice both to the owners of the utility and to the public is assured.[40]

To use a depreciation charge as the measure of the year's consumption of plant, and at the same time reject original cost as the basis of the charge, is inadmissible. It is a perversion of this business device. No method for the ascertainment of the amount of the charge yet invented is workable if fluctuating present values be taken as the basis. Every known method contemplates, and is dependent upon, the accumulation or credit of a fixed amount in a given number of years. The distribution of plant expense expressed in the depreciation charge is justified by the approximation to the fact as to the year's plant consumption which is obtained by applying the doctrine of averages. But if fluctuating present values are substituted for original cost there is no stable base to which the process of averaging can be applied. For thereby the only stable factor involved in fixing a depreciation charge would be eliminated. Each year the present value may be different. The cost of replacement at the termination of the service life of the several units or of the composite life cannot be foretold. To use as a measure of the year's consumption of plant a depreciation charge based on fluctuating present values substitutes conjecture for experience. Such a system would require the consumer of today to pay for an assumed operating expense which has never been incurred and which may never arise.

The depreciation charge is frequently likened to the annual premium in legal reserve life insurance. The life insurance premium is calculated on an agreed value of the human life—comparable to the known cost of plant—not on a fluctuating value, unknown and unknowable. The field of life insurance presented a problem comparable to that here involved. Despite the large experience embodied in the standard mortality tables and the relative simplicity of the problem there presented, the actual mortality was found to vary so widely from that for which the premiums had provided, that their rate was found to work serious injustice either to the insurer or to the insured. The transaction resulted sometimes in bankruptcy of the insurer; sometimes in his securing profits which were extortionate; and rarely, in his receiving only the intended fair compensation for the service rendered. Because every attempt to approximate more nearly the amount of premium required proved futile, justice was sought and found in the system of strictly mutual insurance. Under that system the premium charged is made clearly ample; and the part which proves not to have been needed enures in some form of benefit to him who paid it.

Similarly, if, instead of applying the rule of *Smyth* v. *Ames,* the rate base of a utility were fixed at the amount prudently invested, the inevitable errors incident to estimating service life and net expense in plant consumption could never result in injustice either to the utility or to the community. For, if the amount set aside for depreciation proved inadequate and investment of new capital became necessary, the utility would be permitted to earn a return on the new capital. And if the amount set aside for depreciation proved to be excessive, the income from the surplus reserve would operate as a credit to reduce the capital charge which the rates must earn. If the Railways should ever suffer injustice from adopting cost of plant as the basis for calculating the depreciation charge, it will be an unavoidable incident of applying in valuation the rule of *Smyth* v. *Ames.* This risk, if it exists, cannot be escaped by basing the charge on present value. For this suggested escape, besides being entirely conjectural, is instinct with certainty of injustice either to the community or the Railways. The possibility of such injustice admonishes us, as it did in deciding the constitutional questions concerning interstate commerce, *Foster-Fountain Packing Co.* v. *Haydel,* 278 U.S. 1, 10, *Federal Trade Comm'n* v. *Pacific Paper Ass'n,* 273 U.S. 52, 64, and taxation, *Mountain Timber Co.* v. *Washington,* 243 U.S. 219, 237; *Shaffer* v. *Carter,* 252 U.S. 37, 55; *Farmers Loan & Trust Co.* v. *Minnesota, ante* [280 U.S.], p. 204, decided this day, that rate regulation is an intensely practical matter.[41]

Events have clearly vindicated the analysis made by Mr. Justice Brandeis of the reproduction-cost-minus-depreciation doctrine and have underscored his criticisms. His objection to the doctrine on the score both of economic unreality and social waste, has been reinforced by the reports upon the workings of the public service laws of New York[42] and Massachusetts,[43] the continued uncertainty and costliness of rate litigation,[44] and the growing anxiety of utility leaders over a situation supposedly favorable to their interests.[45] The present drastic drop in commodity prices should conclude the argument.[46] Changing conditions will lead a changed Supreme Court to emphasize other factors than those that have heretofore played a decisive part. The very grab-bag nature of the formula in *Smyth* v. *Ames*[47] will enable the Court to pick some things from the bag and neglect others. The familiar process of accommodating general language to new facts will, one ventures to believe, lead the Court in fact, if not in form, to adopt the "prudent investment" doctrine in the protection of those very interests which in recent years, by resort to the reproduction theory, it had overprotected.

VI

Thus far we have considered action by the States within their reserved spheres, limited merely by the negations of the Fourteenth Amendment and never in direct competition with the affirmative powers of the Federal Government. Where the States and Nation touch a field of legislation wherein both may move, fertile opportunities for conflict arise. The Commerce Clause gives controlling authority to the Nation. But how these conflicts are to be resolved—when the Commerce Clause becomes operative and the States have to stand aside, when the States are still free despite the Commerce Clause or because Congress has not seen fit to invoke its authority—depends ultimately upon the philosophy of the Justices regarding our federalism.

Mr. Justice Brandeis' regard for the States is no mere lip service. He is greatly tolerant of their powers because he believes intensely in the opportunities which they afford for decentralization. And he believes in decentralization not because of any persisting habit of political allegiance or through loyalty to an anachronistic theory of states' rights. His views are founded on deep convictions regarding the manageable size for the effective conduct of human affairs and the most favorable conditions for the exercise of wise judgment.

In the practical adjustments between national rule and local diversities, he is keenly mindful that the Nation spans a continent and that, despite the unifying forces of technology, the States for many purposes remain distinctive communities. As to matters not obviously of common national concern, thereby calling for a centralized system of control, the States have a localized knowledge of details, a concreteness of interest and varieties of social policy, which ought to be allowed tolerant scope.

And so he has closely scrutinized objections to state action based merely on remote or hypothetical encroachments upon that national uniformity which is the concern of the Commerce Clause. The ultimate organic nature of society is not a decree of constitutional centralization. Just because the national government will necessarily absorb more and more power, the States ought to be allowed to manage those activities which bear an essential state emphasis. Even though an enterprise is part of the concatenation that makes up interstate and foreign commerce, its local abuses should be removable by local remedies. The protection which states afford to industries within their borders may properly give rise to the states' taxing power, regardless of a nexus of that industry with interstate business.

The statute is an exertion of the police power of the State. Its evident purpose is to prevent a particular species of fraud and imposition found to have been practiced in Pennsylvania upon persons of small means, unfamiliar with our language and institutions. Much of the immigration into the United States is effected by arrangements made here for remittance of the means of travel. The individual immigrant is often an advance guard. After gaining a foothold here, he has his wife and children, aged parents, brothers, sisters or other relatives follow. To this end he remits steamship tickets or orders for transportation. The purchase of the tickets involves trust in the dealer. This is so not only because of the nature of the transaction, but also because a purchaser when unable to pay the whole price at one time makes successive deposits on account, the ticket or order not being delivered until full payment is made. The facilities for remitting both cash and steamship tickets are commonly furnished by private bankers of the same nationality as the immigrant. It was natural that the supervision of persons engaged in the business of supplying steamship tickets should be committed by the statute to the Commissioner of Banking.

Although the purchase made is of an ocean steamship ticket, the transaction regulated is wholly intrastate—as much so as if the purchase were of local real estate or of local theatre tickets. There is no purpose on the part of the State to regulate foreign commerce. The statute is not an obstruction to foreign commerce. It does not discriminate against foreign commerce. It places no direct burden upon such commerce. It does not affect the commerce except indirectly. Congress could, of course, deal with the subject, because it is connected with foreign commerce. But it has not done so. Nor has it legislated on any allied subject. Thus, there can be no contention that Congress has occupied the field. And obviously, also, this is not a case in which the silence of Congress can be interpreted as a prohibition of state action—as a declaration that in the sale of ocean steamship tickets fraud may be practiced without let or hindrance. If Pennsylvania must submit to seeing its citizens defrauded, it is not because Congress has so willed, but because the Constitution so commands. I cannot believe that it does.[48]

The business of the Narragansett Company is an intrastate one. The only electricity sold for use without the State is that agreed to be delivered to the Attleboro Company. That company takes less than 3 per cent of the electricity produced and manufactured by the Narragansett, which has over 70,000 customers in Rhode Island. The problem is essentially local in character. The Commission found as a fact that continuance of the service to the Attleboro Company at the existing rate would prevent the Narragansett from performing its full duty towards its other customers and would be detrimental to the general public welfare. It issued the order specifically to prevent unjust discrimination and to prevent unjust increase in the price to other customers. The Narragansett, a public service corporation of

Rhode Island, is subject to regulation by that State. The order complained of is clearly valid as an exercise of the police power, unless it violates the Commerce Clause.

The power of the State to regulate the selling price of electricity produced and distributed by it within the State and to prevent discrimination is not affected by the fact that the supply is furnished under a long-term contract. *Union Dry Goods Co.* v. *Georgia Public Service Corporation,* 248 U.S. 372. If the Commission lacks the power exercised, it is solely because the electricity is delivered for use in another State. That fact makes the transaction interstate commerce, and Congress has power to legislate on the subject. It has not done so, nor has it legislated on any allied subject, so there can be no contention that it has occupied the field. Nor is this a case in which it can be said that the silence of Congress is a command that the Rhode Island utility shall remain free from the public regulation— that it shall be free to discriminate against the citizens of the State by which it was incorporated and in which it does business. That State may not, of course, obstruct or directly burden interstate commerce. But to prevent discrimination in the price of electricity wherever used does not obstruct or place a direct burden upon interstate commerce.[49]

From the multitude of cases, this general rule may be educed. The validity of a state tax under the commerce clause does not depend upon its character or classification. It is not void merely because it affects or burdens interstate commerce. The tax is void only if it directly burdens such commerce, or (where the burden is indirect) if the tax discriminates against or obstructs interstate commerce. In this case there is no claim that interstate commerce is discriminated against or obstructed. The contention is that the tax imposes a direct burden. Whether the burden should be deemed direct depends upon the character of plaintiff's occupation and its relation to interstate transactions. . . .

The New Orleans tax is obviously not laid upon property moving in interstate commerce. Nor does it, like a gross-receipts tax, lay a burden upon every transaction. It is simply a tax upon one of the instrumentalities of interstate commerce. It is no more a direct burden, than is the tax on the other indispensable instrumentalities; upon the ship; upon the pilot boat, which she must employ; upon the wharf at which she must load and unload; upon the office which the owner would have to hire for his employees, if, instead of engaging the services of an independent contractor, he had preferred to perform those duties himself. The fact that, in this case, the services are performed by an independent contractor having his own established business, and the fact that the services rendered are not limited to soliciting, differentiate this case from *McCall* v. *California*, 136 U.S. 104. If these differences are deemed insufficient to distinguish that case from the one at bar, it should be frankly overruled as inconsistent with the general trend of later decisions.[50]

The corporation maintains in Washington a branch office and a warehouse. There, it does a large intrastate business. Nearly one-half of the aggregate sales of $1,313,275.74 made within the State were local and were from broken packages. It is subjected to two taxes which are separate and distinct. The filing fee is payable only once and as laid was $545. The annual license fee is $580. The latter results in a charge of about one-tenth of one per cent on the intrastate business. The corporation's pay roll there is more than a hundred times as large. These small taxes are obviously not more than a fair contribution to the necessary expenses of the State government. They are the same for foreign corporations as for domestic. In my opinion both taxes are valid.

If the statute sought to impose a tax on corporations engaged wholly in interstate commerce, or if the taxes laid a direct burden upon interstate commerce, or if they were laid upon property without the State, or if they were unjustly discriminatory, the fact that they are small in amount would, of course, be immaterial. *Sprout* v. *City of South Bend*, 277 U.S. 163, 171. But these taxes are not subject to any of those infirmities. The taxes are not laid upon interstate commerce. They are not measured by the amount of interstate commerce. They do not grow, or shrink, according to the volume of interstate commerce or of the capital used in it. They are not furtively directed against such commerce. The taxes would be precisely the same in amount if the corporation did in Washington no interstate business whatsoever. Nor are they taxes laid upon property without the State. Indeed, they are neither property taxes nor substitutes for property taxes. They are an excise, laid solely for the privilege of doing business as a corporation. An individual doing the same business would not be required to pay either these taxes or any substitute therefor.

It would be unfortunate to hold that merely because a foreign corporation, doing a local business does also interstate business, the State may not lay upon it a reasonable, non-discriminatory excise, necessarily limited to a reasonable amount, to which all domestic corporations similarly situated are subjected and which can affect interstate commerce only indirectly, if at all.[51]

Similar issues are raised by the implied immunity from state taxation enjoyed by federal instrumentalities. The simple doctrine by which States and the Nation are forbidden to hamper one another's agencies of government has steadily been tortured beyond its original purpose. The practical result of inflating this doctrine has been the contraction of the allowable area of state taxation, without any compensating gain to the strength or resources of the Federal Government. Here again the influence of Mr. Justice Brandeis has been on the side of the States.

The property taxed is lead and zinc ore in bins. The land from which the ore was extracted belongs to a Quapaw allottee under the Act of March 2, 1895, c. 188, 28 Stat. 876, 907. Restrictions on alienation of the land will not expire until 1946. Act of March 3, 1921, c. 119, § 26, 41 Stat. 1225, 1248. But the allottee may lease the land for mining and business purposes for ten years unless he is incompetent, in which case the power to lease is vested in the Secretary of the Interior. Act of June 7, 1897, c. 3, 30 Stat. 62, 72. The ore in question had been detached from the soil and is personal property. It is owned wholly by the Mining Company, a private Oklahoma corporation organized for profit. The ore is assessed under the general laws of the State which lays an *ad valorem* property tax on all property, real or personal, not exempt by law from taxation. Payment of the tax will not affect the financial return to the Indian under the lease. No state legislation exempts this property. There is no specific or general provision in any act of Congress which purports to do so. If an exemption exists, it arises directly from the Federal Constitution. Does ownership by an incompetent Indian of the land from which the ore was taken or ownership of the ore by an instrumentality of the Government create an exemption? . . .

The rule that the property of a privately owned government agency is not exempt from state taxation rests fundamentally upon the principle that such a tax has only a remote relation to the capacity of such agencies efficiently to serve the Government. Such a tax, as distinguished from an occupation or privilege tax, does not impose a charge upon the privilege of acting as a government agent and thereby enable a State to control the power of the Federal Government to employ agents and the power of persons to accept such employment. The tax is levied as a charge by the State for rendering services relating to the protection of the property, which services are rendered alike to agents of the Government and of private persons. Such a tax cannot be deemed to be capable of deterring the entry of persons as agents into the employ of the Government. Conceivably an operating company might pay a higher royalty or bonus if it were assured that it would enjoy immunity from taxation for the small quantity of the year's output of the mine which might be in the ore bins on the day as of which property is assessed. Conceivably also, the cattle owner in *Thomas* v. *Gay, supra,* might have paid higher for the grazing rights if the cattle while on the reservation were immune from taxation. But, in either case, the effect of the immunity, if any, upon the Indian's financial return would be remote and indirect. If we are to regard realities we should treat it as negligible.

The difference in the legal effect of acts which are remote causes and of those which are proximate pervades the law. The power of a State to tax property and its lack of power to tax the occupation in which it is used exist in other connections. In *Baltimore Shipbuilding Co.* v. *Baltimore,* 195 U.S. 375, 382, where the State had levied a tax upon property conveyed by the United States to the Shipbuilding Company on the condition that it construct a dry dock there for the use of the United States and that, if such dry dock were not kept in repair, the property should revert to the United States, this Court said: "But, furthermore, it seems to us extravagant to say that an independent private corporation for gain, created by a State, is exempt from state taxation, either in its corporate person, or its property, because it is employed by the United States, even if the work for which it is employed is important and takes much of its time."[52]

In the domain of interstate commerce, the States of course must yield the field to Congress when Congress has occupied it. But these familiar phrases are, after all, figures of speech, and figures of speech are dangerous instruments for constitutional law. Whether Congress has occupied the field is not a problem in mensuration. Too often, it is an exercise of judgment about practical affairs; it calls for accommodation between state and national interests in the interacting areas of state and national power. Mr. Justice Brandeis, here also, eschews loose generalities and catchwords. He subjects federal enactment and its challenged state analogue to sharp, precise and comprehensive examination to ascertain whether both may survive or the national law alone can prevail.

We are admonished also by another weighty consideration not to impute to Congress the will to deny to the States this power. The subject of compensation for accidents in industry is one peculiarly appropriate for state legislation. There must, necessarily, be great diversity in the conditions of living and in the needs of the injured and of his dependents, according to whether they reside in one or the other of our States and Territories, so widely extended. In a large majority of instances they reside in the State in which the accident occurs. Though the principle that compensation should be made, or relief given, is of universal application, the great diversity of conditions in the different sections of the United States may, in a wise application of the principle, call for differences between States, in the amount and method of compensation, the periods in which payment shall be made, and the methods and means by which the funds shall be raised and distributed. The field of compensation for injuries appears to be one in which uniformity is *not* desirable, or at least not essential to the public welfare.

The contention that Congress has, by legislating on one branch of a subject relative to interstate commerce, preëmpted the whole field —has been made often in this court; and, as the cases above cited show, has been repeatedly rejected in cases where the will of Congress to leave the balance of the field open to state action was far less clear than under the circumstances here considered. Tested by those decisions and by the rules which this court has framed for its guidance, I am of opinion, as was said in *Atlantic Coast Line R.R. Co.* v. *Georgia*, 234 U.S. 280, 294, that: "The intent to supersede the exercise of the State's police power with respect to this subject cannot be inferred from the restricted action which thus far has been taken." The field covered by Congress was a limited field of the carrier's liability for negligence, not the whole field of the carrier's obligation arising from accidents. I find no justification for imputing to Congress the will to deny to a large class of persons engaged in a necessarily hazardous occupation and otherwise unprovided for the protection afforded by beneficent statutes enacted in the long-deferred performance of an insistent duty and in a field peculiarly appropriate for state action.[53]

The argument mainly urged by the States in support of the claim that Congress has not occupied the entire field, is that the federal and the state laws are aimed at distinct and different evils; that the federal regulation endeavors solely to prevent accidental injury in the operation of trains, whereas the state regulation endeavors to prevent sickness and disease due to excessive and unnecessary exposure; and that whether Congress has entered a field must be determined by the object sought through the legislation, rather than the physical elements affected by it. Did Congress intend that there might still be state regulation of locomotives, if the measure was directed primarily to the promotion of health and comfort and affected safety, if at all, only incidentally?

The federal and the state statutes are directed to the same subject —the equipment of locomotives. They operate upon the same object. It is suggested that the power delegated to the Commission has been exerted only in respect to minor changes or additions. But this, if true, is not of legal significance. It is also urged that, even if the Commission has power to prescribe an automatic firebox door and a cab curtain, it has not done so; and that it has made no other requirement inconsistent with the state legislation. This, also, if true, is without legal significance. The fact that the Commission has not seen fit to exercise its authority to the full extent conferred, has no bearing upon the construction of the Act delegating the power. We hold that state legislation is precluded, because the Boiler Inspection Act, as we construe it, was intended to occupy the field. The broad scope of the authority conferred upon the Commission leads to that conclusion. Because the standard set by the Commission must prevail, requirements by the States are precluded, however commendable or however different their purpose.[54]

Safeguarding peculiar state interests is one thing; to discriminate against the common national interest is quite another. Through intimate acquaintance with the managerial and financial difficulties of railroads, Mr. Justice Brandeis is firm to check the imposition of gratuitous burdens. And behind the semblance of local regulation he is quick to detect a selfish attempt merely to obstruct interstate commerce.

That the claims against interstate carriers for personal injuries and for loss and damage of freight are numerous; that the amounts demanded are large; that in many cases carriers deem it imperative, or advisable, to leave the determination of their liability to the courts; that litigation in States and jurisdictions remote from that in which the cause of action arose entails absence of employees from their customary occupations; and that this impairs efficiency in operation, and causes, directly and indirectly, heavy expense to the carriers; these are matters of common knowledge. Facts, of which we, also, take judicial notice, indicate that the burden upon interstate carriers imposed specifically by the statute here assailed is a heavy one; and that the resulting obstruction to commerce must be serious. . . .

. . . orderly, effective administration of justice clearly does not require that a foreign carrier shall submit to a suit in a State in which the cause of action did not arise, in which the transaction giving rise to it was not entered upon, in which the carrier neither owns nor operates a railroad, and in which the plaintiff does not reside. The public and the carriers are alike interested in maintaining adequate, uninterrupted transportation service at reasonable cost. . . . Avoidance of waste, in interstate transportation, as well as maintenance of service, has become a direct concern of the public. With these ends the Minnesota statute, as here applied, unduly interferes. By requiring from interstate carriers general submission to suit, it unreasonably obstructs, and unduly burdens, interstate commerce.[55]

. . . It may be assumed that §4 of the state statute is consistent with the Fourteenth Amendment; and also, that appropriate state regulations adopted primarily to promote safety upon the highways and conservation in their use are not obnoxious to the Commerce Clause, where the indirect burden imposed upon interstate commerce is not unreasonable. Compare *Michigan Public Utilities Commission* v. *Duke*, 266 U.S. 571. The provision here in question is of a different character. Its primary purpose is not regulation with a view to safety or to conservation of the highways, but the prohibition of competition. It determines not the manner of use, but the persons by whom the highways may be used. It prohibits such use to some persons while permitting it to others for the same purpose and in the same manner. Moreover, it determines whether the prohibition shall be applied by resort, through state officials, to a test which is peculiarly within the province of federal action—the existence of adequate facilities for conducting interstate commerce. The vice of the legislation is dramatically exposed by the fact that the State of Oregon had issued its certificate which may be deemed equivalent to a legislative declaration that, despite existing facilities, public convenience and necessity required the establishment by Buck of the auto stage line between Seattle and Portland. Thus, the provision of the Washington statute is a regulation, not of the use of its own highways, but of interstate commerce. Its effect upon such commerce is not merely to burden but to obstruct it. Such state action is forbidden by the Commerce Clause. It also defeats the purpose of Congress expressed in the legislation giving federal aid for the construction of interstate highways.[56]

It appears that there was nothing in the new location which could in any wise affect injuriously the health of the Railway's employees. The location of the shops at West Tulsa and the vicinity in which employees may live are sanitary. The removal to West Tulsa had cost $150,000. It had resulted in a monthly saving of at least $33,500. It had effected a vast improvement of the interstate and other service. To restore the shops and division point to Sapulpa and make there the improvements essential to good service would require an outlay of $3,000,000, besides the expenditure of $300,000 for the shops; and it would entail in addition the operating expenses then being saved. Even with such large expenditures, restoration of the shops and division point to Sapulpa would inevitably impair interstate and other passenger and freight service. On these facts, which were established by affidavits filed in opposition to the motion to compel restitution, it must have seemed to the District Court at least probable that upon final hearing a permanent injunction would issue; and that to order restitution meanwhile would be, not merely an idle act, compare *Goltra* v. *Weeks*, 271 U.S. 536, 549, but one imposing unnecessary hardship on the Railway and the public.[57]

But whether state action unduly impinges upon interstate commerce depends more and more upon the particularities of fact in individual cases. If the Court is to adhere to tradition in the administration of constitutional law and avoid hypothetical decisions or abstract pronouncements, the record must contain the details which control the application of general doctrine or the Court must insist on their ascertainment.

The contentions made in the briefs and arguments suggest, among other questions, the following: Where there is congestion of city streets sufficient to justify some limitation of the number of motor vehicles to be operated thereon as common carriers, or some prohibition of stops to load or unload passengers, may the limitation or prohibition be applied to some vehicles used wholly or partly in interstate commerce while, at the same time, vehicles of like character, including many that are engaged solely in local, or intrastate, commerce are not subjected thereto? Is the right in the premises to which interstate carriers would otherwise be entitled, affected by the fact that, prior to the establishment of the interstate lines, the City had granted to a local carrier, by contract or franchise, the unlimited right to use all the streets of the City, and that elimination of the interstate vehicles would put an end to the congestion experienced? May the City's right to limit the number of vehicles, and to prohibit stops to load or unload passengers, be exercised in such a way as to allocate streets on which motor traffic is more profitable exclusively to the local lines and to allocate streets on which the traffic is less profitable to the lines engaged wholly, or partly, in interstate commerce? Is limitation of the number of vehicles, or prohibition of stops to load or unload passengers, of carriers engaged wholly, or partly, in interstate commerce, justifiable, where the congestion could be obviated by denying to private carriers existing parking privileges or by curtailing those so enjoyed? Are the rights of the interstate carrier in the premises dependent, in any respect, upon the dates of the establishment of its lines, as compared with the dates of the establishment of the lines of the local carrier?

These questions have not, so far as appears, been considered by either of the lower courts. The facts essential to their determination have not been found by either court. And the evidence in the record is not of such a character that findings could now be made with confidence. The answer denied many of the material allegations of the bill. The evidence consists of the pleadings and affidavits. The pleadings are confusing. The affidavits are silent as to some facts of legal significance; lack definiteness as to some matters; and present serious conflicts on issues of facts that may be decisive. For aught that appears, the lower courts may have differed in their decisions solely because they differed as to conclusions of fact. Before any of the questions suggested, which are both novel and of far reaching importance, are passed upon by this Court, the facts essential to their decision should be definitely found by the lower courts upon adequate evidence.[58]

VII

MARSHALL could draw with large and bold strokes the boundaries of state and national power; today most crucial issues involve the concrete application of settled, general doctrines. The fate of vast interests and hopeful reforms, the traditional contest between centralization and local rule, now turn on questions of more or less, on matters of degree, on drawing lines, sometimes very fine lines. Decisions therefore depend more and more on precise formulation of the issues embedded in litigation, and on alertness regarding the exact scope of past decisions in the light of their present significance. The Court's conception of its own function and awareness of its processes in constitutional adjudication, determine the Constitution in action.

In his whole temperament, Mr. Justice Brandeis is poles

apart from the attitude of the technically-minded lawyer. Yet no member of the Court invokes more rigorously the traditional limits of its jurisdiction.[59] In view of our federalism and the Court's peculiar function, questions of jurisdiction in constitutional adjudications imply questions of political power. The history of the Court and the nature of its business admonish against needless or premature decisions. It has no greater duty than the duty not to decide, or not to decide beyond its circumscribed authority. And so Mr. Justice Brandeis will decide only if the record presents a *case*—a live, concrete, present controversy between litigants.

When the bill was filed [to enjoin the construction of the Boulder Dam], the construction of the dam and reservoir had not been commenced. Years must elapse before the project is completed. If by operations at the dam any then perfected right of Arizona, or of those claiming under it, should hereafter be interfered with, appropriate remedies will be available. . . . The bill alleges, that plans have been drawn and permits granted for the taking of additional water in Arizona pursuant to its laws. But Wilbur threatens no physical interference with these projects; and the Act interposes no legal inhibitions on their execution. There is no occasion for determining now Arizona's rights to interstate or local waters which have not yet been, and which may never be, appropriated. . . . This Court cannot issue declaratory decrees.[60]

When the record does present a case and judgment must be rendered, constitutional determination must be avoided if a nonconstitutional ground disposes of the immediate litigation.

If protection of the rights of The Chastleton Corporation and Hahn required us to pass upon the constitutionality of the District Rent Acts, I should agree, also, to the procedure directing the lower court to ascertain the facts. But, in my opinion, it does not. For (on facts hereinafter stated which appear by the bill and which were, also, admitted at the bar) the order entered by the Commission is void as to them, even if the Rent Acts are valid. To express an opinion upon the constitutionality of the acts, or to sanction the enquiry directed, would, therefore, be contrary to a long-prevailing practice of the Court.[61]

Moreover, the duty to abstain from adjudicating, particularly in the field of public law, may arise from the restricted nature of the judicial process. The specific claim before the Court may be enmeshed in larger public issues beyond the Court's reach of investigation, or a suitable remedy may exceed judicial resources. Such a situation, even though formally disguised as a case, eludes adjudication. To forego judgment under such circumstances is not abdication of judicial power, but recognition of rational limits to its competence. Law is only partly in the keeping of courts; much must be left to legislation and administration. Nor does the absence of legislation create a vacuum to be occupied by judicial action.

The rule for which the plaintiff contends would effect an important extension of property rights and a corresponding curtailment of the free use of knowledge and of ideas; and the facts of this case admonish us of the danger involved in recognizing such a property right in news, without imposing upon news-gatherers corresponding obligations. A large majority of the newspapers and perhaps half the newspaper readers of the United States are dependent for their news of general interest upon agencies other than the Associated Press. The channel through which about 400 of these papers received, as the plaintiff alleges, "a large amount of news relating to the European war of the greatest importance and of intense interest to the newspaper reading public" was suddenly closed. The closing to the International News Service of these channels for foreign news (if they were closed) was due not to unwillingness on its part to pay the cost of collecting the news, but to the prohibitions imposed by foreign governments upon its securing news from their respective countries and from using cable or telegraph lines running therefrom. For aught that appears, this prohibition may have been wholly undeserved; and at all events the 400 papers and their readers may be assumed to have been innocent. For aught that appears, the International News Service may have sought then to secure temporarily by arrangement with the Associated Press the latter's foreign news service. For aught that appears, all of the 400 subscribers of the International News Service would gladly have then become members of the Associated Press, if they could have secured election thereto. It is possible, also, that a large part of the readers of these papers were so situated that they could not secure prompt access to papers served by the Associated Press. The prohibition of the foreign governments might as well have been extended to the channels through which news was supplied to the more than a thousand other daily papers in the United States not served by the Associated Press; and a large part of their readers may also be so located that they cannot procure prompt access to papers served by the Associated Press.

A legislature, urged to enact a law by which one news agency or newspaper may prevent appropriation of the fruits of its labors by another, would consider such facts and possibilities and others which appropriate enquiry might disclose. . . .

Courts are ill-equipped to make the investigations which should precede a determination of the limitations which should be set upon any property right in news or of the circumstances under which news gathered by a private agency should be deemed affected with a public interest. Courts would be powerless to prescribe the detailed regulations essential to full enjoyment of the rights conferred or to introduce the machinery required for enforcement of such regulations. Considerations such as these should lead us to decline to establish a new rule of law in the effort to redress a newly-disclosed wrong, although the propriety of some remedy appears to be clear.[62]

The decisions to be made [regarding the allocations of West Virginia natural gas as between West Virginia consumers and those of other States] would be of the character which calls for the informed judgment of a board of experts. The tribunal would have to determine, among other things, whether inadequate service was due in the several States to inadequate supply or to improvident use by some consumers; whether to overcome inadequacy of supply new territory should be developed or more wells be sunk in old territory; whether, in view of prospective needs of the several communities, it would not be better that the reserves should be husbanded and that the uses to which gas may be put be curtailed. It would, thus, be called upon to review—and perhaps to control—the business judgment of those managing the companies. Pro rata distribution among all users of the gas from time to time available would obviously not result in equitable distribution. For domestic users, and also many industrial ones, would, if their gas supply were uncertain, find it necessary to assure themselves of an adequate supply for heating, cooking and power, of either oil or some other kind of fuel; and the expense of producing the necessary alternative appliances would be large. The tribunal would have to decide, also, many other serious questions of the character usually committed for determination to public utility commissions, and the difficulties involved in these decisions would be much enhanced by differences in the laws, rules and practices of the several States regarding the duties of natural gas companies to furnish adequate service.

Clearly, this Court could not undertake such determinations. To make equitable distribution would be a task of such complexity and difficulty that even an interstate public service commission with broad powers, perfected administrative machinery, ample resources, practical experience and no other duties, might fail to perform it satisfactorily. As this Court would be powerless to frame a decree and provide machinery by means of which such equitable distribution of the available supply could be effected, it should, according to settled practice, refuse to entertain the suits.[63]

Even though the abstract conditions for judicial competence exist, the Supreme Court may not be the fittest tribunal for its exercise. When cases depend on subtle appreciation of complicated local arrangements or the interpretation of state enactments not yet interpreted by state courts nor yielding their meaning merely to a reading of English, original interpretations by the Supreme Court are likely to be *in vacuo*. The local court, whether state or federal, has judicial antennae for local situations seldom vouchsafed to the tribunal at Washington. The Supreme Court should draw on the experience and judgment of the local courts before giving ultimate judgment upon local law.

If it be true that the Railway is not bound by the fare provisions, unless the City had power to bind itself in that respect, it is necessary to determine whether the City had that power and whether the parties did in fact contract as to the rate of fare. Whether the City had the power is, of course, a question of state law. In California, the constitution and the statutes leave the question in doubt. Counsel agree that there is no decision in any court of the State directly in point. They reason from policy and analogy. In support of their several contentions they cite, in the aggregate, 30 decisions of the California courts, 15 statutes of the State, besides 3 provisions of its code and 7 provisions of its constitution. The decisions referred to occupy 308 pages of the official reports; the sections of the constitution, code and statutes, 173 pages. Moreover, the 102 franchises here involved were granted at many different times between 1886 and 1927. And during that long period, there have been amendments both of relevant statutes and of the constitution. The City or the County may have had the power to contract as to the rate of fare at one time and not at another. If it is held that the City or the County ever had the power to contract as to rate of fare, it will be necessary to examine the 102 franchises to see whether the power was exercised. It may then be that some of the franchises contain valid fare contracts, while others do not. In that event, the relief to be granted will involve passing also on matters of detail.

In my opinion, these questions of statutory construction, and all matters of detail, should, in the first instance, be decided by the trial court. To that end, the judgment of the District Court should be vacated and the case remanded for further proceedings, without costs to either party in this Court. Pending the decision of the trial court an interlocutory injunction should issue. Compare *City of Hammond v. Schappi Bus Line*, 275 U.S. 164; *City of Hammond v. Farina Bus Line & Transportation Co.*, 275 U.S. 173; *Ohio Oil Co. v. Conway*, 279 U.S. 813. It is a serious task for us to construe and apply the written law of California. Compare *Gilchrist v. Interborough Rapid Transit Co.*, 279 U.S. 159, 207–209. To "one brought up within it, varying emphasis, tacit assumptions, unwritten practices, a thousand influences gained only from life, may give to the different parts wholly new values that logic and grammar never could have got from the books." *Diaz v. Gonzalez*, 261 U.S. 102,

106. This Court is not peculiarly fitted for that work. We may properly postpone the irksome burden of examining the many relevant state statutes and decisions until we shall have had the aid which would be afforded by a thorough consideration of them by the judges of the District Court, who are presumably more familiar with the law of California than we are. The practice is one frequently followed by this Court.

In the case at bar, there are persuasive reasons for adopting the course suggested. The subject matter of this litigation is local to California. The parties are all citizens of that State and creatures of its legislature. Since the Railway denies that there ever was a valid contract governing the rate and asserts that if any such existed they have been abrogated, the contract clause of the Federal Constitution is not involved. The alleged existence of contracts concerning the rate of fare presents the fundamental issue of the case. Whether such contracts exist, or ever existed, depends wholly upon the construction to be given to laws of the State. Upon these questions, the decision of the Supreme Court of California would presumably have been accepted by this Court, if the case had come here on appeal from it. . . .

The constitutional claim of confiscation gave jurisdiction to the District Court. We may be required, therefore, to pass, at some time, upon these questions of state law. And we may do so now. But the special province of this Court is the Federal law. The construction and application of the Constitution of the United States and of the legislation of Congress is its most important function. In order to give adequate consideration to the adjudication of great issues of government, it must, so far as possible, lessen the burden incident to the disposition of cases, which come here for review.[64]

And when, finally, a constitutional decision is rendered not the language in explanation of it, but the terms of the controversy which called it forth alone determine the extent of its sway. This is merely the common-law lawyer's general disrespect for dicta; but in constitutional adjudications dicta are peculiarly pernicious usurpers. To let even accumulated dicta govern, is to give the future no hearing. And immortality does not inhere even in constitutional decisions. The Constitution owes its continuity to a continuous process of revivifying changes. "The Constitution can not make itself; some body made it, not at once but at several times. It is alterable; and by that draweth nearer Perfection; and without suiting itself to differing Times and Circumstances, it could not live. Its Life is prolonged by changing seasonably the several Parts of it at several times."[65] So wrote the shrewd Lord Halifax, and it is as true of our written Constitution as of that strange medley of imponderables which is the British Constitution. A ready and delicate sense of the need for alteration is perhaps the most precious talent required of the Supreme Court. Upon it depends the vitality of the Constitution as a vehicle for life.

I suspect that my brethren would agree with me in sustaining this tax on ore in the bins but for *Gillespie v. Oklahoma*, 257 U.S. 501. The question there involved was different. Any language in the opinion which may seem apposite to the case at bar, should be disregarded as inconsistent with the earlier decisions. It is a peculiar virtue of our system of law that the process of inclusion and exclusion, so often employed in developing a rule, is not allowed to end with its enunciation and that an expression in an opinion yields later to the impact of facts unforeseen. The attitude of the Court in this respect has been especially helpful when called upon to adjust the respective powers of the States and the Nation in the field of taxation.[66]

The recent legislation of Congress seeks, in a statesmanlike manner, to limit the practical scope and effect of our decisions in *Southern Pacific Co.* v. *Jensen*, 244 U.S. 205; *Knickerbocker Ice Co.* v. *Stewart*, 253 U.S. 149, and later cases, by making them hereafter applicable only to the relations of the ship to her master and crew. To hold that Congress can effect this result by sanctioning the application of state workmen's compensation laws to accidents to any other class of employees occurring on the navigable waters of the State would not, in my judgment, require us to overrule any of these cases. It would require merely that we should limit the application of the rule therein announced, and that we should declare our disapproval of certain expressions used in the opinions. Such limitation of principles previously announced, and such express disapproval of *dicta*, are often necessary. It is an unavoidable incident of the search by courts of last resort for the true rule. The process of inclusion and exclusion, so often applied in developing a rule, cannot end with its first enunciation. The rule as announced must be deemed tentative. For the many and varying facts to which it will be applied cannot be foreseen. Modification implies growth. It is the life of the law.

If the Court is of opinion that this act of Congress is in necessary conflict with its recent decisions, those cases should be frankly overruled. The reasons for doing so are persuasive. Our experience in attempting to apply the rule, and helpful discussions by friends of the Court, have made it clear that the rule declared is legally unsound; that it disturbs legal principles long established; and that if adhered to, it will make a serious addition to the classes of cases which this Court is required to review. Experience and discussion have also made apparent how unfortunate are the results, economically and socially. It has, in part, frustrated a promising attempt to alleviate some of the misery, and remove some of the injustice, incident to the conduct of industry and commerce. These far-reaching and unfortunate results of the rule declared in *Southern Pacific Co.* v. *Jensen* cannot have been foreseen when the decision was rendered. If it is adhered to, appropriate legislative provision, urgently needed, cannot be made until another amendment of the Constitution shall have been adopted. For no federal workmen's compensation law could satisfy the varying and peculiar economic and social needs incident to the diversity of conditions in the several States.

The doctrine of *stare decisis* should not deter us from overruling that case and those which follow it. The decisions are recent ones. They have not been acquiesced in. They have not created a rule of property around which vested interests have clustered. They affect solely matters of a transitory nature. On the other hand, they affect seriously the lives of men, women and children, and the general welfare. *Stare decisis* is ordinarily a wise rule of action. But it is not a universal, inexorable command. The instances in which the Court has disregarded its admonition are many. The existing admiralty jurisdiction rests, in large part, upon like action of the Court in *The Genesee Chief*, 12 How. 443, 456. In that case the Court overruled *The Thomas Jefferson*, 10 Wheat. 428, and *The Steamboat Orleans v. Phoebus*, 11 Pet. 175; and a doctrine declared by Mr. Justice Story with the concurrence of Chief Justice Marshall, and approved by Chancellor Kent, was abandoned when found to be erroneous, although it had been acted on for twenty-six years.[67]

It is usually more important that a rule of law be settled, than that it be settled right. Even where the error in declaring the rule is a matter of serious concern, it is ordinarily better to seek correction by legislation. Often this is true although the question is a constitutional one. The human experience embodied in the doctrine of *stare decisis* teaches us, also, that often it is better to follow a precedent, although it does not involve the declaration of a rule. This is usually true so far as concerns a particular statute whether the error was made in construing it or in passing upon its validity. But the doctrine of *stare decisis* does not command that we err again when we have occasion to pass upon a different statute. In the search for truth through the slow process of inclusion and exclusion, involving trial and error, it behooves us to reject, as guides, the decisions upon such questions which prove to have been mistaken. This course seems to me imperative when, as here, the decision to be made involves the delicate adjustment of conflicting claims of the Federal Government and the States to regulate commerce. The many cases on the Commerce Clause in which this Court has overruled or explained away its earlier decisions show that the wisdom of this course has been heretofore recognized. In the case at bar, also, the logic of words should yield to the logic of realities.[68]

VIII

A PHILOSOPHY of intellectual humility determines Mr. Justice Brandeis' conception of the Supreme Court's function: an instinct against the tyranny of dogma and skepticism regarding the perdurance of any man's wisdom, though he be judge. No one knows better than he how slender a reed is reason— how recent its emergence in man, how powerful the countervailing instincts and passions, how treacherous the whole rational process. But just because the efforts of reason are tenuous, a constant process of critical scrutiny of the tentative claims of reason is essential to the very progress of reason. Truth and knowledge can function and flourish only if error may freely be exposed. And error will go unchallenged if dogma, no matter how widely accepted or dearly held, may not be questioned. Man must be allowed to challenge it by speech or by pen, not merely by silent thought. Thought, like other instincts, will atrophy unless formally exercised. If men cannot speak or write freely, they will soon cease to think freely. Limits there are, of course, even to this essential condition of a free society. But they do not go beyond the minimum requirements of an imminent and substantial threat to the very society which makes individual freedom significant. Together with his colleagues, Mr. Justice Brandeis has refused to make freedom of speech an absolute. But the test of freedom of speech is readiness "to allow it to men whose opinions seem to you wrong and even dangerous."[69]

The extent to which Congress may, under the Constitution, interfere with free speech was in *Schenck* v. *United States*, 249 U.S. 47, 52, declared by a unanimous court to be this:—"The question in every case is whether the words used are used in such circumstances and are of such a nature as to create a clear and present danger that they will bring about the substantive evils that Congress has a right to prevent. It is a question of proximity and degree."

This is a rule of reason. Correctly applied, it will preserve the right of free speech both from suppression by tyrannous, well-meaning majorities and from abuse by irresponsible, fanatical minorities. Like many other rules for human conduct, it can be applied correctly only by the exercise of good judgment; and to the exercise of good judgment, calmness is, in times of deep feeling and on subjects which excite passion, as essential as fearlessness and honesty. The question whether in a particular instance the words spoken or written fall within the permissible curtailment of free speech is, under the rule enunciated by this court, one of degree. And because it is a question of degree the field in which the jury may exercise its judgment is, necessarily, a wide one. But its field is not unlimited. The trial provided for is one by judge *and* jury; and the judge may not abdicate his function. If the words were of such a nature and were used under such circumstances that men, judging in calmness, could not reasonably say that they created a clear and present danger that they would bring about the evil which Congress sought and had a right to prevent, then it is the duty of the trial judge to withdraw the case from the consideration of the jury; and if he fails to do so, it is the duty of the appellate court to correct the error. In my opinion, no jury acting in calmness could reasonably say that any of the publications set forth in the indictment was of such a character or was made under such circumstances as to create a clear and present danger either that they would obstruct recruiting or that they would promote the success of the enemies of the United States.[70]

A verdict should have been directed for the defendants on these counts also because the leaflet was not distributed under such circumstances, nor was it of such a nature, as to create a clear and present danger of causing either insubordination, disloyalty, mutiny or refusal of duty in the military or naval forces. The leaflet contains lurid and perhaps exaggerated pictures of the horrors of war. Its arguments as to the causes of this war may appear to us shallow and grossly unfair. The remedy proposed may seem to us worse than the evil which, it is argued, will be thereby removed. But the leaflet, far from counselling disobedience to law, points to the hopelessness of protest, under the existing system, pictures the irresistible power of the military arm of the Government, and indicates that acquiescence is a necessity. Insubordination, disloyalty, mutiny and refusal of duty in the military or naval forces are very serious crimes. It is not conceivable that any man of ordinary intelligence and normal judgment would be induced by anything in the leaflet to commit them and thereby risk the severe punishment prescribed for such offences. Certainly there was no clear and present danger that such would be the result. . . .

The fundamental right of free men to strive for better conditions through new legislation and new institutions will not be preserved, if efforts to secure it by argument to fellow citizens may be construed as criminal incitement to disobey the existing law—merely, because the argument presented seems to those exercising judicial power to be unfair in its portrayal of existing evils, mistaken in its assumptions, unsound in reasoning or intemperate in language. No objections more serious than these can, in my opinion, reasonably be made to the arguments presented in "The Price We Pay."[71]

As the Minnesota statute is in my opinion invalid because it interferes with federal functions and with the right of a citizen of the United States to discuss them, I see no occasion to consider whether it violates also the Fourteenth Amendment. But I have difficulty in believing that the liberty guaranteed by the Constitution, which has been held to protect against state denial the right of an employer to discriminate against a workman because he is a member of a trade union, *Coppage* v. *Kansas*, 236 U.S. 1, the right of a business man to conduct a private employment agency, *Adams* v. *Tanner*, 244 U.S. 590, or to contract outside the State for insurance of his property, *Allgeyer* v. *Louisiana*, 165 U.S. 578, 589, although the legislature deems it inimical to the public welfare, does not include liberty to teach, either in the privacy of the home or publicly, the doctrine of pacifism; so long, at least, as Congress has not declared that the public safety demands its suppression. I cannot believe that the liberty guaranteed by the Fourteenth Amendment includes only liberty to acquire and to enjoy property.[72]

Freedom of speech and freedom of assembly are empty phrases if their exercise must yield to unreasonable fear. Great social convulsions like the Russian Revolution are bound to have their repercussion of panic among the timid and humorless, particularly panic stimulated by all the modern incitements to mass feeling. Such times present the decisive occasions for a stern enforcement of the right to air grievances, however baseless, and to propose remedies even more cruel than the grievances.

This Court has not yet fixed the standard by which to determine when a danger shall be deemed clear; how remote the danger may be and yet be deemed present; and what degree of evil shall be deemed sufficiently substantial to justify resort to abridgement of free speech and assembly as the means of protection. To reach sound conclusions on these matters, we must bear in mind why a State is, ordinarily, denied the power to prohibit dissemination of social, economic and political doctrine which a vast majority of its citizens believes to be false and fraught with evil consequence.

Those who won our independence believed that the final end of the State was to make men free to develop their faculties; and that in its government the deliberative forces should prevail over the arbitrary. They valued liberty both as an end and as a means. They believed liberty to be the secret of happiness and courage to be the secret of liberty. They believed that freedom to think as you will and to speak as you think are means indispensable to the discovery and spread of political truth; that without free speech and assembly discussion would be futile; that with them, discussion affords ordinarily adequate protection against the dissemination of noxious doctrine; that the greatest menace to freedom is an inert people; that public discussion is a political duty; and that this should be a fundamental principle of the American government. They recognized the risks to which all human institutions are subject. But they knew that order cannot be secured merely through fear of punishment for its infraction; that it is hazardous to discourage thought, hope and imagination; that fear breeds repression; that repression breeds hate; that hate menaces stable government; that the path of safety lies in the opportunity to discuss freely supposed grievances and proposed remedies; and that the fitting remedy for evil counsels is good ones. Believing in the power of reason as applied through public discussion, they eschewed silence coerced by law—the argument of force in its worst form. Recognizing the occasional tyrannies of governing majorities, they amended the Constitution so that free speech and assembly should be guaranteed.

Fear of serious injury cannot alone justify suppression of free speech and assembly. Men feared witches and burnt women. It is the function of speech to free men from the bondage of irrational fears. To justify suppression of free speech there must be reasonable ground to fear that serious evil will result if free speech is practiced. There must be reasonable ground to believe that the danger apprehended is imminent. There must be reasonable ground to believe that the evil to be prevented is a serious one. Every denunciation of existing law tends in some measure to increase the probability that there will be violation of it. Condonation of a breach enhances the probability. Expressions of approval add to the probability. Propagation of the criminal state of mind by teaching syndicalism increases it. Advocacy of law-breaking heightens it still further. But even advocacy of violation, however reprehensible morally, is not a justification for denying free speech where the advocacy falls short of incitement and there is nothing to indicate that the advocacy would be immediately acted on. The wide difference between advocacy and incitement, between preparation and attempt, between assembling and conspiracy, must be borne in mind. In order to support a finding of clear and present danger it must be shown either that immediate serious violence was to be expected or was advocated, or that the past conduct furnished reason to believe that such advocacy was then contemplated.

Those who won our independence by revolution were not cowards. They did not fear political change. They did not exalt order at the cost of liberty. To courageous, self-reliant men, with confidence in the power of free and fearless reasoning applied through the processes of popular government, no danger flowing from speech can be deemed clear and present, unless the incidence of the evil apprehended is so imminent that it may befall before there is opportunity for full discussion. If there be time to expose through discussion the falsehood and fallacies, to avert the evil by the processes of education, the remedy to be applied is more speech, not enforced silence. Only an emergency can justify repression. Such must be the rule if authority is to be reconciled with freedom. Such, in my opinion, is the command of the Constitution. It is therefore always open to Americans to challenge a law abridging free speech and assembly by showing that there was no emergency justifying it.[73]

Utterance also has responsibility. To misrepresent fact is to corrupt the source of opinion. No compensating social gain demands the right to such misrepresentation. But the free exchange of opinion upon complicated issues must not be turned into crime by treating the prevailing view as a fact and proscribing unpopular dissent.

To prove the falsity of this statement the Government introduced the address made by the President to Congress on April 2, 1917, which preceded the adoption of the Joint Resolution of April 6, 1917, declaring that a state of war exists between the United States and the Imperial German Government (c. 1, 40 Stat. 1). This so-called statement of fact—which is alleged to be false—is merely a conclusion or a deduction from facts. True it is the kind of conclusion which courts call a conclusion of fact, as distinguished from a conclusion of law; and which is sometimes spoken of as a finding of ultimate fact as distinguished from an evidentiary fact. But, in its essence it is the expression of a judgment—like the statements of many so-called historical facts. . . .

The cause of a war—as of most human action—is not single. War is ordinarily the result of many coöperating causes, many different conditions, acts and motives. Historians rarely agree in their judgment as to what was the determining factor in a particular war, even when they write under circumstances where detachment and the availability of evidence from all sources minimize both prejudice and other sources of error. For individuals, and classes of individuals, attach significance to those things which are significant to them. And, as the contributing causes cannot be subjected, like a chemical combination in a test tube, to qualitative and quantitative analysis so as to weigh and value the various elements, the historians differ necessarily in their judgments. One finds the determining cause of war in a great man, another in an idea, a belief, an economic necessity, a trade advantage, a sinister machination, or an accident. It is for this reason largely that men seek to interpret anew in each age, and often with each new generation, the important events in the world's history.[74]

The press is the most important vehicle for the dissemination of opinion. The Constitution precludes its censorship. Equally inadmissible should be all oblique methods to censor the press. Particularly offensive is the coercive power of unregulated administrative control.

This case arose during the World War; but it presents no legal question peculiar to war. It is important, because what we decide may determine in large measure whether in times of peace our press shall be free.

The denial to a newspaper of entry as second-class mail, or the revocation of an entry previously made, does not deny to the paper admission to the mail; nor does it deprive the publisher of any mail facility. It merely deprives him of the very low postal rates, called second class, and compels him to pay postage for the same service at the rate called third class, which was, until recently, from eight to fifteen times as high as the second-class rate. Such is the nature and the only effect of an order denying or revoking the entry.

In conclusion I say again—because it cannot be stressed too strongly—that the power here claimed is not a war power. There is no question of its necessity to protect the country from insidious domestic foes. To that end Congress conferred upon the Postmaster General the enormous power contained in the Espionage Act of entirely excluding from the mails any letter, picture or publication which contained matter violating the broad terms of that act. But it did not confer—and the Postmaster General concedes that it did not confer—the vague and absolute authority practically to deny circulation to any publication which in his opinion is likely to violate in the future any postal law. The grant of that power is construed into a postal rate statute passed forty years ago which has never before been suspected of containing such implications. I cannot believe that in establishing postal classifications in 1879 Congress intended to confer upon the Postmaster General authority to issue the order here complained of. If, under the Constitution, administrative officers may, as a mere incident of the peace time administration of their departments, be vested with the power to issue such orders as this, there is little of substance in our Bill of Rights and in every extension of governmental functions lurks a new danger to civil liberty.[75]

IX

His deep consciousness of the imperfections of reason leads Mr. Justice Brandeis to observe rigorously the conditions which alone assure the fair working of even disinterested judgment. Truth may be beyond mortals, but law should at least satisfy the requirements for truth-seeking. Laymen, and even lawyers who are not historically-minded, are too apt to identify procedure with obstructive technicalities.[76] But there are technicalities and technicalities. The fundamental aspects of judicial procedure have the support of enduring human interests.

English criminal justice rightly serves as a shining contrast to our own. Yet those features in our Bill of Rights which it is now fashionable to regard as unduly favorable to the accused, are even more securely embedded in the texture of English feeling than they are secured through the written words in our Constitution. Here the third degree is widely practiced and too often condoned.[77] In England the suggestion that Scotland Yard applied the third degree aroused the condemnation of all the parties in the House of Commons.[78] Mr. Justice Brandeis has been true to the civilized standards of the British tradition.

The Court of Appeals appears to have held the prisoner's statements admissible on the ground that a confession made by one competent to act is to be deemed voluntary, as a matter of law, if it was not induced by a promise or a threat; and that here there was evidence sufficient to justify a finding of fact that these statements were not so induced. In the federal courts, the requisite of voluntariness is not satisfied by establishing merely that the confession was not induced by a promise or a threat. A confession is voluntary in law if, and only if, it was, in fact, voluntarily made. A confession may have been given voluntarily, although it was made to police officers, while in custody, and in answer to an examination conducted by them. But a confession obtained by compulsion must be excluded whatever may have been the character of the compulsion, and whether the compulsion was applied in a judicial proceeding or otherwise. *Bram* v. *United States*, 168 U.S. 532. None of the five statements introduced by the Government as admissions or confessions was made until after Wan had been subjected for seven days to the interrogation. The testimony given by the superintendent of police, the three detectives and the chief medical officer left no room for a contention that the statements of the defendant were, in fact, voluntary. The undisputed facts showed that compulsion was applied. As to that matter there was no issue upon which the jury could properly have been required or permitted to pass. The alleged oral statements and the written confession should have been excluded.[79]

Anxiety over the deep shadows which crime casts upon the American scene should not tempt relaxation of the moral restraints which painful history has prescribed for law officers. Our own days furnish solemn reminders that police and prosecutors and occasionally even judges will, if allowed, employ illegality and yield to passion, with the same justification of furthering the public weal as their predecessors relied upon for the brutalities of the seventeenth and eighteenth centuries.

Plaintiff's private papers were stolen. The thief, to further his own ends, delivered them to the law officer of the United States. He, knowing them to have been stolen, retains them for use against the plaintiff. Should the court permit him to do so?

That the court would restore the papers to plaintiff if they were still in the thief's possession is not questioned. That it has power to control the disposition of these stolen papers, although they have passed into the possession of the law officer, is also not questioned. But it is said that no provision of the Constitution requires their surrender and that the papers could have been subpoenaed. This may be true. Still I cannot believe that action of a public official is necessarily lawful, because it does not violate constitutional prohibitions and because the same result might have been attained by other and proper means. At the foundation of our civil liberty lies the principle which denies to government officials an exceptional position before the law and which subjects them to the same rules of conduct that are commands to the citizen. And in the development of our liberty insistence upon procedural regularity has been a large factor. Respect for law will not be advanced by resort, in its enforcement, to means which shock the common man's sense of decency and fair play.[80]

I am aware that courts—mistaking relative social values and forgetting that a desirable end cannot justify foul means—have, in their zeal to punish, sanctioned the use of evidence obtained through criminal violation of property and personal rights or by other practices of detectives even more revolting. But the objection here is of a different nature. It does not rest merely upon the character of the evidence or upon the fact that the evidence was illegally obtained. The obstacle to the prosecution lies in the fact that the alleged crime was instigated by officers of the Government; that the act for which the Government seeks to punish the defendant is the fruit of their criminal conspiracy to induce its commission. The Government may set decoys to entrap criminals. But it may not provoke or create a crime and then punish the criminal, its creature.[81]

Will this Court by sustaining the judgment below sanction such conduct [wire-tapping] on the part of the Executive? The governing principle has long been settled. It is that a court will not redress a wrong when he who invokes its aid has unclean hands. The maxim of unclean hands comes from courts of equity. But the principle prevails also in courts of law. Its common application is in civil actions between private parties. Where the Government is the actor, the reasons for applying it are even more persuasive. Where the remedies invoked are those of the criminal law, the reasons are compelling. . . .

Decency, security, and liberty alike demand that government officials shall be subjected to the same rules of conduct that are commands to the citizen. In a government of laws, existence of the government will be imperilled if it fails to observe the law scrupulously. Our Government is the potent, the omnipresent teacher. For good or for ill, it teaches the whole people by its example. Crime is contagious. If the Government becomes a law-breaker, it breeds contempt for law; it invites every man to become a law unto himself; it invites anarchy. To declare that in the administration of the criminal law the end justifies the means—to declare that the Government may commit crimes in order to secure the conviction of a private criminal—would bring terrible retribution. Against that pernicious doctrine this Court should resolutely set its face.[82]

The possession of political power assumes subtler forms of temptation than its vulgar abuse. The love of power grows by what it feeds on. To Mr. Justice Brandeis, as to Lincoln, concentration of power is a standing threat to liberty; and to him liberty is a greater good than efficiency. So it was to the Age of Reason, and the Constitution is a product of that age. It is in the light of his prejudice for liberty that Mr. Justice Brandeis construes the Constitution.

The separation of the powers of government did not make each branch completely autonomous. It left each, in some measure, dependent upon the others, as it left to each power to exercise, in some respects, functions in their nature executive, legislative and judicial. Obviously the President cannot secure full execution of the laws, if Congress denies to him adequate means of doing so. Full execution may be defeated because Congress declines to create offices indispensable for that purpose. Or, because Congress, having created the office, declines to make the indispensable appropriation. Or, because Congress, having both created the office and made the appropriation, prevents, by restrictions which it imposes, the appointment of officials who in quality and character are indispensable to the efficient execution of the law. If, in any such way, adequate means are denied to the President, the fault will lie with Congress. The President performs his full constitutional duty, if, with the means and instruments provided by Congress and within the limitations prescribed by it, he uses his best endeavors to secure the faithful execution of the laws enacted. Compare *Kendall* v. *United States*, 12 Pet. 524, 613, 626.

Checks and balances were established in order that this should be "a government of laws and not of men." As White said in the House, in 1789, an uncontrollable power of removal in the Chief Executive "is a doctrine not to be learned in American governments." Such power had been denied in Colonial Charters, and even under Proprietary Grants and Royal Commissions. It had been denied in the thirteen States before the framing of the Federal Constitution. The doctrine of the separation of powers was adopted by the Convention of 1787, not to promote efficiency but to preclude the exercise of arbitrary power. The purpose was, not to avoid friction, but, by means of the inevitable friction incident to the distribution of the governmental powers among three departments, to save the people from autocracy. In order to prevent arbitrary executive action, the Constitution provided in terms that presidential appointments be made with the consent of the Senate, unless Congress should otherwise provide; and this clause was construed by Alexander Hamilton in *The Federalist*, No. 77, as requiring like consent to removals. Limiting further executive prerogatives customary in monarchies, the Constitution empowered Congress to vest the appointment of inferior officers, "as they think proper, in the President alone, in the Courts of Law, or in the Heads of Departments." Nothing in support of the claim of uncontrollable power can be inferred from the silence of the Convention of 1787 on the subject of removal. For the outstanding fact remains that every specific proposal to confer such uncontrollable power upon the President was rejected. In America, as in England, the conviction prevailed then that the people must look to representative assemblies for the protection of their liberties. And protection of the individual, even if he be an official, from the arbitrary or capricious exercise of power was then believed to be an essential of free government.[83]

X

PASSIONATE convictions are too often in the service of the doctrinaire. In Mr. Justice Brandeis they are the offspring of an extraordinarily penetrating mind and intense devotion to the commonweal. He never flinches from stubborn reality. Facts, not catchwords, are his sovereigns. Of course, a lifelong study of history and deep immersion in affairs have bent him to certain preferences. And since cases are not just cases, but imply alternative social policies, his predilections may decide cases. But Mr. Justice Brandeis is the very negation of a dogmatist. He has remained scrupulously flexible, constantly subjecting experience to the test of wider experience. All men have some ultimate postulates by which they wrest a private world of order from the chaos of the world. The essential postulate of Mr. Justice Brandeis is effective and generous opportunity for the unflagging operation of reason. He is not theory-ridden himself and would not impose theories on others.

And so his opinions reveal consciousness of a world for which no absolute is adequate. It is a world of more or less, of give and take, of live and let live. Interests clash, but no single one must yield. Self-willed power must be guarded against, but government cannot be paralyzed. And even liberty has its bounds.

Knowledge of the facts of industry has made him realize that centralization in the organization of workingmen is a necessary counterpoise to centralization in the control of business. And in the contests between them, the courts ought not to be partisan. But thereby the right of combat is not introduced into the constitutional structure. Society may evolve an adjustment comprehending the specialized interests of both sides.

Members of the Journeymen Stone Cutters' Association could not work anywhere on stone which had been cut at the quarries by "men working in opposition" to it, without aiding and abetting the enemy. Observance by each member of the provision of their constitution which forbids such action was essential to his own self-protection. It was demanded of each by loyalty to the organization and to his fellows. If, on the undisputed facts of this case, refusal to work can be enjoined, Congress created by the Sherman Law and the Clayton Act an instrument for imposing restraints upon labor which reminds of involuntary servitude. The Sherman Law was held in *United States* v. *United States Steel Corporation,* 251 U.S. 417, to permit capitalists to combine in a single corporation 50 per cent of the steel industry of the United States dominating the trade through its vast resources. The Sherman Law was held in *United States* v. *United Shoe Machinery Co.,* 247 U.S. 32, to permit capitalists to combine in another corporation practically the whole shoe machinery industry of the country, necessarily giving it a position of dominance over shoe-manufacturing in America. It would, indeed, be strange if Congress had by the same Act willed to deny to members of a small craft of workingmen the right to coöperate in simply refraining from work, when that course was the only means of self-protection against a combination of militant and powerful employers. I cannot believe that Congress did so.[84]

Because I have come to the conclusion that both the common law of a State and a statute of the United States declare the right of industrial combatants to push their struggle to the limits of the justification of self-interest, I do not wish to be understood as attaching any constitutional or moral sanction to that right. All rights are derived from the purposes of the society in which they exist; above all rights rises duty to the community. The conditions developed in industry may be such that those engaged in it cannot continue their struggle without danger to the community. But it is not for judges to determine whether such conditions exist, nor is it their function to set the limits of permissible contest and to declare the duties which the new situation demands. This is the function of the legislature which, while limiting individual and group rights of aggression and defense, may substitute processes of justice for the more primitive method of trial by combat.[85]

Mr. Justice Brandeis does not regard all concentration of economic power as a decree of nature, nor even as the inevitable consequence of modern technology. Some of its phases, according to his analysis, are the results of socially inimical practices. These excesses are "a curse of bigness."[86] But recognition of a limit to the economic and social advantages of combination does not lead him to read the Sherman Law as a policy of anarchic *laissez faire*. One who was the first to espouse business as a profession[87] naturally found no legal obstacles to the efforts of business to rationalize its processes.

The Sherman Law does not prohibit every lessening of competition; and it certainly does not command that competition shall be pursued blindly, that business rivals shall remain ignorant of trade facts or be denied aid in weighing their significance. It is lawful to regulate competition in some degree. *Chicago Board of Trade* v. *United States*, 246 U.S. 231. But it was neither the aim of the Plan, nor the practice under it, to regulate competition in any way. Its purpose was to make rational competition possible by supplying data not otherwise available and without which most of those engaged in the trade would be unable to trade intelligently. . . .

Surely it is not against the public interest to distribute knowledge of trade facts, however detailed. Nor are the other features of the

Plan—the market letters and the regional conferences, an unreasonable interference with freedom in trade. Intelligent conduct of business implies not only knowledge of trade facts, but an understanding of them. To this understanding editorial comment and free discussion by those engaged in the business and by others interested are aids. Opinions expressed may be unsound; predictions may be unfounded; but there is nothing in the Sherman Law which should limit freedom of discussion, even among traders. . . .

But surely Congress did not intend by the Sherman Act to prohibit self-restraint—and it was for self-restraint that the only appeal was made. The purpose of the warnings was to induce mill owners to curb their greed—lest both they and others suffer from the crushing evils of overproduction. Such warning or advice whether given by individuals or the representatives of an association presents no element of illegality.

It is urged that this was a concerted effort to enhance prices. There was at no time uniformity in prices. So far as appears every mill charged for its product as much as it could get. There is evidence that the hardwood mills expected, by adopting the Plan, to earn more in profits; and to do so, at least in part, by getting higher prices for their product. It may be that the distribution of the trade data, the editorial comment and the conferences enabled the producers to obtain, on the average, higher prices than would otherwise have been possible. But there is nothing in the Sherman Law to indicate that Congress intended to condemn coöperative action in the exchange of information, merely because prophecy resulting from comment on the data collected may lead, for a period, to higher market prices. Congress assumed that the desire to acquire and to enjoy property is the safest and most promising basis for society. And to that end it sought, among other things, to protect the pursuit of business for private profit. Its purpose, obviously, was not to prevent the making of profits or to counteract the operation of the law of supply and demand. Its purpose was merely to prevent restraint. The illegality of a combination under the Sherman Law lies not in its effect upon the price level, but in the coercion thereby effected. It is the limitation of freedom, by agreements which narrow a market, as in *Addyston Pipe & Steel Co.* v. *United States*, 175 U.S. 211, and *Montague & Co.* v. *Lowry*, 193 U.S. 38, or by organized boycott, as in

Loewe v. *Lawlor*, 208 U.S. 274, and *Eastern States Retail Lumber Dealers' Association* v. *United States*, 234 U.S. 600, or by the coercive power of rebates, as in *Thomsen* v. *Cayser*, 243 U.S. 66, which constitutes the unlawful restraint.[88]

Every judicial proceeding, however preliminary its determination, must observe the essential requirements of a fair hearing. This safeguard courts can assure. But the protection of individual liberty, due to oppressive enforcement of the criminal law, does not lie wholly within the power of courts.

. . . by refusing to hear and consider evidence introduced or offered which bore upon the existence of probable cause [in a hearing for removal of an accused person], the Commissioner did not merely commit error, but deprived the petitioner of his liberty without due process of law in violation of the Fifth Amendment, because he was denied a fair hearing.[89]

Protection against unjustifiable vexation and harassment incident to repeated arrests [for extradition] for the same alleged crime must ordinarily be sought, not in constitutional limitations or treaty provisions, but in a high sense of responsibility on the part of the public officials charged with duties in this connection.[90]

The extensive governmental control now so widely exercised by administrative agencies over business and professions is giving rise to a new system of law. Mr. Justice Brandeis has been very hospitable to the necessity for this new development. His opinions in this field are helping to evolve a coherent body of administrative law. He recognizes the informality of procedure which these agencies must be allowed to adopt, and accords deference to the findings of experts.[91] But even experts cannot disregard evidence or dispense with the logic of relevance.

The statute provides that the examination shall be before a board of practicing dentists; that the applicant must be a graduate of a reputable dental school; and that he must be of good moral character. Thus, the general standard of fitness and the character and scope of the examination are clearly indicated. Whether the applicant posesses the qualifications inherent in that standard is a question of fact. Compare *Red "C" Oil Mfg. Co.* v. *North Carolina,* 222 U.S. 380, 394. The decision of that fact involves ordinarily the determination of two subsidiary questions of fact. The first, what the knowledge and skill is which fits one to practice the profession. The second, whether the applicant possesses that knowledge and skill. The latter finding is necessarily an individual one. The former is ordinarily one of general application. Hence, it can be embodied in rules. The legislature itself may make this finding of the facts of general application, and by embodying it in the statute make it law. When it does so, the function of the examining board is limited to determining whether the applicant complies with the requirements so declared. But the legislature need not make this general finding. To determine the subjects of which one must have knowledge in order to be fit to practice dentistry; the extent of knowledge in each subject; the degree of skill requisite; and the procedure to be followed in conducting the examination; these are matters appropriately committed to an administrative board. *Mutual Film Corporation* v. *Ohio Industrial Commission,* 236 U.S. 230, 245–246. And a legislature may, consistently with the Federal Constitution, delegate to such board the function of determining these things, as well as the functions of determining whether the applicant complies with the detailed standard of fitness.[92]

The log traffic is limited substantially to the section of the State lying west of the Cascade Mountains. The average length of its haul on each of these roads is not more than 32 miles. The three principal carriers presented evidence tending to show that their existing rates were so low as not to yield any return upon the property employed in the business; and that the rates did not defray fully the operating costs of the traffic and its proportion of the taxes payable. This evidence was in character persuasive. It was fairly specific, direct, and comprehensive. If the facts warranted, the shippers and the public officials might, of course, have shown by evidence of similar character that the carriers' evidence was inherently untrustworthy; or it might have been overcome by more persuasive evidence to the contrary. Little attempt was made to show that any testimony introduced by the carriers was inherently untrustworthy. Little conflict with the evidence of the carriers was developed by the evidence as to specific facts introduced for the shippers and the public. Apparently necessary inferences from specific facts established by the carriers were not explained away. The Department's findings concerning operating costs rested largely upon deductions from data found in published reports of the carriers and in their exhibits filed in this case. Instead of attempting to show by evidence, reasonably specific and direct, what the actual operating cost of this traffic was to the several carriers, the Department created a composite figure representing the weighted average operating cost per 1,000 gross ton miles of all revenue freight carried on the four systems and made that figure a basis for estimating the operating cost of the log traffic in Washington. This was clearly erroneous.

A precise issue was the cost on each railroad of transporting logs in carload lots in western Washington, the average haul on each system being not more than 32 miles. In using the above composite figure in the determination of this issue the Department necessarily ignored, in the first place, the differences in the average unit cost on the several systems; and then the differences on each in the cost incident to the different classes of traffic and articles of merchandise, and to the widely varying conditions under which the transportation is conducted. In this unit cost figure no account is taken of the differences in unit cost dependent, among other things, upon differences in the length of haul; in the character of the commodity; in the configuration of the country; in the density of the traffic; in the daily loaded car movement; in the extent of the empty car movement; in the nature of the equipment employed; in the extent to which the equipment is used; in the expenditures required for its maintenance. Main line and branch line freight, interstate and intrastate, car load and less than car load, are counted alike. The Department's error was fundamental in its nature. The use of this factor in computing the operating costs of the log traffic vitiated the whole process of reasoning by which the Department reached its conclusion.[93]

XI

To quote from Mr. Justice Brandeis' opinions is not to pick plums from a pudding but to pull threads from a pattern.

He achieves not by epigrammatic thrust but through powerful exposition. His aim is not merely to articulate the grounds
of his judgment, but to reach the mind even of the disap-
pointed suitor, deeming it essential for defeated interests to
know that their claims have adequately entered the judicial
process. His opinions march step by step toward demonstra-
tion, with all the auxiliary reinforcement of detailed proof.
The documentation of his opinions is one aspect of his reliance
on reason. To sever text from accompanying footnotes is
therefore to dismember an organic whole.[94]

The style of his opinions befits their aim. The dominant
note is Doric simplicity. Occasionally, as in the terrible case
of Ziang Sung Wan,[95] his restraint attains austerity. And
sometimes the majesty of his theme stirs him to eloquence.
When the issue is freedom of speech, he gives noble utterance to his faith and to the meaning of our institutions as the
embodiment of that faith.

In truth, Mr. Justice Brandeis is a moral teacher, who follows Socrates in the belief that virtue is the pursuit of enlightened purpose. His long years of intimate connection
with the history of the Harvard Law School symbolize his
dominant impulse. Problems, for him, are never solved.
Civilization is a sequence of new tasks. Hence his insistence
on the extreme difficulty of government and its dependence
on sustained interest and effort, on the need for constant
alertness to the fact that the introduction of new forces is accompanied by new difficulties. This, in turn, makes him
mindful of the limited range of human foresight, and leads
him to practice humility in attempting to preclude the freedom of action of those who are to follow.

The Justice himself, while at the bar, disavowed allegiance
to any general system of thought or hope. "I have no rigid
social philosophy; I have been too intent on concrete problems of practical justice." Devotion to justice is widely pro-
fessed. By Mr. Justice Brandeis it has been given concrete

expression in a long effort toward making the life of the commonplace individual more significant. His zest for giving significance to life is not sentimentality; it arises from a keen sensitiveness to quality. He not only evokes the best qualities in others; he exacts the best in himself. Stern self-discipline of a mind preternaturally rich and deep has fashioned a judge who, by common consent, is a great and abiding figure of the world's most powerful court.

IV

THE INDUSTRIAL LIBERALISM OF
MR. JUSTICE BRANDEIS

BY

DONALD R. RICHBERG

THE INDUSTRIAL LIBERALISM OF
MR. JUSTICE BRANDEIS

IN his introduction to that brilliant volume of Jerome Frank on *Law and the Modern Mind*,[1] Judge Mack observes that "the last two decades have made it abundantly clear that the just decision of causes requires a careful weighing of social and economic considerations not to be found in the strict body of the law itself." And he commends Mr. Frank for demonstrating that not only must we consider "the social and economic facts upon which legal decisions should properly be predicated, but that the very thought processes of the judge and jurist himself must be tested and freed from persistently childish notions that have no place in an adult civilization."

It may be generally conceded that Mr. Justice Brandeis has so constantly and carefully tested his own thought processes as to free them to an exceptional degree from those "childish notions" which seem to persist to some extent in all adult thought—and which commonly become radio-active when the judicial conservative rebukes the legislative radical. It is, therefore, not only interesting but comforting to examine, behind the social and economic facts upon which the Brandeis opinions have been predicated, the thought processes from which they have arisen. One is free from any embarrassing fear that the investigation may expose a philosophy of life that never developed beyond the day dreams of childhood. But there is a question which must be fairly faced in reviewing his views of industry, with their disturbing consistency over a period of sweeping industrial change: Will Justice Brandeis be time-justified in his persistent protest against "bigness"; or is bigness the product of an irresistible force which if now misdirected should be harnessed and wisely directed in the service of mankind?

It may be well to restate the question in the clear language of Professor Beard:[2] "Is the America of tomorrow to be the society of 'the new freedom' so effectively portrayed by Mr. Brandeis and the President who appointed him? Or will the march of integration in finance and industry override the small enterprises which they sought to preserve against extinction?"

For more than twenty years, at least, whether discussing the problems of worker, manager or consumer, Mr. Justice Brandeis has opposed monopoly and concentration and advocated competition and the preservation of small business units. He has pointed out the inefficiencies as well as the oppressions of big business operations. He has steadfastly sought to maintain the individual satisfactions and social advantages of a multiplicity of units of production and distribution, which should insure a competitive incentive for improvement and progress and a competitive check on excessive individual gain. The consequences of these thought processes are written deep into his judicial opinions. If these ideas are progressive, our civilization must refuse submission to its conquering enemy. If these ideas are reactionary, our civilization must protect itself against the destructive experiments now being carried on by its well-meaning but ruthless friend.

It is probably fair to assume that the industrial liberalism of Mr. Justice Brandeis arises out of a deep rooted individualism, which is not only intensely concerned with his own freedom of thought and act, but is profoundly sympathetic with the desire of any other human being to stand erect, to tower above environment, to maintain an individual sovereignty subject to no political or economic Caesars.

The makers of our Constitution undertook to secure conditions favorable to the pursuit of happiness. They recognized the significance of man's spiritual nature, of his feelings and of his intellect. They knew that only a part of the pain, pleasure and satisfactions of life are to be found in material things. They sought to protect

Americans in their beliefs, their thoughts, their emotions and their sensations. They conferred, as against the Government, the right to be let alone—the most comprehensive of rights and the right most valued by civilized men.[3]

But political freedom is not enough. "Can any man be really free who is constantly in danger of becoming dependent upon somebody and something else than his own exertion and conduct?"[4] The answer is quite clear: "You cannot have true American citizenship, you cannot preserve political liberty, you cannot secure American standards of living unless some degree of industrial liberty accompanies it."[5]

For the wage earner this liberty can only be obtained through participation in the responsibilities of a business enterprise:

The social justice for which we are striving is an incident of our democracy, not the main end. It is rather the result of democracy—perhaps its finest expression—but it rests upon democracy, which implies the rule by the people. And, therefore, the end for which we must strive is the attainment of rule by the people, and that involves industrial democracy as well as political democracy. That means that the problems of a trade should no longer be the problems of the employer alone. The problems of his business, and it is not the employer's business alone, are the problems of all in it. The union cannot shift upon the employer the responsibility for conditions, nor can the employer insist upon determining, according to his will, the conditions which shall exist.[6]

For the business man this liberty can only be obtained through preserving his responsibility for the welfare of an industrial unit. The extinction of a multitude of small units and the transformation of their independent owners into dependent employees of "big business" extinguishes economic democracy upon which political democracy—and liberty—depend.

Already the displacement of the small independent business man by the huge corporation with its myriad of employees, its absentee ownership, and its financier control presents a grave danger to our democracy. The social loss is great; and there is no economic gain. But the process of capitalizing free Americans is not an inevitable one. It is largely the result of unwise, man-made, privilege creating law, which has stimulated existing tendencies to inequality instead of discouraging them.[7]

Thus we find clearly stated a common interest of employer and employee, who would be free citizens of a democracy, in combating the tendency toward concentration and monopoly. Each loses not only his individual freedom but his capacity to coöperate with the other—a capacity dependent on the opportunity for personal relations.

The grave objection to the large business is that, almost inevitably, the form of organization, the absentee stock holdings, and its remote directorship prevent participation, ordinarily, of employees in such management. The executive officials become stewards in charge of the details of the operation of the business, they alone coming into direct relation with labor. Thus we lose that necessary coöperation which naturally flows from contact between employers and employees—and which the American aspirations for democracy demand. It is in the resultant absolutism that you will find the fundamental cause of prevailing unrest; no matter what is done with the superstructure, no matter how it may be improved in one way or the other, unless we eradicate that fundamental difficulty, unrest will not only continue, but, in my opinion, will grow worse.[8]

This loss of liberty, this degradation of democracy, is accompanied, according to Mr. Justice Brandeis, by "no economic gain"—a conclusion which will incite heated opposition. But the inefficiency of large organizations, their drift into bureaucracy, red tape, inertia and decadence is a favorite theme of this champion of "smallness." When he argued against the railroad demand for an advance in freight rates, in 1911, he massed his statistics to prove that scientific management, instead of seeking higher rates, would produce lower costs and increased business. But, he argued, scientific management had been sacrificed to "bigness":

I ask the Commission to consider whether there is not a causal connection between the fact of bigness, the fact of this extraordinary gross,and the fact of the reduced net; whether it is not a fact that the Pennsylvania system, the New York Central system, and indeed, to a less extent, the Baltimore & Ohio system have not exceeded what may be called the limit of greatest efficiency. Because, obviously, in all human institutions there must be a limit of greatest efficiency. These railroads are run by men; and, preëminently, they are determined by one or two men. Everybody in his experience knows his own limitations; knows how much less well he can do many things than a few things. There undoubtedly is a limit with a railroad, as in the case of other institutions, where they may be too small; but there is another limit where they may be too large—where the centrifugal force will be greater than the centripetal, and where, by reason of the multiplicity of problems and the distance to the circumference, looseness of administration arises that overcomes any advantage from size, overcomes it so far as to make it relatively a losing proposition. . . .

I say, therefore, may not that be one of the causes of the trouble which some of the railroads believe themselves to be in? And this question, this bigness, or, as I would be inclined to call it, this curse of bigness, has other incidents than the ones I have mentioned.[9]

These political-economic views of Mr. Justice Brandeis are of the utmost importance in a consideration of his contribution to the development of American law. No doctrine of *laissez faire* permits him to isolate industrial evolution from the making and enforcement of the law. The legislatures and the courts do not sit idly by while through concentration and utilization of economic power, strong-willed industrialists make over our civilization. This transformation "is largely the result of unwise, man-made, privilege creating law." It is because of what our law-makers have *done*, as well as because of what they have failed to do, that monopolies have grown great. "The small man needs the protection of the law; but the law becomes the instrument by which he is destroyed."[10]

The point of the lawyer's argument was emphasized in the dissenting opinion of the judge filed six years later:

The refusal to permit a multitude of small rivals to co-operate, as they have done here, in order to protect themselves and the public from the chaos and havoc wrought in their trade by ignorance, may result in suppressing competition in the hardwood industry. These keen business rivals, who sought through co-operative exchange of trade information to create conditions under which alone rational competition is possible, produce in the aggregate about one-third of the hardwood lumber of the country. This Court held in *United States* v. *U.S. Steel Corporation*, 251 U.S. 417, that it was not unlawful to vest in a single corporation control of 50 per cent of the steel industry of the country; and in *United States* v. *United Shoe Machinery Co.*, 247 U.S. 32, the court held that it was not unlawful to vest in a single corporation control of practically the whole shoe machinery industry. May not these hardwood lumber concerns, frustrated in their efforts to rationalize competition, be led to enter the inviting field of consolidation? And if they do, may not another huge trust with highly centralized control over vast resources, natural, manufacturing and financial, become so powerful as to dominate competitors, wholesalers, retailers, consumers, employees and, in large measure, the community?[11]

Not even in the field of public utilities should there be an acceptance of private monopoly, according to this philosophy.

It has been suggested that we accept the proposed monopoly in transportation but provide safeguards.

This would be like surrendering liberty and substituting despotism with safeguards. There is no way in which to safeguard people from despotism except to prevent despotism. There is no way to safeguard the people from the evils of a private transportation monopoly except to prevent the monopoly. The objections to despotism and to monopoly are fundamental in human nature. They rest upon the innate and ineradicable selfishness of man. They rest upon the fact that absolute power inevitably leads to abuse. They rest upon the fact that progress flows only from struggle.[12]

Some years ago Mr. Justice Brandeis made an effort to summarize certain of his views in a letter which can be quoted with propriety here as an aid in the interpretation of more public expressions:

Refuse to accept as inevitable any evil in business (*e.g.*, irregularity of employment). Refuse to tolerate any immoral practice (*e.g.*, espionage). But do not believe that you can find a universal remedy for evil conditions or immoral practices in effecting a fundamental change in society (as by State Socialism). And do not pin too much faith in legislation. Remedial institutions are apt to fall under the control of the enemy and to become instruments of oppression.

Seek for betterment within the broad lines of existing institutions. Do so by attacking evil *in situ;* and proceed from the individual to the general. Remember that progress is necessarily slow; that remedies are necessarily tentative; that because of varying conditions there must be much and constant enquiry into facts . . . and much experimentation; and that always and everywhere the intellectual, moral and spiritual development of those concerned will remain an essential —and the main factor—in real betterment.

This development of the individual is, thus, both a necessary means and the end sought. For our objective is the making of men and women who shall be free, self-respecting members of a democracy— and who shall be worthy of respect. Improvement in material conditions of the worker and ease are the incidents of better conditions —valuable mainly as they may ever increase opportunities for development.

The great developer is responsibility. Hence no remedy can be hopeful which does not devolve upon the workers participation in responsibility for the conduct of business; and their aim should be the eventual assumption of full responsibility—as in coöperative enterprises. This participation in and eventual control of industry is likewise an essential of obtaining justice in distributing the fruits of industry.

But democracy in any sphere is a serious undertaking. It substitutes self-restraint for external restraint. It is more difficult to maintain than to achieve. It demands continuous sacrifice by the individual and more exigent obedience to the moral law than any other form of government. Success in any democratic undertaking must proceed from the individual. It is possible only where the process of perfecting the individual is pursued. His development is attained mainly in the processes of common living. Hence the industrial struggle is essentially an affair of the Church and is its imperative task.[13]

It may be a dangerous, even a presumptuous, effort to attempt a distillation of the utterances of a keen and subtle thinker in order to isolate the essence of a philosophy. All intelligent reasoning, and particularly that of a lawyer or a judge, proceeds from a multitude of uncertain generalizations to a particular conclusion which may be described as an expedient certainty. In order to give this conclusion the sanction of apparent inevitableness the uncertainties of its origin cannot be too clearly revealed. In the classic language of Justice Holmes: "The decision will depend on a judgment or intuition more subtle than any articulate major premise."[14] For this very reason the "instinctive preferences and inarticulate syllogisms" of a jurist are of greater importance than the language of particular opinions—if they can be discovered.

Lawyers and laymen casually acquainted with the life and works of Mr. Justice Brandeis might assume that he was possessed by instinctive sympathy with the under dog, and that the onward and ruthless march of big business, the rapid growth in his generation of political and economic despotism with increasing submergence of the "little fellow," invoked this sympathy and drove him to pull the big man down in order to lift the little man up. Without questioning the existence of this sympathy, it may be suggested that a love of equity is at least secondary in the Brandeis philosophy to a passion for liberty and a faith in democracy as the political method of its production.

Is there not a flash from the inmost life in his plea for "the right to be let alone—the most comprehensive of rights and the right most valued by civilized men."[15] Here is the reckless superlative of passion and faith.

Why should workers have a voice in the control of industry? There is little materialistic reasoning in his answer; no mere economic advantage that is stressed. He is not content with any program that runs the "great risk of improving their material condition and reducing their manhood . . . the United States is a democracy and . . . we must have above all things, men. It is the development of manhood to which any industrial and social system should be directed. . . . Men must have industrial liberty as well as good wages."[16]

Why should independent business be saved from absorption into monopolistic combinations? It is because "the United States Steel Corporation and these other trusts have stabbed industrial liberty in the back. . . . The trust problem can never be settled right for the American people by looking at it through the spectacles of bonds and stocks. You must study it through the spectacles of people's rights and people's interests; must consider the effect upon the development of the American democracy."[17] The writer of these lines understands that democracy is not a political program. It is a religion.

It is interesting to note how "individualistic" and non-"socialistic" are the justifications for social legislation which proceed from this exponent of liberty and democracy.

The liberty of each individual must be limited in such a way that it leaves to others the possibility of individual liberty; the right to develop must be subject to that limitation which gives everybody else the right to develop; the restriction is merely an adjustment of the relations of one individual to another.[18]

There is no sublimation of society, as a composite being of

greater worth than the individual human, in this argument. There is no artificial concept of the State as an entity whose health and happiness is more important than individual health and happiness. The primary obligation whose fulfilment must be compelled by law is not that of individuals to society, but of society to individuals. The distinction is fundamental and there is no confusion in the mind of a real individualist. "Universal suffrage necessarily imposes upon the State the obligation of fitting its governors—the voters—for their task; and the freedom of the individual is as much an essential condition of successful democracy as his education."[19]

The function of our Government as viewed by Mr. Justice Brandeis is not merely the preservation of an assumed "natural" liberty, but a positive duty through coöperative aid to set men free from the tyrannies that otherwise might be imposed by nature and other human beings. Here is the authority and the reason for both social legislation and antitrust legislation; for permitting "industrial combatants to push their struggle to the limits of the justification of self-interest," or for setting "the limits of permissible contest."[20] In the opinion just quoted he wrote: "All rights are derived from the purposes of the society in which they exist; above all rights rises duty to the community." But this is no deification of society. It is merely a reference to the liberties of the many which may not be infringed by arbitrary exercises of individual liberty. The purposes of our society are vigorously asserted in another opinion:

Those who won our independence believed that the final end of the State was to make men free to develop their faculties; and that in its government the deliberative forces should prevail over the arbitrary. They valued liberty both as an end and as a means. They believed liberty to be the secret of happiness and courage to be the secret of liberty.[21]

If this be a faithful description of the original purposes of our society—and who will question it?—there can be little doubt of the value and steadfastness of the work of Mr. Justice Brandeis as an expounder and defender of the Constitution of the United States and the government which "we, the people," undertook to establish thereunder. And if the trend of the times is moving contrary to the current of his thought, must we not conclude that his is the historic American spirit and that the rulers of modern industrial empires are aliens to that spirit?

With his realistic approach to all problems, with his patient researches into actualities, Mr. Justice Brandeis cannot be unaware that the independent worker or business man, for whom he would preserve liberty, shows precious little of the courage that is the "secret of liberty." He must observe the hordes of "white collar men" who, lacking the vigor and self-reliance to organize themselves for self-improvement, give support to the claim that their services are not worth more than their miserable wages. He must observe the hundreds of "company unions" of wage earners who demonstrate their incapacity for any greater responsibility than that of taking orders. He must observe the decadent futility of many old and anciently militant national unions. He must observe the thousands of once independent merchants and manufacturers, who, after a few years of feeble protesting against "trusts" and "chain-stores," have resigned themselves to life-time dependence upon the favor of remote controllers.

After years of such observations how often may the liberty-loving judge wonder for whom the American democracy is to be preserved? To one who could see but a little way ahead (and behind) the prospect (and retrospect) might be discouraging. But to the reader of history, who, in its reflected light, seeks also to look beyond tomorrow and tomorrow, there may be a more cheerful view.

Every generation has known a receding and an oncoming enemy of freedom. The man on horseback has come and conquered and has been defeated, time and time again. The new tyrannies of economic power will likewise rise and fall. Happily there is already much evidence that banker control is a passing phase. The huge vertical and horizontal "trusts" of the present day must have great directors to survive. They require double Napoleons, who as yet have not been found. The dinosaur perished not from lack of power, but from lack of brain. Perhaps the already demonstrated incapacity of human beings to administer wisely their superhuman organizations may bring about decentralization and revive democracy. Or, without disintegration, a redistribution of the control of vast enterprises may be achieved as the product of industrial-social engineering. Man, who survived the monstrosities of the prehistoric era, may survive the monstrosities of his own creation in the era of megalomania.

The industrial ideals of Mr. Justice Brandeis may remain shining long after the lights of modern business have gone out, and may aid generations yet unborn to move forward on the world-old path toward liberty.

V

Mr. Justice Brandeis and the Regulation of Railroads

BY

Henry Wolf Biklé

Mr. Justice Brandeis and the Regulation of Railroads

TO undertake to isolate the influence of a single Justice of the United States Supreme Court upon a given portion of the law involves obvious difficulties; difficulties that should, perhaps, have persuaded to a declination of the task; but the gracious suggestion of the editors of the *Harvard Law Review* that the attempt be made to study the relation of Mr. Justice Brandeis to the law of railroad regulation was directed toward a quarter all too ready to give it hospitable reception, and "the only way to get rid of a temptation is to yield to it."

The part played by Mr. Justice Brandeis in the famous *Five Per Cent Case*[1] is not forgotten. The brief which he filed in that proceeding in his capacity as attorney for the Interstate Commerce Commission disclosed a thorough understanding of the railroad problem, not only as to its traffic aspect, but also as to its accounting and operating features; an understanding that did not content itself with criticism, but concerned itself also with constructive suggestion. Inevitably he became associated in the public mind with the railroads; and when he was appointed to the Supreme Court of the United States, it was anticipated that the opinions filed by him as an Associate Justice would evidence his intimate acquaintance with the federal plan for the regulation of railroads and with the practical significance of its operation. How this anticipation has been realized presents a fascinating subject of study to a railroad lawyer. It is hoped that it may interest others also.

It is true, of course, that the extent to which a single member of the Court may influence the development of the law is not measured solely by the text of his own opinions. Indeed, his theories may find their way into the opinions of his brethren and his own opinions may be colored or materially modified by the views of his associates. As Mr. Chief Justice Hughes recently said, when he responded to the address of Attorney-General Mitchell presenting the resolutions adopted by the Bar of the Supreme Court upon the death of Mr. Justice Sanford:

> The strength of the Court is the resultant of the interaction and coöperation of individual forces, and the successful performance of its function depends upon the discharge of individual responsibility by Justices of equal authority in the decision of all matters that come before the Court.[2]

But, notwithstanding this interaction and coöperation, the individual contribution remains, and it is deemed reasonable to regard the opinions filed by a Justice as the best available materials for the character of study here undertaken.

Accordingly the assumption is made that the opinions of Mr. Justice Brandeis in those cases in which he has voiced the opinion of the Court, or concurred specially, or dissented, constitute a reasonable and proper basis for an examination of his part in the development of the law relating to the regulation of the railroads.

That law is, of course, almost wholly statutory, consisting of the Interstate Commerce Act and related legislation; and the opinions interpreting and enforcing the provisions of these acts reflect the characteristics found in opinions dealing with questions of statutory interpretation, that is to say, they are devoted primarily to the examination of the language of the statute in the light of accepted aids to statutory construction. But in the case of important statutes the decisions, as a rule, soon begin to take on another aspect, becoming themselves the generating source of new principles and producing a coherent body of law having the same essential vitality as other portions of the law whose roots are not embedded in statutes. This tendency has found abundant illustration in the decisions interpreting and enforcing the Interstate Commerce Act and related legislation.

When Mr. Justice Brandeis took his seat on the bench in June, 1916, this development of judicial interpretation of the Interstate Commerce Act had made material progress. It will be remembered that the Act, passed in 1887, had been extensively amended in 1906 and again in 1910, with other amendments of importance at other times. The story has been told elsewhere,[3] and even a summary of the history of the changes in the statute would be out of place here; but by the process of judicial construction sundry principles had been recognized as underlying the new *régime* of governmental regulation. Among these some of the more important were:

(*a*) That the tariffs of a railroad filed with the Interstate Commerce Commission as required by the statute prescribe the terms on which its interstate transportation service must be conducted.

(*b*) That primary resort must be had to the Commission— not to the courts—for the determination of administrative questions.

(*c*) That the courts are not only deprived of jurisdiction to consider initially the administrative questions confided to the Commission, but have only a limited power to review the decisions of the Commission, a power which does not permit the substitution of their views regarding administrative questions for those of the Commission.

(*d*) That intrastate railroad rates may prejudice interstate commerce, or shippers and communities engaged in such commerce; and that, to the extent that they do so, they are subject to federal authority and have been brought within the jurisdiction of the Interstate Commerce Commission by the Interstate Commerce Act.

These principles furnish, to a substantial extent, the basis of present-day railroad regulation. All had been established before 1916, but they find important illustration in the opinions of Mr. Justice Brandeis. They will be briefly explored in the light of these opinions.

That the tariffs of a railroad filed with the Interstate Commerce Commission prescribe the terms on which the interstate transportation service must be conducted is a natural corollary of the rule of non-preferential treatment of all shippers.[4] To insure such treatment the railroad must be required to publish what it offers its patrons, and the offer so made cannot be modified in favor of some particular shipper. This principle, embedded in the legislation, is illustrated in *Texas & Pac. Ry.* v. *Mugg*.[5] In this case the Court held the shipper liable to pay the published rate on an interstate shipment, irrespective of the fact that he had relied on, and based sales upon, a lower rate quoted by the railroad's agent. The hardship upon the shipper is obvious, and yet there seems to be no alternative if fair treatment as among shippers is to be attained. In theory, the shipper is able to consult the tariffs and ascertain the correct rate: in practice, except in the case of large industries, he frequently relies on the agent of the railroad. But in legal effect he is charged with notice because of the provisions of the filed tariff.[6]

Now, it is manifest that this theory applies not only to the rates charged for the transportation service, but to all privileges and practices required by law to be published in tariffs and which affect the amount or character of the service rendered or the charges for such service.[7] So, it soon became apparent that the provisions of the tariffs, and not contractual arrangements, control almost every aspect of the relation between the shipper and the carrier,[8] and that such provisions cannot be waived or varied.[9] In *Davis* v. *Henderson*,[10] a case in which an intending shipper orally notified an agent of a railroad that he wished cars to ship cattle when the tariff required written notice, Mr. Justice Brandeis said: "There is no claim that the rule requiring written notice was void. The contention is that the rule was waived. It could not be. The transportation service to be performed was that of a common carrier under published tariffs. The rule was a part of the tariff."[11] In *Galveston, Harrisburg & San Antonio Ry.* v. *Woodbury*, he applies the principle to the matter of liability: "Since the transportation [of certain baggage] here in question was subject to the Act to Regulate Commerce, both carrier and passenger were bound by the provisions of the published tariffs."[12] In *Texas & Pac. Ry.* v. *Leatherwood*, he presses the proposition to its logical conclusion, and, speaking of the terms of a bill of lading and a rate properly filed, says: "Each has in effect the force of a statute, of which all affected must take notice."[13] This principle is simple and understandable, but it gives scant recognition to the older rule that the terms of the relation between the carrier and the shipper are determined by their contract; that the relation is a kind of bailment, and that bailment is a kind of contract. The principle is reminiscent of the older cases that dealt with the legality of limiting carriers' liability by notice, but those cases sought their justification, such as it was, in contractual theory:[14] the present doctrine finds its more solid foundation in the policy of the statute. And, while in particular cases this doctrine sometimes seems to involve hardship—a result apparently inescapable when important objectives are deemed essential on a large scale—such hardship is mitigated by the fact that all rates, practices and privileges required to be filed with the Commission are subject to challenge under the provisions of the Interstate Commerce Act.[15] Here is encountered the second principle in the development of the present law of railroad regulation referred to above.

When a shipper seeks to challenge rates, privileges, and practices, duly published in the filed tariffs, his attack almost invariably is based upon the contention that such rates, privileges or practices are unreasonable, discriminatory, unduly prejudicial or preferential.[16] In all such cases the Supreme

Court has held that the Interstate Commerce Act requires primary resort to the Interstate Commerce Commission and to this extent disestablishes such court jurisdiction as may theretofore have existed. This principle finds its first important exposition in *Texas & Pac. Ry.* v. *Abilene Cotton Oil Co.*[17] In this case a shipper brought an action in a state court against a railroad seeking to recover on account of the exaction of transportation charges on interstate shipments alleged to be excessive. The Court held that such an action could not be maintained in the absence of a finding by the Interstate Commerce Commission that the rates charged were unreasonable. This decision was made in the face of the provision in section 22 of the Act to Regulate Commerce that ". . . Nothing in this act contained shall in any way abridge or alter the remedies now existing at common law or by statute, but the provisions of this Act are in addition to such remedies." The Court held that the important purpose of the statute, to secure equality to all shippers, could be achieved only by confining to the Commission the initial jurisdiction to determine whether or not rates were unreasonable. Court jurisdiction might result in awards to different shippers on different bases. "In other words, the act cannot be held to destroy itself."[18] The principle found rapid extension to other classes of cases involving so-called administrative questions. It was well established when Mr. Justice Brandeis came to the bench. By that time the cases began to present the question whether certain issues necessitate administrative consideration and therefore come within the rule. In *Northern Pac. Ry.* v. *Solum,*[19] a shipper sued to recover damages on the ground that the carrier had not forwarded his shipment *via* the cheapest route available. Mr. Justice Brandeis says:

Whether the practice of the carrier of shipping over the interstate route was reasonable, when a lower intrastate route was open to it, presents an administrative question, one of perhaps considerable complexity. . . .

The fact that the administrative question presented involves an intrastate as well as interstate route does not prevent the application of the rule, that the courts may not be resorted to until the administrative question has been determined by the Commission.[20]

Likewise the construction of a tariff may involve an administrative question, but not necessarily so. The principle is thus stated by Mr. Justice Brandeis in *Great Northern Ry.* v. *Merchants Elevator Co.:*

When the words of a written instrument are used in their ordinary meaning, their construction presents a question solely of law. But words are used sometimes in a peculiar meaning. Then extrinsic evidence may be necessary to determine the meaning of words appearing in the document. This is true where technical words or phrases not commonly understood are employed. Or extrinsic evidence may be necessary to establish a usage of trade or locality which attaches provisions not expressed in the language of the instrument. Where such a situation arises, and the peculiar meaning of words, or the existence of a usage, is proved by evidence, the function of construction is necessarily preceded by the determination of the matter of fact. Where the controversy over the writing arises in a case which is being tried before a jury, the decision of the question of fact is left to the jury, with instructions from the court as to how the document shall be construed, if the jury finds that the alleged peculiar meaning or usage is established. But where the document to be construed is a tariff of an interstate carrier, and before it can be construed it is necessary to determine upon evidence the peculiar meaning of words or the existence of incidents alleged to be attached by usage to the transaction, the preliminary determination must be made by the Commission; and not until this determination has been made, can a court take jurisdiction of the controversy. If this were not so, that uniformity which it is the purpose of the Commerce Act to secure could not be attained. For the effect to be given the tariff might depend, not upon construction of the language—a question of law—but upon whether or not a particular judge or jury had found, as a fact, that the words of the document were used in the peculiar sense attributed to them or that a particular usage existed.[21]

It is not difficult to discover in the test here laid down opportunity for further debate.

The reasonableness of a practice in regard to the distribution of coal cars to mines presents an administrative question;[22] and, under the amendments incorporated in the Interstate Commerce Act by Transportation Act, 1920, the establishment of junctions between the main lines of independent carriers and the interchange of car services is confided primarily to the exclusive jurisdiction of the Interstate Commerce Commission.[23]

The cases which have followed *Texas & Pac. Ry.* v. *Abilene Cotton Oil Co.* are an excellent illustration of the tendency to develop from a statute a principle, which then seems to establish its own claim to an independent existence and becomes the progenitor of vigorous offspring. The stock from which it was bred is almost forgotten and it asserts its position as a principle in its own right. The doctrine that administrative questions arising under the Interstate Commerce Act are confided to the primary and exclusive jurisdiction of the Interstate Commerce Commission seems almost to have become a principle of general jurisprudence.

The sweep of the jurisdiction thus confided to the Interstate Commerce Commission is seldom realized. The monetary stake is frequently tremendous. In the 1920 *Rate Case*[24] the advances sought and authorized by the Commission were estimated to amount to more than $1,000,000,000 per annum. The reductions in the 1922 *Rate Case*[25] were estimated to amount to several hundred millions per annum. In the *Pullman Surcharge Investigation*[26] the amount at stake was approximately $35,000,000 to $40,000,000 per annum; and the amount involved in the *Interchangeable Mileage Ticket Case*[27] approximately $20,000,000 to $30,000,000 per

annum. These proceedings are cited merely by way of illustration, though the first two cases were, of course, exceptional. Ordinary court litigation is a mere bagatelle in point
of monetary stake as compared with proceedings before the
Commission, particularly when it is remembered that action
by the Commission in rate cases continues to have its effect
from year to year.

Furthermore, by virtue of its jurisdiction of controversies
involving undue prejudice and preference in railroad rates,
as distinguished from unreasonableness, the Commission exercises a power of profound significance in its effect upon the
economic status of competing communities.[28] Its decisions
abound in illustrations of this power. The perennial contests
over the so-called port-differentials,[29] over the grain and
flour rates between Chicago, Buffalo, Minneapolis, Duluth,
and other points,[30] over the rates on citrus fruit and lumber
as between the south and the west,[31] over the lake-cargo coal
rates applicable from the so-called northern and southern
coal fields,[32] come to mind at once. The list might be extended almost indefinitely, since most rate cases represent
the vocalization of the economic dolor resulting from the
stress of competition between industries and localities. The
slightest reflection will indicate the immense importance to
the public of the extraordinary power which is involved in
adjudicating these controversies; and, when consideration is
given to the powers confided to the Commission by the Interstate Commerce Act in addition to those over rates, such as
the powers with respect to service, the issuance of securities,
the extension and abandonment of lines, the establishment of
divisions between carriers, and so forth, the magnitude of its
authority is at once manifest. And this authority is enhanced,
on the one hand, by the primary jurisdiction of the Commission over administrative questions, with its consequent effect
upon court jurisdiction, and, on the other hand, by the limited court review of Commission action permitted by the stat-

ute. For, if the Commission is to perform its functions effectively, not only must it have primary jurisdiction of matters coming within the scope of its activities, but a proper balance must be secured between the maintenance of its authority and protection to the interested parties when it passes the boundaries of its domain.

So, the third of the important principles referred to above as lying at the foundation of present-day railroad regulation —namely, the limitation imposed upon the courts with respect to Commission action—becomes a central feature in the whole scheme of regulation, a fact emphatically testified to by the extensive volume of literature that has been developed on this subject.[33] Perhaps the most satisfactory general statement of the rule regarding the power of the courts to review action by the Interstate Commerce Commission is found in *Interstate Commerce Comm.* v. *Union Pac. R.R.*,[34] in which the Supreme Court said:

> There has been no attempt to make an exhaustive statement of the principle involved, but in cases thus far decided, it has been settled that the orders of the Commission are final unless (1) beyond the power which it could constitutionally exercise; or (2) beyond its statutory power; or (3) based upon a mistake of law. But questions of fact may be involved in the determination of questions of law, so that an order, regular on its face, may be set aside if it appears that (4) the rate is so low as to be confiscatory and in violation of the constitutional prohibition against taking property without due process of law; or (5) if the Commission acted so arbitrarily and unjustly as to fix rates contrary to evidence, or without evidence to support it; or (6) if the authority therein involved has been exercised in such an unreasonable manner as to cause it to be within the elementary rule that the substance, and not the shadow, determines the validity of the exercise of the power.[35]

It is believed that this statement summarizes with accuracy the law with respect to court review of action by the Commission under the Interstate Commerce Act.[36] Subsequent decisions disclose the application of these principles in numerous situations.[37] In many of these cases the opinions have been by Mr. Justice Brandeis: indeed, he has contributed substantially to the law on this subject; and while the decisions are frequently unanimous, it is not without significance that where difference of opinion arises as between the different members of the Court the tendency of Mr. Justice Brandeis seems to be to support the Commission, although he is quite ready, if error of law appears, to join in setting aside the Commission's orders. Reference is made in the notes to his opinions bearing upon this matter.[38] Here brief comments upon a few of the more important will suffice.

How far the Court will go in declining to interfere with Commission action is well illustrated by the *New England Divisions Case*.[39] This proceeding originated before the Interstate Commerce Commission with a complaint filed by the New England railroads invoking the provisions of the Interstate Commerce Act as amended by Transportation Act, 1920, and demanding increased divisions out of the joint rates in which they participated with the railroads west of the Hudson River. Before the Commission special emphasis was laid upon the fact that the low net railway operating income of the New England railroads must have been a material factor in persuading the Commission to authorize the increases in rates approved in 1920,[40] but that the New England lines had not received increases in revenue commensurate with their needs although they were commensurate with the increases permitted in the joint rates. In brief, the New England roads did not wish to seek increases in rates within New England or in rates applying to or from that territory sufficient to meet what they conceived to be their needs. Traffic considerations, they thought, argued otherwise. But they joined with the lines west of the Hudson and east of the Mississippi in seeking an increase on a uniform basis for this entire territory, including New England; and the Commission acted in accordance with this proposal and authorized an advance generally of 40 per cent in the freight rates in this so-called Eastern Group. Obviously, the subsequent demand of the New England railroads for increased divisions suggested, somewhat bluntly, that localities outside New England should help to support the New England roads through the medium of increases in the divisions of joint rates; in other words, that the division of joint rates should be influenced, to a substantial extent, by the respective "needs" of the carriers participating in such rates. The action of the Court in sustaining the decision of the Commission, illustrates the reach of the Commission's authority. Mr. Justice Brandeis, who wrote the opinion, said:

> It is contended that if the act be construed as authorizing such apportionment of a joint rate on the basis of the greater needs of particular carriers, it is unconstitutional. There is no claim that the apportionment results in confiscatory rates, nor is there in this record any basis for such a contention. The argument is that the division of a joint rate is essentially a partition of property; that the rate must be divided on the basis of the services rendered by the several carriers; that there is no difference between taking part of one's just share of a joint rate and taking from a carrier part of the cash in its treasury; and, thus, that apportionment according to needs is a taking of property without due process. But the argument begs the question. What is its just share?—It is the amount properly apportioned out of the joint rate. That amount is to be determined, not by an agreement of the parties or by mileage. It is to be fixed by the Commission; fixed at what that board finds to be just, reasonable and equitable. Cost of the service is one of the elements in rate making. It may be just to give the prosperous carrier a smaller proportion of the increased rate than of the original rate. Whether the rate is reasonable may depend largely upon the disposition which is to be made of the revenues derived therefrom.[41]

The approach of the action of the Commission to socialistic theory is apparent: but the Court finds its decision within the scope of its jurisdiction and holds that "to consider the weight of the evidence, or the wisdom of the order entered, is beyond our province."[42]

Moreover, the case illustrates the tendency of the Court to accept as adequate support for the Commission's order evidence of limited scope found by the Commission to be typical,[43] a tendency emphasized in the *Assigned Car Cases*[44] in which the Court, again speaking through Mr. Justice Brandeis, said:

> The contention that findings of the Commission concerning discrimination were unsupported by evidence, or that findings essential to the order are lacking, rests largely upon a misconception. This objection was directed particularly to the finding that the existing practice in regard to assigned cars results in giving to the mines enjoying assigned cars an unjust and unreasonable share of railroad services and of facilities other than cars. The claim is that the evidence, upon which the finding of the resulting discrimination in these other transportation facilities rests, relates to only a few carriers, and that the general finding to that effect is without support, because the evidence introduced was not shown to be typical. Compare *New England Divisions Case*, 261 U.S. 184, 196–197; *United States* v. *Abilene & Southern Ry. Co.*, 265 U.S. 274, 291. The argument overlooks the difference in the character between a general rule prescribed under paragraph (12) and a practice for particular carriers ordered or prohibited under §§1, 3, and 15 of the Interstate Commerce Act. In the cases cited, the Commission was determining the relative rights of the several carriers in a joint rate. It was making a partition; and it performed a function quasi-judicial in its nature. In the case at bar, the function exercised by the Commission is wholly legislative. Its authority to legislate is limited to establishing a reasonable rule. But in establishing a rule of general application, it is not a condition of its validity that there be adduced evidence of its appropriateness in respect to every railroad to which it will be applicable. In this connection, the Commission, like other legislators, may reason from the particular to the general.[45]

Whether it is intended to suggest that there is a difference between the so-called "legislative" function of the Commission and its customary administrative functions is not wholly clear. In the *Chicago Junction Case*[46] Mr. Justice Brandeis had said: "Rate orders are clearly legislative."[47] Probably, therefore, the language quoted does not mean to suggest greater freedom of action, so far as dependence on formal records is concerned, than in the ordinary case where the Commission exercises its administrative authority, but to distinguish, as the context seems to show is intended, between its administrative and its quasi-judicial functions. It would imply, apparently, that in the exercise of its quasi-judicial authority—as, for example, in passing upon claims for reparation—it must find more definite and complete support in the record than when it prescribes rates for the future.[48]

The opinions filed by Mr. Justice Brandeis in cases involving the validity of orders of the Commission cover a wide variety of action by the Commission, but probably none are more important than those dealing with alleged undue preference and prejudice. As already stated, controversies turning on the significance of the provisions of the law prohibiting such undue preference and prejudice are of the greatest practical significance. The fate of an industry or of a community may be determined by what the Commission does under this power. Furthermore, it is here[49] that the Commission finds the great authority under which, in certain cases, it may control intrastate railroad and express rates and establish them on a level in direct conflict with the requirements of state commissions, state statutes, or state constitutions. Under this power the Commission, within prescribed limits, may invalidate state action. The power resembles a limited judicial review of unconstitutional legislation. Although bitterly challenged at the outset, the propriety of this authority is now recognized on all hands: in no other way can the Commission make its authority over interstate rates effective.

As is well known, the jurisdiction was upheld in the famous decision, popularly known as the *Shreveport Case.*[50] It was given broader scope by the amendments incorporated in the Interstate Commerce Act by Transportation Act, 1920;[51] so that now there is effective authority in the Interstate Commerce Commission not only to protect interstate traffic against intrastate rates improperly related to interstate rates, but also to see that intrastate traffic produces "a proportionate and equitable share of the income of the carriers."[52]

Here the recent opinion of Mr. Justice Brandeis, in *Georgia Public Serv. Comm.* v. *United States,*[53] constitutes an important contribution to the solution of the delicate questions arising in connection with the application of these principles. This opinion deals with the difficult matter of the sufficiency of the proof of unjust discrimination against interstate commerce. He says:

> The order here challenged is state-wide in operation; and it governs a vast multitude of rates. Because of divergent conditions, a doubt may well arise in applying the rule prescribed to some particular situation. But possible uncertainty of application in isolated instances is not a sufficient ground for setting aside in its entirety, by judicial process, a carefully drawn order, otherwise valid and practicable of operation over a wide territory. . . .
>
> The appellants contend that the order is void because there are no adequate findings of undue disparity between the rates charged for intrastate transportation in Georgia and the rates actually in force for interstate transportation; and also because there was no finding that the intrastate rates imposed an undue burden upon the carriers' interstate revenues or that the alteration of the intrastate rates would produce additional revenue. The findings in the report are definite and comprehensive. There are, moreover, illustrative specific findings which confirm the general ones and show that in a real sense, and to a substantial degree, undue prejudice and discrimination to interstate shippers and localities have resulted and will result. The requirement of definiteness to which attention was called in *Beaumont, S. L. & W. Ry. Co.* v. *United States*, 282 U.S. 74, 86 and in *Florida* v. *United States*, 282 U.S. 194, 208, is also met.

The appellants contend that the findings are unsupported by the evidence. When an investigation involves shipments from and to many places under varying conditions, typical instances justify general findings. *Railroad Commission* v. *Chicago, B. & Q. R. Co.,* 257 U.S. 563, 579. Compare *Beaumont, S. L. & W. Ry. Co.* v. *United States,* 282 U.S. 74, 83. While the order relates only to a few commodities, the scales of rates are statewide in operation; and they apply to shipments between hundreds of points of origin and destination. To require specific evidence and separate adjudication in respect to each would be tantamount to denying the possibility of granting relief. Compare *New England Divisions Case,* 261 U.S. 184; *Railroad Commission* v. *Chicago, B. & Q. R. Co., loc. cit. supra.* The evidence was comprehensive in scope.[54]

It thus appears that Mr. Justice Brandeis has had occasion to contribute, through his opinions in important cases, to the development of the four principles of railroad regulation which had been established by decisions of the Court before he became a member and which lie at the foundation of present-day railroad regulation. But it was not long after his elevation to the bench that there came the "strange interlude" of federal control with its perplexing questions. Was the Government operating the railroads through the legal personality of the Director General or through the legal personalities of the corporate owners of the property? Important practical results followed from either answer: and the question was actively debated for some months. The Court's decision in *Missouri Pac. R.R.* v. *Ault*[55] cleared the atmosphere. The opinion of Mr. Justice Brandeis is unequivocal: the railroads were operated, not through the owner-companies, but by a Director General:

By the establishment of the Railroad Administration and subsequent orders of the Director General, the carrier companies were completely separated from the control and management of their systems. . . . It is obvious, therefore, that no liability arising out of the operation of these systems was imposed by the common law upon the owner-companies as their interest in and control over the systems were completely suspended.[56]

"The Government operated this railroad not as lessee, but under a right in the nature of eminent domain," he said in *North Carolina R.R. v. Lee.*[57]

It seems of little use to refer to other questions arising during this era, although at the time they seemed of great importance. Was the Director General one person or did he have as many legal personalities as the companies whose properties he controlled?[58] And what if these companies were interrelated?[59] What constituted the taking possession of a railroad?[60] To what extent did state statutes, suspended during federal control in their application to railroads, become operative thereafter?[61] Could the Director General be substituted as defendant in place of a railroad corporation erroneously sued?[62] These and other similar questions[63] troubled the minds of counsel for the shippers and the railroads for several years after federal control had ceased and the new provisions of Transportation Act, 1920, had become operative. "*Quis, talia fando, . . . temperet a lacrimis?*"[64]

The provisions of this last named Act introduced a new policy into the regulation of railroads. As Mr. Justice Brandeis said in his opinion in the *New England Divisions Case:*

Transportation Act, 1920, introduced into the federal legislation a new railroad policy. *Railroad Commission of Wisconsin* v. *Chicago, Burlington & Quincy R. R. Co.*, 257 U.S. 563, 585. Theretofore, the effort of Congress had been directed mainly to the prevention of abuses; particularly, those arising from excessive or discriminatory rates. The 1920 Act sought to ensure, also, adequate transportation service. That such was its purpose, Congress did not leave to inference. The new purpose was expressed in unequivocal language. And to attain it, new rights, new obligations, new machinery, were created. The new provisions took a wide range. Prominent among them are those specially designed to secure a fair return on capital devoted to the transportation service. Upon the

Commission, new powers were conferred and new duties were imposed.

The credit of the carriers, as a whole, had been seriously impaired. To preserve for the nation substantially the whole transportation system was deemed important.[65]

The significance of the new legislation is further illustrated by his opinion in *Texas & Pac. Ry.* v. *Gulf, Colorado & Santa Fe Ry.*[66] He there decides, first, that one railroad may challenge in court the construction of proposed additional trackage by another railroad, irrespective of the fact that the Interstate Commerce Commission has not decided whether such proposed additional trackage constitutes an extension of road within the meaning of the Interstate Commerce Act; and, second, that in such case it is a question of law as to what constitutes an extension. He then points out that the meaning of the word should be sought in the light of the context and policy of Transportation Act, 1920, and says:

By that measure, Congress undertook to develop and maintain, for the people of the United States, an adequate railway system. It recognized that preservation of the earning capacity, and conservation of the financial resources, of individual carriers is a matter of national concern; that the property employed must be permitted to earn a reasonable return; that the building of unnecessary lines involves a waste of resources and that the burden of this waste may fall upon the public; that competition between carriers may result in harm to the public as well as in benefit; and that when a railroad inflicts injury upon its rival, it may be the public which ultimately bears the loss. See *Railroad Commission* v. *Chicago, Burlington & Quincy R. R. Co.*, 257 U.S. 563; *The New England Divisions Case*, 261 U.S. 184; *The Chicago Junction Case*, 264 U.S. 258; *Railroad Commission* v. *Southern Pacific Co.*, 264 U.S. 331. The Act sought, among other things, to avert such losses.[67]

He then proceeds to contrast an extension of line with industrial side tracks.

Tracks of that character are commonly constructed either to improve the facilities required by shippers already served by the carrier or to supply the facilities to others, who being within the same territory and similarly situated are entitled to like service from the carrier. The question whether the construction should be allowed or compelled depends largely upon local conditions which the state regulating body is peculiarly fitted to appreciate. Moreover, the expenditure involved is ordinarily small. But where the proposed trackage extends into territory not theretofore served by the carrier, and particularly where it extends into territory already served by another carrier, its purpose and effect are, under the new policy of Congress, of national concern. For invasion through new construction of territory adequately served by another carrier, like the establishment of excessively low rates in order to secure traffic enjoyed by another, may be inimical to the national interest. If the purpose and effect of the new trackage is to extend substantially the line of a carrier into new territory, the proposed trackage constitutes an extension of the railroad within the meaning of paragraph 18, although the line be short and although the character of the service contemplated be that commonly rendered to industries by means of spurs or industrial tracks. Being an extension, it cannot be built unless the federal commission issues its certificate that public necessity and convenience require its construction. The Hale-Cement Line is clearly an extension within this rule.[68]

These opinions emphasize the new policy initiated by Congress in 1920 with respect to the regulation of the railroads, and the excerpts quoted constitute a succinct statement of the economic philosophy which underlies this policy.

Indeed, considerations drawn from his theories as to the economic aspect of the matter play a large part in his views on that most controversial of subjects, railroad valuation. There is no purpose, however, to make this discussion an excuse for participating in this dispute. It seems long ago to have ceased to be a private controversy and to have become a fight open to anyone, as the Irishman suggested. But, since it presents an issue closely related to that involved in the valuation of public utilities generally, and since the articles heretofore produced on the subject do not seem to have tended to promote a reconciliation of opposing views or a solution of the problem, the writer of this article must hold himself excused from engaging in what to him would seem a work of futility, viz., submitting a critique of Mr. Justice Brandeis' famous dissenting opinion in the so-called *O'Fallon Case*.[69] Suffice it to say that that opinion, taken in conjunction with his opinion in the *Southwestern Bell Tel. Co.* v. *Public Serv. Comm.*,[70] presents the ablest available discussion of the so-called prudent investment theory of valuation. It constitutes a contribution to the literature on the subject which must be reckoned with whenever new questions arise in this field.

In like fashion his dissenting opinion in *United Railways* v. *West*,[71] by virtue of its elaborate discussion of the part depreciation plays in valuation cases, furnishes abundant material that is provocative, not only of controversy, but of thought also; and while this case did not specifically relate to the problem of depreciation in the matter of railroad valuation, his opinion evidences his full understanding of the special character of the questions involved as they affect the railroads. He outlines in clear detail the considerations advanced by the railroads in support of the contention that no depreciation, in the proper sense of the term, inheres in a railroad property currently and adequately maintained;[72] and says:[73] "We have no occasion to decide now whether the view taken by the Interstate Commerce Commission in *Telephone and Railroad Depreciation Charges*, 118 I.C.C. 295, or the protest of the railroads, gas and electric companies should prevail."[74]

But whether there is agreement or disagreement with Mr. Justice Brandeis on these issues involved in valuation cases, the importance of his opinions is evidenced by the fact that they have become the shining target at which those with contrary views undertake to aim their answering shafts—the best kind of compliment, it is believed, to their intellectual texture.

Passing to less controversial matters, his opinions with respect to the scope and significance of the prohibition of undue preference and prejudice furnish a clear definition of a tort which has sometimes caused confusion in the judicial mind. In *Central R.R. of New Jersey* v. *United States* he says:

> Discrimination may, of course, be practiced by a combination of connecting carriers as well as by an individual railroad; and the Commission has ample power under §3 to remove discrimination so practiced. See *St. Louis Southwestern Ry. Co.* v. *United States,* 245 U.S. 136, 144. But participation merely in joint rates does not make connecting carriers partners. They can be held jointly and severally responsible for unjust discrimination only if each carrier has participated in some way in that which causes the unjust discrimination; as where a lower joint rate is given to one locality than to another similarly situated.[75]

The essential and fundamental character of discrimination is thus authoritatively established: it involves diverse treatment of two patrons by a single carrier. In no other way can "each carrier" participate "in that which causes the unjust discrimination."

Further light on the nature of the wrong is found in the following excerpt from his opinion in *United States* v. *Illinois Cent. R.R.:*[76]

> Self-interest of the carrier may not override the requirement of equality in rates. It is true that the law does not attempt to equalize opportunities among localities. *Interstate Commerce Commission* v. *Diffenbaugh,* 222 U.S. 42, 46; and that the advantage which comes to a shipper merely as a result of the position of his plant does not constitute an illegal preference. *Ellis* v. *Interstate Commerce Commission,* 237 U.S. 434, 445. To bring a difference in rates within the prohibition of §3, it must be shown that the discrimination practiced is unjust when measured by the transportation standard. In other

words, the difference in rates cannot be held illegal, unless it is shown that it is not justified by the cost of the respective services, by their values, or by other transportation conditions. But the mere fact that the Knoxo rate is inherently reasonable, and that the rate from competing points is not shown to be unreasonably low, does not establish that the discrimination is just. Both rates may lie within the zone of reasonableness and yet result in undue prejudice. *American Express Co.* v. *Caldwell,* 244 U.S. 617, 624.[77]

In like fashion, his construction of the statutory provisions regarding the famous long-and-short-haul clause in *Skinner & Eddy Corp.* v. *United States*[78] affords substantial help to those who must toil in this rather barren field—too barren to justify the exposition of their difficulties here. But this opinion is also noteworthy as indicating with succinct clearness the practical importance of a minimum rate power, a power conferred upon the Commission the following year.

His opinion in *Baltimore & Ohio S.W. R.R.* v. *Settle*[79] deals with a question of great practical difficulty: When is transportation which, isolatedly considered, takes place wholly within a state, part of interstate commerce because of its relation to a prior or subsequent movement of the same traffic? And what facts establish such relationship? An adequate discussion of these questions would involve the writing of another article, a task which for some years the writer of this one has held before his eager eyes without being able to accomplish it. *The Daniel Ball*[80] is the great progenitor of this hardy and contentious race; but some of the progeny bear little resemblance to their ancestor. Suffice it to say that in the *Settle* case, which has become a leading case, the decision is made to turn largely on the intention of the shipper, a test for which much can be said. But much can be said against it, especially if one is asked to advise a railroad what rate to apply on a given shipment. It is likely to be difficult for the railroad to ascertain the intention of the shipper.[81] But it is required under heavy penalty to charge the proper rate.

As to the person liable for charges, his opinion in *Louisville & Nashville R.R.* v. *Central Iron Co.*[82] summarizes the matter as follows:

But delivery of goods to a carrier for shipment does not, under the Interstate Commerce Act, impose upon a shipper an absolute obligation to pay the freight charges. The tariff did not provide when or by whom the payment should be made. As to these matters carrier and shipper were left free to contract, subject to the rule which prohibits discrimination. The carrier was at liberty to require prepayment of freight charges; or to permit that payment to be deferred until the goods reached the end of the transportation. *Wadley Southern Ry. Co.* v. *Georgia*, 235 U.S. 651, 656. Where payment is so deferred, the carrier may require that it be made before delivery of the goods; or concurrently with the delivery; or may permit it to be made later. Where the payment is deferred, the contract may provide that the shipper agrees absolutely to pay the charges; or it may provide merely that he shall pay if the consignee does not pay the charges demanded upon delivery of the goods. Or the carrier may accept the goods for shipment solely on account of the consignee; and, knowing that the shipper is acting merely as agent for the consignee, may contract that only the latter shall be liable for the freight charges. Or both the shipper and the consignee may be made liable. Nor does delivery of goods to a carrier necessarily import, under the general law, an absolute promise by the shipper to pay the freight charges. We must, therefore, determine what promise, if any to pay freight charges was, in fact, made by the Central Company.[83]

On the other hand, his opinions regarding the right of shippers to reparation furnish a noteworthy contribution to this difficult subject; but in view of the fact that the questions arising here are highly specialized, it seems inadvisable to undertake a discussion of the decisions. The more important are referred to in the notes.[84]

Other opinions might be cited, but enough has been said to indicate that Mr. Justice Brandeis has had occasion to express his views on practically every part of the Interstate Commerce Act that has required interpretation by the Supreme Court; and his views have now become part and parcel of the principles daily applied in the enforcement of the statute.

The outstanding impression created by a study of his work is that of a judge seeking, through the maze of conflicting contentions, to find "the logic of realities"[85] on which he may safely build his judicial conclusions. In these railroad cases the terrain is not unfamiliar. He had himself practiced before the Commission prior to his appointment to the Court and had handled cases of importance.[86] As stated above, he had been selected by the Commission to represent it in the *Five Per Cent Case*—up to that time one of the most important cases to come before it. He had been asked "to undertake the task of seeing that all sides and angles of the case are presented of record." This duty he discharged with signal ability. So he had come to understand the vast power of the Commission: he had an intimate understanding of its procedure:[87] he was thoroughly familiar with railroad terminology and the concepts which that terminology connotes.

All of this appears in his opinions. He understands the different classes of rates and their economic functions and significance.[88] He has a clear conception of that seemingly simple, but in reality highly complex, matter of railroad demurrage.[89] To him undue preference is not a legal concept only, but a matter of vital business significance in its bearing on the relation of industries and communities. And the interest of the community as related to the interest of the railroad is fully appreciated whether the question be as to the divisions of rates, or the mistaken policy of unduly low rates, the extension of new lines, or any other of the multitudinous issues that come before the Commission. He knows well that, "Transportation conditions are not static; the oppressor of today may tomorrow be the oppressed."[90]

Indeed, this ready comprehension of the whole background of the situation makes it a peculiar pleasure to argue a railroad case before him. The questions he puts invariably serve to illuminate the picture, the apparently unconscious nods of comprehension infuse the eager advocate with renewed confidence, albeit he may know that these nods may signify clear understanding of the argument rather than agreement with it.[91] It is always regrettable to lose a case, but there is some consolation to the vanquished when the court's opinion indicates that at least the trusted contentions have been fully understood. It is more difficult to be philosophic when the feeling persists that the court, like the lady celebrated by Mr. Kipling, "did not understand"—a fairly common complaint of defeated litigants, but one that the writer has never heard made in reference to the opinions of Mr. Justice Brandeis. And, at least in the matter of railroad cases, he has been in a position to hear them if any there have been.

Along with this thorough comprehension of the particular subject matter with which the railroad cases necessarily deal, there is disclosed in his opinions that thoroughgoing acquaintance with business methods generally which is a necessary corollary to a comprehension of the problems of the railroads; and it is but trite to say that his familiarity with the social and economic forces that underlie the modern world has won him unique recognition, whether it comes from those who agree with him or from those who disagree. He must be reckoned with because he is searching for "the logic of realities." As he says in another case: "*Ex facto jus oritur.* That ancient rule must prevail in order that we may have a system of living law."[92]

His attitude to the high responsibilities which have been devolved upon him seems essentially that of the scientist in the world of today. He must be on the lookout for the legal concepts, which have been "encysted in phrases"[93] so that they have ceased "to provoke further analysis." He must avoid assumption—indeed, the most generally accepted assumption must be as open to challenge as the newest theory. They must all be brought to the same test: Are they justified by the facts? So, in his opinions—and in this regard his railroad opinions are excellent illustrations—there is elaborate documentation by reference to the literature other than judicial which tends to remove obscurity from the problem to which he applies the judicial solution. Only in this way will the principle of evolution which has been the life of the common law develop in the direction most consistent with the genius of the people and with their best interest.

In the famous aphorism of Mr. Justice Holmes: "The life of the law has not been logic: it has been experience."[94] And, as one concludes a review of the opinions of Mr. Justice Brandeis, there comes to mind what his brilliant associate said as far back as 1897: "For the rational study of the law the black-letter man may be the man of the present, but the man of the future is the man of statistics and the master of economics."[95]

VI

THE JURIST'S ART

BY

WALTON H. HAMILTON

THE JURIST'S ART

*Ex facto jus oritur. That ancient rule must prevail in order that
we may have a system of living law.* Mr. Justice Brandeis[1]

I

IF jurists have the feelings of other men, Monday, the
fifth of January, nineteen hundred and thirty-one, must
have been a day of consequence in the life of Mr. Justice
Brandeis. On that day he handed down the judgment of the
United States Supreme Court in the *O'Gorman* case.[2] The
cause was a simple suit in contract; the result depended upon
the validity of a New Jersey statute regulating the commissions to be paid by insurance companies to their agents for
securing business. The more general question was the tolerance to be accorded to legislative price-fixing under the Fourteenth Amendment. And, as the fortunes of litigation broke,
the issue came to be the intellectual procedure by which the
constitutionality of the acts which make up the public control
of business are to be determined. Upon that day the views of
Brandeis became "the opinion of the Court," and a new chapter in judicial history began to be written.

The judgment was clearly an act of deliberation. In a test
suit the statute had been found valid by the Court of Errors
and Appeals of New Jersey.[3] It had been argued before the
United States Supreme Court; restored to the docket for reargument, probably because a bench of eight had divided
evenly;[4] and, after reargument, found valid by a bare majority of one. The dissent found a unique expression in "a
separate opinion" which bears the names of four of the Justices;[5] they insisted that the decision overlooked the established presumption in favor of freedom of contract, that it
went against compelling precedents, that "the restrictions
were novel" and lacked "the sanction of general assent and
practical experience," and that the statute was "arbitrary, un-

reasonable, and beyond the power of the legislature." The language of the official opinion bears every evidence of a studied statement, subjected to close scrutiny, and carefully worded to express the views of the majority of the court.

In form "the opinion of the Court" is a very simple and unpretentious document. It begins with a statement of the issue and a history of the case, continues with a brief summary of the reasons for the statute and a statement that "the business of insurance is so affected with a public interest that the state may regulate the rates," and concludes with a declaration of the test for validity. As "underlying questions of fact may condition the constitutionality of legislation of this character," it follows that "the presumption of constitutionality must prevail in the absence of some factual foundation of record for overthrowing the statute." It did not appear "upon the face of the statute, or from any facts of which the Court must take judicial notice" that in New Jersey "evils did not exist," for which the statute was "an appropriate remedy." Accordingly the court was compelled to declare the statute valid; in fact it was left with no alternative.

Yet the simple lines of a short opinion present a superb example of the jurist's art. The catalogue of precedents is left to the dissent; the technique of distinction would do no more than serve the current need. There is no attempt to make out a case; an elaborate argument, concerned with the insurance business, filled with citations, and buttressed in footnotes would save a single statute. The demand is to find an escape from the recent holdings[6] predicated upon "freedom of contract" as "the rule," from which a departure is to be allowed only in exceptional cases.[7] The occasion calls not for the deft use of tactics, but for a larger strategy. The device of presumption is almost as old as law; Brandeis revives the presumption that acts of a state legislature are valid and applies it to statutes regulating business activity. The factual brief has many times been employed to make a case for social

legislation; Brandeis demands of the opponents of legislative
acts a recitation of fact showing that the evil did not exist or
that the remedy was inappropriate. He appeals from precedents to more venerable precedents;[8] reverses the rules of
presumption and proof in cases involving the control of industry; and sets up a realistic test of constitutionality. It is all
done with such legal verisimilitude that a discussion of particular cases is unnecessary; it all seems obvious—once Brandeis has shown how the trick is done.[9] It is attended with so
little of a fanfare of judicial trumpets that it might have
passed almost unnoticed,[10] save for the dissenters, who usurp
the office of the chorus in a Greek tragedy and comment upon
the action.[11] Yet an argument which degrades "freedom of
contract" to a constitutional doctrine of the second magnitude
is compressed into a single compelling paragraph.

This judgment is a single specimen from the workshop of
a distinguished jurist. In form it is not cut to a pattern; the
opinions are suited to the variable task and the changing occasion. In spirit it is representative; the techniques which are
law are given employment in the service of judicial statesmanship.

II

In justice, as in every craft, the creative artist leaves his distinctive mark upon his work. The critic of art can distinguish
the paintings of Raphael and Michelangelo; the musician,
even at a first hearing, can separate the compositions of Mo-
zart and Beethoven, Debussy and Stravinsky. The student of
letters needs only brief excerpts to discover the characteristics which set Scott off from Fielding, Dickens from Thack-
eray, and Thomas Hardy from Edith Wharton. In law, even
when rules are compelling and cases come along in dull mo-
notony, the manner of the judge appears in the interstices of
opinion. In constitutional decision, law encounters the problems of a culture in the making and its path must be broken;

judges must find their ways as best they can, through tangles of imperfectly understood situations, past the conflict of values which cannot be resolved, to answers which will do. The jurist, even as the spokesman for a court, cannot escape from being himself.

The annals of constitutional law attest an almost infinite variety of judicial workmanship. Marshall moves along with a majestice sweep an argument which will make no compromise with the word "peradventure."[12] Field turns expediencies into verities and identifies his righteous convictions with the supreme law and with God's commandments.[13] Harlan, quite without stint, transfers to the reports all that is on his mind.[14] White, in interminable sentences filled with polysyllables, sweeps aside opposing argument as self-contradictory.[15] Moody applies a Constitution, which embodies "the spirit of the nation-builder and not the code-maker," to "the infinite variety of the changing conditions of our national life."[16] Stone pries critically into a concept and wonders if it is not in itself question begging.[17] Even Holmes and Brandeis may look upon each other's work and find it good; but their opinions come out of different workshops. It is probably the conception of law as "the law" which has thrown into obscurity the fine art of the jurist.

The art of judgment is of its own kind. Unlike the poet, the historian, or the essayist, the jurist cannot listen to the promptings of his own heart, choose the subject upon which he would write, say as he would all that is in his mind, and follow his interest to a fresh theme. Instead, as a member of a court, his decisions are a mere step in the process of disposing of litigation. He cannot speak until the appropriate cause comes along, he can address himself to the larger issue only so far as a suit at law allows, he must express a partial opinion and wait for a suitable occasion to continue. Even when his concern is with constitutional issues, and in granting or withholding approval to statutes he is declaring public policy, his manner of speech cannot be that of the statesman. His place is in the institution of the judiciary; he is bound by its usages and procedures; he addresses himself, not directly to a social question, but to a matter of policy translated into the language of law; he cannot escape the values, rules, and intellectual ways of the discipline he professes. On the frontier where a changing social necessity impinges upon the established law, the jurist must possess a double competence; he must employ alike legal rule and social fact, and where they clash, as inevitably they will in a developing culture, he must effect the best reconciliation that may lie between them. The judge must become the statesman without ceasing to be the jurist; the quality of his art lies in the skill, the intelligence, and the sincerity with which he manages to serve two masters.

An art, whose concern is mediation, is evident in Mr. Justice Brandeis' judicial style. It has been deliberately contrived to serve its unique purpose. His private conversation is marked by the veiled word, the pointed thrust, the neat characterization; and he possesses a gift of happy phrasing not incomparable to Holmes. Although his early opinions hold much of literary charm,[18] he presently committed himself to a direct, straightforward style as the most effective judicial utterance. He aims at simplicity of statement, clarity of meaning, and persuasiveness of argument; he tries to attain these qualities without resort to colorful words or rhetorical flourish. The use of exposition to do duty as argument has an effectiveness all its own; in the *Wan* case[19] he employs a bare recitation of the facts to make out a convincing indictment of "the third degree" methods of the police; in the *O'Fallon* case[20] he challenges the rule of the cost of reproduction new in the valuation of public utilities by a mere enumeration of the practical difficulties which attend its operation. The lawyer finds his opinions written in conventional language, concerned with legal questions, and filled with citations to the reports. The layman, after penetrating the outward form, discovers the facts, problems, and arguments from the universe he knows. Yet the stuff of the world seems at home in the habitat of law; there is no intellectual fault-line between constitutional issue and social problem. Above all his writing is communication, rather than self-expression;[21] it conveys to you his meaning, rather than provides verbal receptacles for your own thought.

In the use of the tricks of the legal trade,[22] Mr. Justice Brandeis is a master. His skilful use of extra-legal material has somewhat obscured the fact that he is probably the best technical lawyer on his bench. There is hardly a device or usage of intellectual method or judicial procedure which he does not employ. If he is less zealous than some of his brethren in keeping unworthy causes away, he knows how, on occasion, to put his knowledge of the jurisdiction of the Court to very purposive use. In an original suit the states of Ohio and Pennsylvania prayed the Court for an order restraining the state of West Virginia from giving effect to a statute granting to its own citizens a priority in the use of natural gas.[23] The case was novel, the records barren of precedents. Brandeis feared judicial interference in a matter which might be handled more constructively by some other agency of control. So he argued[24] that "the bills present neither a 'case' nor a 'controversy' within the meaning of the Federal Constitution"; that, in the absence of the gas-producing companies and the consumers, "there is a fatal lack of the necessary parties," and that the Court, sitting in equity, lacked the power to grant effective relief. Thus the question was shifted from the constitutionality of the statute to the validity of judicial discretion in an industrial matter. Although his view did not prevail, it was only after the raising of new issues had led to the argument of the case for the third time that the Court made up its mind. Moreover, it is evident that Mr. Justice Van Devanter reformed his argument; for, point by point, "the opinion of the Court" is addressed to the Brandeis dissent.

In like manner, he puts to effective use the usages of procedure. The primary question before the Court is always the disposition of the case; it is only as the exigencies of litigation demand that the Constitution is expounded. A neat example of the advantage taken of a suit at law to settle a substantive question is the opinion of Brandeis in the *Live-stock Commission* case.[25] In accordance with the provisions of an act of Congress, the Secretary of Agriculture had issued an order fixing the rates to be charged by "market agencies" at the Omaha stockyards, and in a test case a lower federal court had found the regulation valid. The appeal to the Supreme Court alleged a number of errors, relating to the process of notice, the interpretation of the statute, and its validity under the due process clause. It was easy for the bench to vote to affirm the judgment below; but the argument was hard going, for on a number of recent occasions the Court had in very broad language declared price-fixing to be an improper deprivation of liberty of contract.[26] The difficulty was met by putting in the foreground the allegations of error and insisting that they had not been proved. The device served to relegate substantive questions to a less conspicuous place in the argument, where Brandeis by deft strokes robbed former holdings of their compulsions. Even if the logical difficulties could not be escaped, the shift from major to minor theme made the rhetorical going much easier.[27] The task was for Brandeis the harder because he had not concurred[28] in decisions which in behalf of the Court he was now called upon to distinguish.[29] The need for such a device grows out of the conflict between the judicial theory that the decisions of a Court have logical continuity and the fact that a judicial body must on occasion overrule former holdings. The need to reconcile reality with appearance is most acute when changes in personnel bring changes in policy. In law, as elsewhere, an exercise of discretion must often wear the mask of compulsion.

Quite as adroit is Brandeis' employment of the legal device, "the facts of the case." He knows that in law there is a minor as well as a major premise, that the issue turns not only upon the categories invoked but also upon the classification of the particulars. He never confuses the statement of facts and their legal connotations into a single narrative, nor does he allow preconceived judicial notions to determine what facts are relevant. In his opinions the tangles which come out of society are fully and realistically presented before the legal issues are raised. It often happens that the student, after reading "the opinion of the Court" and passing on to "Mr. Justice Brandeis, dissenting," finds himself in another intellectual world. In "the printing press case,"[30] which is typical, an employer is asking for an order restraining a labor organization and the affiliates from using the secondary boycott in a campaign to organize its shop. Mr. Justice Pitney, who speaks for the Court, deals with the two parties as if they were strangers, regards union program and policy as irrelevant, and recognizes no motive in the activities other than the malicious injury of the employer. It is only from the dissent[31] that we learn that there are in the country four manufacturers of printing presses, that all save the Duplex Company are organized, that the effectiveness of the organization is threatened by the non-union shop, and that the purpose of the boycott is the preservation of the wages and working conditions of the union employees. The relevance of this single item, ignored by Pitney and put to the fore by Brandeis, is the vital point in the case; it determines whether the matter is to be approached in terms of a common-law rule surviving from the days of handicraft or as a problem of the legal limits of group activity in an industrial society. Present or withdraw this one salient fact, and the rest of the erudite and fine-spun argument, concerned with rules of law, the pertinence of precedents, the ways of interpretation, and the meaning of statutes, stands or falls. In his judicial strategy Mr. Justice Brandeis does not forget that a case may be won or lost before a legal question is ever raised.

The knack of distinction is probably the neatest trick of the jurist's trade; and Brandeis employs it in his own distinctive way. Any lawyer who knows the indices can muster precedents in imposing array; the length of his list of citations is limited only by his industry. It takes a capacity for analysis to separate holding from dicta and to limit it to its specific meaning; it requires a sense of historical reality to see that precedents are not lifted across factual and ideological gulfs to be given novel applications. The dissenting opinion of Brandeis in "the news-stealing case,"[32] is an elaborate exercise in the art of separating lines of decision which are only verbally alike. The Associated Press was applying for an injunction against the International News Service. The complaint was that items, copied from early morning editions of its clientele in the East, were published in the supporting western newspapers of the rival organization. Brandeis passes in review[33] the several series of cases in which the courts have accorded a limited protection against disclosure or republication to common-law copyright, ticker service, and to trade secrets, and against unfair competitive practices; he shows, in each instance, the difference from the instant case in the factual situation, the interests of the parties, and the incidence of judicial interference upon the conduct of the business. There is nothing unprecedented in a Court of Equity doing an unprecedented thing; but the dissent robs of its foundation in formidable precedents the restraining order which the Court grants, and makes it clear that a property right is being created by judicial process. Here, as in like instances,[34] an ordinary usage becomes an instrument of a realistic jurisprudence.

But the touch of the artist is most apparent in Mr. Justice Brandeis' creative use of judicial notice. The judgment of the

Court is predicated not only upon the law but also upon the matter to which it relates. The constitutionality of a statute depends upon its reasonableness, and reason invites a pragmatic test. An informed judgment awaits alike a knowledge of the conditions out of which legislation emerged and of the way in which it may be expected to operate. It was not Brandeis who first introduced realistic discussions of the matters to which statutes relate into the law reports; but he, more than any other person, has domesticated the device to judicial service. The state of Nebraska, by official act, allowed a leeway of no more than two ounces in the pound in the weight of loaves of bread; the constitutional issue of "the taking of property" and "due process of law" became the practical question of whether the technique of baking had attained such perfection as to make the tolerance sufficient.[35] Brandeis examined the literature of a branch of the culinary art, concluded that the restriction was justified by prevailing practice, and forced the spokesman for the Court to justify his decision by a like resort to the lay word.[36] The state of Washington forbade private employment agencies to charge fees from employees for whom they found jobs;[37] Brandeis made an exhaustive study of their operation, discovered their method to be exploitative, found their function adequately performed by public agencies, and concluded that the magnitude of the evil justified the drastic remedy.[38] To the spokesman of the Court this was "not enough to justify destruction of one's right to follow a distinctly useful calling in an upright way."[39] A case turning upon the power of the President to remove an executive officer led him to an exhaustive research out of which emerged a historical essay upon senatorial and presidential control of federal officeholders.[40] The challenge, in the name of "the equal protection of the laws," of an act of Pennsylvania imposing upon the corporate operators of taxicabs taxes from which individuals were exempt led him to inquire how it had come about that privileges conferred upon chartered companies by the state had ripened into constitutional rights.[41] In a suit concerned with the proper valuation of a street railway property, Brandeis discovered the questionable item in the capital account, examined all the books on accounting in the Library of Congress, and wrote perhaps the best discussion of the basis of depreciation to be found in print.[42] Among many skills this is distinctly his—to contrive to make terms between the law and the secular subjects upon which it operates.

But a mere sample must do duty for a catalogue of the techniques with which Brandeis does his work. The lines of argument may be one or many, simple or complex; the manner, the device, the combination of skills varies from opinion to opinion.[43] In the southern lumber case,[44] he does no more than recite the conditions which attend an uncontrolled competition in the industry, and show the need for a trade association;[45] in the *Di Santo* case, he is content to show the necessity for the legislative protection of immigrants against the fraud of unscrupulous sellers of steamship tickets.[46] On the contrary, when exigency commands, he employs an elaborate strategy. In the *Hitchman* case,[47] an employer prays for an injunction against the officials of a labor organization who are attempting to unionize its mine; in opposing the writ,[48] Brandeis examines the concepts of contract, property, and conspiracy; interprets the common-law and the anti-trust act, and inquires into the usages and limits of equitable relief. The opinion ranges from a technical examination of the meaning of "the contract," by which workingmen were bound to their employer not to affiliate with a labor union, to a realistic consideration of organization as an agency of economic security among coal miners. In the *Frost* case, he elaborates a legal discussion of a license, the privileges it confers, and the legal protection to which it is entitled; adds a financial argument that capital stock, dividends, and service to non-members cannot be used as criteria in separating business ventures from mutual benefit societies; and employs the whole complex dialectic to refute the argument that the granting of permits to gin cotton to private corporations and to farmers' coöperatives upon different terms is a denial of "the equal protection of the laws."[49] But no enumeration of its elements can reveal a way of work. As with all creative effort, it is not the device, but the skilled use of the device, not the procedure, but the procedure suited to the occasion, which reveals the craftsman. The workmanship of Brandeis, to be appreciated, must be studied in its native habitat—the reports.

For the key to the judicial technique of Mr. Justice Brandeis is not far to seek. In ordinary cases his mind moves along with the decorous processes of law; in great constitutional questions, where the words of a document must be adapted to the changing circumstances of society, the supreme question is what difference it makes whether the decision goes the one way or the other. He knows that usages employed in the process of judgment are inventions contrived to serve the ends of justice; he regards them as instruments to be employed, rather than compulsions to be obeyed; and as conditions change and common sense gives way to its better, he would keep them alive by fresh contact with reality. To him the great constitutional doctrines are formulas; and, as cause follows cause, their antithetical terms of public welfare and private inconvenience must be given weights from the stuff of life before a balance can be struck. Here rule and concept, fact and precedent, are to him henchmen who serve the greater and more enduring values of jurisprudence. In Brandeis' opinions one must look beyond the deft employment of the tricks of the jurist's trade for the secret of their use.

III

In the art of the jurist the thought and its words, the substance and its form, the man and the Justice are inseparable. The lines and the larger meaning of the Constitution abide; but, as bench succeeds bench with the passing years, different

winds of doctrine blow through its classic phrases. The how
and the why in the opinions of Bradley and Waite, of Brewer
and Gray, of McKenna and Pitney run back of judicial utterance to ways of thought which they shared with the laity.
Although he is intellectually aware and the most self-re-
strained of judges, the universe of ideas which lives in Mr.
Justice Holmes' head is an essential ingredient in his constitutional law. The very conception of the instrumental
character of the mechanism of justice makes the intellectual
views of the man dominant in the opinions of Mr. Justice
Brandeis.

At the very heart of his juristic theory lies the idea of the
worth of the individual. The spirit of the Constitution is to
be found in the amendments which make up the Bill of
Rights. Its makers "recognized the significance of man's
spiritual nature," "sought to protect Americans in their beliefs, their thoughts, their emotions, and their sensations,"
and thus "undertook to secure conditions favorable to the
pursuit of happiness."[50] In a democracy "harmony in national
life is a resultant of the struggle between contending forces";
for that reason "the full and free exercise" by the citizen of
the right to speak or write about public affairs is a duty; and
"in the frank expression of conflicting opinion lies the greatest
promise of wisdom in governmental action."[51] In economic
matters he recognizes "the fundamental right of free men to
strive for better conditions through new legislation and new
institutions"; he would not have argument suppressed merely
because it seems "to those exercising the judicial power to be
unfair in its portrayal of existing evils, mistaken in its assumptions, unsound in reasoning, or intemperate in language."[52]
To him a greater danger, in fact "the greatest danger to
liberty, lurks in insidious encroachment by men of zeal, well-
meaning, but without understanding."[53] He protests against
the fuller protection accorded to "property" than to "liberty"
in constitutional interpretation.[54] The recent decision of the

Court, announced by Mr. Chief Justice Hughes, that a state statute providing for the suppression of newspapers as nuisances is an infringement of the freedom of the press comprehended within the Fourteenth Amendment, epitomizes[55] a doctrine to which he is firmly committed.[56] Even if all justiciable questions resolve themselves into matters of degree,[57] and constitutional law has no absolutes, the rights of free men must have the utmost protection against legislative action.

It is, however, not an abstract individual, but man in an organized society, who occupies this unique distinction. In a culture as complex as ours there can be few laws "of universal application." In fact, "it is of the nature of our law that it has dealt, not with man in general, but with him in relationships."[58] The legislature, therefore, must be allowed wide latitude in classification, in order that its statutes may be neatly accommodated to the variety of enterprises which variously serve the community. He would not, in the name of "the equal protection of the laws," visit judicial disapproval upon statutes taxing corporations and exempting individuals,[59] imposing higher franchise taxes upon chain stores than upon individual merchants,[60] and making the way easier for farmers' coöperatives than for ordinary business ventures.[61] He favors the trade association as a "commendable effort by concerns engaged in a chaotic industry to make possible its intelligent conduct under competitive conditions";[62] he sees in the trade union an instrument for the maintenance of conditions of work and standards of living by workingmen.[63] The use of similar language to justify the activities of trade associations and of labor unions[64] attests a concern in economic order deeper than sympathy with a particular interest. But it is the less strategic group and little business, rather than large-scale production and combination, which has his support. He has, as occasion gave opportunity,[65] noted that his Court has held that "it was not unlawful to vest" in single corporations "control of fifty per cent of the steel"[66] and "practically the whole of the shoe machinery industry."[67] His tolerance of coöperation is associated with a distrust of centralization. To him mere size is never a virtue; the giant enterprise substitutes routine for discretion; its overorganized activities are not easily accommodated to changing conditions. His values belong to a theory of society which discounts advertising, skyscrapers, and "the bigger and better," and exalts the individual and personal enterprise.

Out of such values and trends of thought Brandeis' theory of constitutionality emerges. He makes a sharp separation between the rights of individuals of flesh and blood and the privileges of corporations, artificial persons, created by the Government. The contrast between the two appears in cases involving freedom of speech and freedom of contract. The right to a free and full expression of personal opinion has such value that only a positive case will justify its abridgment; the right of free contract is a business usage which has its important but limited function. The interference by the state, to regulate hours, to set standards of safety in hazardous employments, to keep inferior wares out of the market, and even to fix prices, is rather a modification of the arrangements under which industry is carried on than a deprivation of individual rights. As culture advances, "rights of property and the liberty of the individual must be remolded, from time to time, to meet the changing needs of society."[68] In the practical effort to improve institutions, which are of human contrivance, the state, as well as other institutions of control must be employed. The task is essentially experimental; and great latitude must be allowed to the legislature in adapting remedial measures to economic maladjustment. It is, therefore, essential that the legal formulas in which constitutional questions are stated should not obscure the conflict of social values with which they are concerned. Although "*stare decisis* is ordinarily a wise rule of action"[69] it "does not command that we err again when we pass upon a different statute."[70] This view led him, in days when the presumption was in favor of freedom of contract, to present a factual argument for a challenged statute. It leads him, now that the presumption favors legislative action, to demand a recitation of fact from its opponents. His concern, in constitutional issues, is that current necessity shall not be judged by the borrowed merits of former causes.

It follows, almost as of course, that he assigns to the judiciary a limited province in the social order. The legislature, the administrative commission, the court, the voluntary association within industry, are complementary agencies of control; each has its structure, its peculiar domain, its distinctive way of work. The business of the court must be limited to tasks which it can intelligently and constructively perform. It may well be that news collected at great expense needs to be protected against piracy; but "courts are ill-equiped to make the investigations which should precede" positive action and "powerless to prescribe the detailed regulations essential to the full enjoyment of the rights conferred" by judicial protection.[71] The struggle between employers and employed falls far short of industrial order, but so long as militancy prevails, "it is not for judges" to "set the limits of permissible contest and to declare the duties which the new situation demands."[72] The Interstate Commerce Commission has an acquaintance with, and an appreciation of, the values involved in the determination of railroad rates and valuations which a busy judiciary cannot bring to so alien a task.[73] The legislature can inquire into evils, examine experience, contrive remedies, and revise its measures of reform as expendiency dictates. The ways of courts, and the remedies at their disposal, are still too much in the service of suits between litigants, to be given the dominant rôle in the government of industry.[74] The Supreme Court must not elevate "the performance of the constitutional function of judicial review" into "an exercise of the powers of a super-legislature."[75]

A kindred value is his conception of the office of jurist. When he speaks for the Court, he is their spokesman—so far as his own integrity will allow. The views he sets forth are the common opinion which compromise makes possible; they represent, not what any member would like to say, but what all who concur are willing to accept. It is here that Brandeis exhibits in greatest variety the technique of the jurist; he employs great ingenuity in bringing the sanctions of law to common-sense judgment;[76] he distinguishes, quite neatly, contrary holdings. If the procedure seems at times to the layman to border upon verbal magic, it must be remembered that it serves a rhetorical, rather than a logical, purpose, and that Brandeis is not responsible for a theory of judicial work which has no place for trial and error. Accordingly, it is no accident that the great opinions of Mr. Justice Brandeis are dissents. The cause has for the moment been lost; the little questions will presently cease to be of moment; the larger issue alone is important; the task is to set forth in argument the values which have not had recognition.[77] In dissent Brandeis sharply and clearly states the question, presents from the law reports and secular literature all that he finds relevant and brings to judgment everything of information and understanding which he possesses. His workmanship, to quote a favorite phrase of his, is "painstaking"; his opinions are written and rewritten until they convey his studied conception of the problem; the dissenting opinion in the *O'Fallon* case[78] is said to have gone through thirty drafts. The dissent is his own utterance, unconfused by the need of voicing the opinions of others; it is not the law, but the law as he would have it be. Brandeis does not overvalue immediate victory. He contrives an informed and reasoned argument, spreads it upon the record—and is content to leave to the future the final verdict. His great dissents attest his most dominant value; he has a profound belief in the power of truth ultimately to prevail.

It is this scheme of values which gives quality to his workmanship; in them is the source of the strength of his judicial utterance. His art is the employment of the technique of the advocate in the service of the jurist. His opinions seem to reveal a mind rather quickly made up, a process of judging by the reference of facts to his scheme of values, a use of legal devices to secure the right answer to the dominant question. A great many of his dissenting opinions read like briefs; they put forward the arguments which might—if only attorneys had been abler and better informed—have been presented in behalf of the losing causes. But it is pleading of a very high order, free from cheap appeal, in a sense detached, aiming to convince rather than merely to persuade, resting upon information and understanding, and prompted by a sincere belief in the goodness of his cause. In a word, it is the art of the advocate, subdued to intellectual inquiry, and directed to the ends of social justice.

If the quest for the secret of Brandeis' art runs further, it is to be found in the manner of the man. He was born in Kentucky, in 1856, when the state was ringing with the clash of interests and of values which attended the conflict over slavery. He is of Jewish faith; in his family the great tradition of social righteousness had long been cherished. His parents, natives of Prague, were members of a band of "Pilgrims of '48";[79] the failure of revolution in Europe led them to emigrate to America. They brought with them democratic notions and grand pianos, hard sense in their heads and verses from the romantic poets upon their lips. Brandeis went to school in Germany and came away with his head full of the lines and the ideas of Goethe. He attended the Harvard Law School when the dogmatism of the text was being discarded, and Langdell was beginning to find out the actual ways of the courts by the case-method. In a unique law practice, he came to be a kind of general counsel for the public, taking cases affected with a social interest, and arguing the cause of the shipper, the laborer, or the consumer. He was among its ablest and most distinguished members, when he was transferred from the bar to the bench of the United States Supreme Court.

In appointing him a Justice of our highest court, Woodrow Wilson set down his judicial qualities. The President referred to "his impartial, impersonal, orderly, and constructive mind," to his "rare analytical power and deep human sympathy," to "his profound acquaintance with the historical roots of our institutions," to "his devotion to our American ideals of justice and equality of opportunity," and to "his knowledge of modern economic conditions and the way they bear upon the masses of the people."[80] Among these traits a faith in intellectual procedure yields place only to a ruling passion for social righteousness. This is a superb equipment for a jurist; the opinions in the reports attest how well it has been put to use. The language Brandeis speaks is that of the Justice; the thought he expresses is that of the man.

IV

IT is much too early to appraise the work of Mr. Justice Brandeis, and to assign to him a place among jurists. Among the men who have sat in his court, perhaps among the great judges of all time, his rank will be high. But what that place will be, and what contributions will be conceded as distinctly his no man may certainly say. In the development of our culture we cannot tell what lies around the corner; the thought we regard as common sense may give way to its better or worse; in the immediate future even constitutional law cannot escape taking its chances.[81] Yet the worth of any product of the mind depends upon what the future makes of it.

Already the course of judicial events has given increasing importance to the work of Brandeis. When the Court condemned the practices of the trade association, Brandeis dissented;[82] when in time the issue reappeared, he was silent, for the Court had come around to his way of thinking.[83] A decision which denied to a coöperative association a chance to win its experimental way drew from him a studied protest;[84] when another case, involving an almost identical factual situation came along, the decision went the other way, and a colleague easily distinguished the former holding on a legal issue.[85] An argument that in matters of taxation it was proper for the legislature to make industrial differences a basis for classification[86] has passed from dissent into official utterance.[87] He protested in vain against a judicial interpretation which left stevedores without work accident benefits;[88] the protection against industrial injury has since been extended to harbor workers and to longshoremen by Congressional act.[89] The decisions in a number of cases, involving in one way or another "freedom of speech"[90] failed to win his support;[91] he has just concurred in an opinion which finds the guarantees of the First Amendment in the word "liberty" in the Fourteenth.[92] The critic may easily separate holdings; but the values which have impelled the members of the bench to judgment lie far deeper than the criteria of legal distinction. Brandeis has seen a presidential nomination to his Court rejected, because the appointee as a federal judge did not follow his dissent in a labor case;[93] he has just participated in the grant of an injunction to preserve the integrity of a process of collective bargaining.[94] In the two bulky volumes which record the work of the last term, one looks in vain for the once familiar line, "Mr. Justice Brandeis, dissenting."[95] One can but wonder, whether in his new rôle, Brandeis will be as effective in declaring the law as he has been in blazing its path.

Another generation must discover the lasting qualities in Brandeis' work; but already his contribution to the doctrine of constitutionality appears to be significant. Others have contended that law supplies only the formula whose terms of public policy and private rights must be weighted with social facts, and have agreed with him that not even the exposition of the supreme law of the land is above the experimental attitude.[96] Brandeis' distinctive work has been in converting these secular intellectual procedures into the technique of the jurist's trade. His court has of late agreed with him about the factual foundations of public policy; it has even accepted the idea of trial and error, and during its last term has reconsidered, "in the light of actual experience,"[97] two statutes upon the validity of which it had already passed.[98] It chances, however, that the currency of the realistic test is not firmly established, for it has the support of a bare majority of the court.

But, even if there is a reversion to older doctrine, the way of Brandeis seems destined to prevail. Our ways of thought are changing, and the individualistic values of a pioneer society have served their day. The words "liberty" and "property," "natural law," and "individual right," no longer suffice for a statement of the problem of economic order. The problem of "the state and industry" does not present a choice between "restraint" and "freedom"; government and business are alike schemes of control whose compulsions we must obey and within whose arrangements we may do as we will. Social legislation is not an abridgment, nor "free enterprise" a realization, of "industrial liberty"; they are alike rules of the game of making a living, alike in being of human contrivance and subject to improvement. We are, rather empirically than by deliberate choice, beginning to face the problem of making an instrument of national welfare out of a rather unruly industrial system. Even if we succeed in having business contrive for itself an adequate organization, the state must have a place in the scheme of control. As statutes are passed, the Supreme Court, by separating the valid from the invalid, must continue to mark out the limits of the province of government. In an approach toward planning for national life, it is no small asset to have the question of constitutionality stated in terms of the interests and values of a developing society. The supreme task of the jurist is to square changing social necessity with the established law. In this abiding process a living law owes no mean debt to the art of Mr. Justice Brandeis.

NOTES

II

1. "Introduction" by Ernest Poole to Brandeis, *Business—A Profession* (1914), p. xii.

2. It is significant that most of the writers in the excellent collection of tributes to Mr. Justice Holmes find in him something to confirm their own faiths. Thus Mr. Justice Cardozo finds him a philosophical jurist, Frankfurter a legal statesman, Dewey a pragmatist, Cohen a lonely thinker, and Miss Sergeant a gallant gentleman whose flame is fed by subterranean fires.

3. This has, however, not kept some Supreme Court opinions from reading like Herbert Hoover's *American Individualism* (1922).

4. For an interesting exposition of these limitations on the judicial process, see Judge Hutcheson's review of Lief, *The Social and Economic Views of Mr. Justice Brandeis* (1930), 40 *Y.L.J.* (1931), p. 1116.

5. For the biographical material on which the interpretation of Mr. Justice Brandeis' earlier career in this section is based, the writer has drawn chiefly upon Ernest Poole's introduction to Brandeis, *Business—A Profession*, *supra* note 1. See also De Haas, *Louis Dembitz Brandeis* (1929), Norman Hapgood's penetrating "Justice Brandeis: Apostle of Freedom," 125 *Nation* (1927), p. 330, and Charles Beard's admirable introduction to Lief, *op. cit.*, *supra* note 4. The most valuable source material is to be found in the records of the Senate Judiciary Committee that held hearings on the appointment of Mr. Justice Brandeis in 1916.

6. The story of the emigration of the Goldmark and Brandeis families is recounted with considerable charm in Goldmark, *Pilgrims of '48* (1930).

7. This is pointed out clearly in Santayana, *Character and Opinion in the United States* (1924).

8. Wallas, "Bentham as Political Inventor," 129 *Contemporary Review* (1926), p. 308.

9. *Other People's Money* (1914). This originally appeared as a series of articles in *Harper's Weekly* (1913–14).

10. See the reprint in Hapgood's introduction to *Other People's Money*, *supra* note 9, of Hapgood's editorial for *Harper's Weekly* entitled "Arithmetic."

11. For an account of this genteel tradition that can be set up in illuminating contrast to the turmoil of the "social justice" period, see Santayana's essay on "The Genteel Tradition in American Philosophy" in his *Winds of Doctrine* (1913).

12. "We are sure to have for the next generation an ever-increasing contest between those who have and those who have not—." *Business—A Profession, supra* note 1, pp. li–lii. This book is a collection of articles and occasional speeches by Mr. Brandeis.

13. "If you search for the heroes of peace, you will find many of them among those obscure and humble workmen who have braved idleness and poverty in devotion to the principle for which their union stands." *Business —A Profession, supra* note 1, p. 84.

14. *Muller* v. *Oregon,* 208 U.S. 412, 28 Sup. Ct. 324 (1908).

15. See the account of this arbitration, its difficulties and consequences, in Lorwin, *The Women's Garment Workers* (1924).

16. *Business—A Profession, supra* note 1, pp. 109–197.

17. These articles, especially those on the size of the corporate unit and on the failure of banker-management, are brilliant economic analyses that have scarcely been surpassed in the literature. See note 9, *supra.*

18. U.S. Congress, Senate Committee on the Judiciary, *Testimony Relating to the Appointment of Hon. Louis D. Brandeis* (1916).

19. Mr. Justice Holmes has also in a sense broken with the classical tradition. But while he rejects the rhetoric of constitutional laws as "a fiction intended to beautify what is disagreeable to the sufferers" (*Tyson* v. *Banton,* 273 U.S. 418, 446, 47 Sup. Ct. 426, 434 (1927), and has few if any "fighting faiths" of his own for time to destroy, his deepest attitude is still one of social skepticism. "I think the proper course is to recognize that a state legislature can do whatever it sees fit to do unless it is restrained by some express prohibition in the Constitution of the United States or of the State, and that Courts should be careful not to extend such prohibitions beyond their obvious meaning by reading into them conceptions of public policy that the particular Court may happen to entertain." *Ibid.* Few would accuse Mr. Justice Brandeis of making too ascetic a dissociation between his views of public policy and his opinions.

20. See T. R. Powell, "The Logic and Rhetoric of Constitutional Law," 5 *Jour. of Philos., Psychol. and Sci. Meth.* (1918), pp. 645–658.

21. This is not intended to exclude other bases for comparison. For an admirable treatment of these two liberal figures, see Hamilton, "Mr. Justice Holmes and Mr. Justice Brandeis Dissenting," 33 *Current History* (1931), p. 654.

22. *United Railways and Electric Co.* v. *West,* 280 U.S. 234, 266, 50 Sup. Ct. 123, 130 (1930).

23. *Adams* v. *Tanner,* 244 U.S. 590, 597, 613, 37 Sup. Ct. 662, 665, 671 (1917): "The problem which confronted the people of Washington was far more comprehensive and fundamental than that of protecting

workers applying to the private agencies. It was the chronic problem of unemployment,—perhaps the gravest and most difficult problem of modern industry. . . ."

24. Among the changes that Mr. Brandeis recommended was "the recognition of the true nature of the life insurance business; namely, that its sole province is to manage temporarily with absolute safety and at a minimum cost the savings of the people deposited to make appropriate provision in case of death. . . ." *Business—A Profession, supra* note 1, p. 139.

25. There is of course no intent to convey the idea that such a scheme is either explicit or unique in Mr. Justice Brandeis' thought.

26. *Supra* note 14. This case involved an Oregon statute which limited the working day for women to ten hours. It is interesting to note that the mass of material which the brief presented as "the world's experience upon which the legislation limiting the hours of labor for women is based" was offered to the Court as "facts of common knowledge of which the Court may take judicial notice." Mr. Justice Brewer, for the Court, said, "We take judicial cognizance of all matters of general knowledge." The "economic briefs" were thus admitted into the mansions of the law through a side entrance.

27. *Adams* v. *Tanner, supra* note 23, p. 615, 37 Sup. Ct., p. 672:

There is reason to believe that the people of Washington not only considered the collection by the private employment offices of fees from employees a social injustice; but that they considered the elimination of the practice a necessary preliminary to the establishment of a constructive policy for dealing with the subject of unemployment.

28. *Di Santo* v. *Pennsylvania*, 273 U.S. 34, 37, 47 Sup. Ct. 267, 268 (1927).

29. *Quaker City Cab Co.* v. *Pennsylvania*, 277 U.S. 389, 403, 410, 48 Sup. Ct. 553, 555, 558 (1928):

There are still intelligent, informed, just-minded and civilized persons who believe that the rapidly growing aggregation of capital through corporations constitutes an insidious menace to the liberty of the citizen; that it tends to increase the subjection of labor to capital; that, because of the guidance and control necessarily exercised by great corporations upon those engaged in business, individual initiative is being impaired and creative power will be lessened; that the absorption of capital by corporations, and their perpetual life, may bring evils similar to those which attended mortmain. . . .

30. 254 U.S. 443, 479, 41 Sup. Ct. 172, 181 (1921).

31. *Jay Burns Baking Co.* v. *Bryan*, 264 U.S. 504, 517, 44 Sup. Ct. 412, 415 (1924).

32. *American Column and Lumber Co.* v. *United States,* 257 U.S. 377, 413, 42 Sup. Ct. 114, 121 (1921).

33. *Truax* v. *Corrigan,* 257 U.S. 312, 354, 42 Sup. Ct. 124, 137 (1921).

34. *Frost* v. *Corporation Commission,* 278 U.S. 515, 528, 49 Sup. Ct. 235, 240 (1929).

35. The opinion in *American Column and Lumber Co.* v. *United States, supra* note 32, is an example of Mr. Justice Brandeis' style at its best.

36. *Truax* v. *Corrigan, supra* note 33, p. 357, 42 Sup. Ct., p. 138.

37. See, for example, *Gilbert* v. *Minnesota,* 254 U.S. 325, 338, 41 Sup. Ct. 125, 129 (1920); *Whitney* v. *California,* 274 U.S. 357, 373, 47 Sup. Ct. 641, 647 (1927); *Schaefer* v. *United States,* 251 U.S. 466, 483, 40 Sup. Ct. 259, 264 (1920); *Pierce* v. *United States,* 252 U.S. 239, 273, 40 Sup. Ct. 205, 217 (1920).

38. A discussion of Mr. Justice Brandeis' economic thought in terms of the orthodox categories would be unfruitful. It is interesting to note however that he speaks of "the operation of the law of supply and demand." *American Column and Lumber Co., supra* note 32, p. 417, 42 Sup. Ct., p. 123.

39. The remainder of this paragraph is partly based on the able and subtle reasoning of Mr. Justice Brandeis in *International News Service* v. *Associated Press,* 248 U.S. 215, 248, 39 Sup. Ct. 68, 75 (1918).

40. The International News Services case, *supra* note 39, involved the copying of Associated Press bulletins by the International News Service. Because the Associated Press had unusual and even exclusive advantages in the gathering of foreign news, Justice Brandeis felt that in the absence of legislative regulation, no new property right should be vested in news.

41. For an enumeration of the dangers of corporate control, see the eloquent passage in *Quaker City Cab Co.* v. *Pennsylvania, supra,* partially quoted above in note 29. The setting of the Sherman, Clayton and Federal Trade Commission Acts in the history of American economic opinion is well presented in *Federal Trade Commission* v. *Gratz,* 253 U.S. 421, 429, 40 Sup. Ct. 572, 575 (1920).

42. *Chicago Board of Trade* v. *United States,* 246 U.S. 231, 238, 38 Sup. Ct. 242, 244 (1918). See also *Federal Trade Commission* v. *Gratz, supra* note 41, p. 438, 40 Sup. Ct., p. 578: "A method of competition fair among equals may be very unfair if applied where there is inequality of resources."

43. *American Column and Lumber Co.* v. *United States, supra* note 32, p. 415, 42 Sup. Ct., p. 122.

44. *Chicago Board of Trade* v. *United States, supra* note 42; *Boston Store* v. *American Graphophone Co.*, 246 U.S. 8, 27, 38 Sup. Ct. 257, 261 (1918).

45. *Chicago Board of Trade* v. *United States, supra* note 42.

46. *Boston Store* v. *American Graphophone Co., supra* note 44. See also Mr. Justice Brandeis' utterances on this question before his appointment; his statement before the House Committee on Patents, May 15, 1912 (excerpt in Lief, *op. cit., supra* note 4, pp. 400–403); his article in *Harper's Weekly* (November 15, 1913), p. 10, attacking the opinion of the Court in *Dr. Miles Medical Co.* v. *Park and Sons Co.*, 220 U.S. 373, 31 Sup. Ct. 376 (1910), and *Bauer* v. *O'Donnell*, 229 U.S. 1, 33 Sup. Ct. 616 (1912) (excerpt in Lief, *op. cit., supra*, pp. 403–408); and his statement before the House Committee on Interstate Commerce, January 9, 1915, attacking *Bauer* v. *O'Donnell, supra* (excerpt in Lief, *op. cit., supra*, pp. 398–399).

47. *American Column and Lumber Co.* v. *United States, supra* note 32. For Mr. Justice Brandeis' views on this question before his appointment, see his statement before the Federal Trade Commission, April 30, 1915 (excerpt in Lief, *op. cit., supra* note 4, pp. 411–415), urging it to take upon itself the function of spreading trade information.

48. *Federal Trade Commission* v. *Gratz, supra* note 41.

49. "The investor agrees, by embarking capital in a utility, that its charges to the public shall be reasonable. His company is the substitute for the State in the performance of the public service, thus becoming a public servant." *Southwestern Bell Telepone Co.* v. *Public Service Commission of Missouri*, 262 U.S. 276, 290, 43 Sup. Ct. 544, 547 (1923). It will be noted that this rationalization differs from that given above in which regulation is based on the competitionless character of public utilities.

50. See the brilliant historical analysis in *Southwestern Bell Telephone Co.* v. *Public Service Commission, supra* note 49.

51. Especially in his attempts to find in economic theory a satisfactory definition of value. *Southwestern Bell Telephone Co.* v. *Public Service Commission, supra* note 49, p. 292, 43 Sup. Ct., p. 548.

52. Especially in his discussion of functional depreciation in *United Railways* v. *West*, 280 U.S. 234, 255, 50 Sup. Ct. 123, 127 (1930).

53. *Southwestern Bell Telephone* case, *supra* note 49, p. 291, 43 Sup. Ct., p. 547.

54. *Southwestern Bell Telephone* case, *supra* note 49, p. 292, 43 Sup. Ct., p. 548.

55. In *St. Louis and O'Fallon Ry. Co.* v. *United States*, 279 U.S. 461, 488, 494, 49 Sup. Ct. 384, 389, 391 (1929).

56. *Railroad Commission* v. *Los Angeles Railway*, 280 U.S. 145, 158, 50 Sup. Ct. 71, 74 (1929).

57. For an interesting study of the relation between legal rules and capitalistic organization see Commons, *Legal Foundations of Capitalism* (1924). See also the chapter on law and politics in Veblen, *The Theory of Business Enterprise* (1904).

58. The way of life that informs the common law is that of a rural and bourgeois society. But the ideas evolved in such a society have adapted themselves tolerably to the purposes of the successive stages of capitalist development.

59. *McCulloch* v. *Maryland*, 4 Wheat. 316, 407 (U.S. 1819).

60. *Dorchy* v. *Kansas*, 272 U.S. 306, 311, 47 Sup. Ct. 86, 87 (1926), where a strike was called "to collect a stale claim due to a fellow member of the union who was formerly employed in the business."

61. "Organized Labor and Efficiency" in *Business—A Profession, supra* note 1, pp. 37–50.

62. At hearings before the Interstate Commerce Commission on a proposed advance in railroad rates in 1911 Mr. Brandeis as counsel for shippers introduced evidence indicating that the railroads could save $1,000,000 a day by "scientific managament." This represented the first use of the term. For Mr. Justice Brandeis' views on the subject see his brief and argument at this hearing, January 3, 1911, and his foreword to Gilbreth, *Primer of Scientific Management* (1912). See also Drury, *Scientific Management: A History and Criticism* (1915).

63. See notes 46 and 47, *supra*.

64. See the title essay in *Business—A Profession, supra* note 1.

65. For a tantalizingly brief suggestion of the relation of legal status to class structure and philosophy see Alvin Johnson's review of Hoxie, *Trade Unionism in the United States* (1919) in 13 *New Republic* (1917), p. 319:

Existing law is the embodiment of one philosophy of life, a middle class philosophy. Labor is working out another philosophy of life. The laborer's conception of right locks horns with yours: labor is therefore the lawbreaker. Labor is the lawbreaker, for the present: as to the future, who knows what philosophies will prevail?

See also Blum, *Labor Economics* (1925) and Pound, "Liberty of Contract," 18 *Y.L.J.* (1909), p. 454.

66. See Seagle, "The Martyrdom of Mr. Justice Brandeis," 132 *Nation* (1931), p. 156, for the view that Mr. Justice Brandeis' position on the Court is more helpless than the liberals suspect.

67. For a recent statement of the extent of the development see Laidler,

Concentration of Control in American Industry (1931). The review of this book by Stuart Chase in 68 *New Republic* (1931), p. 238, supports the view that the almost complete control of American industry by the large mergers is a matter of common knowledge and acceptance.

68. His psychological thought comes close to that expressed in Follett, *Creative Experience* (1924).

69. "The old method of distribution and developing of the great resources of the country is creating a huge privileged class that is endangering liberty. There cannot be liberty without financial independence, and the greatest danger to the people of the United States today is in becoming, as they are gradually more and more, a class of employees"—from Mr. Brandeis' argument at the Ballinger investigation, May 27, 1910.

70. See Llewellyn, "Case Law," *Encyclopaedia of the Social Sciences* (1930), III, 249.

71. For Mr. Justice Holmes's experimentalism, a comparison with which is of interest, see John Dewey's contribution to the symposium on *Mr. Justice Holmes*, ed. Felix Frankfurter (1931).

72. Brandeis, "The Living Law," 10 *Ill. L. Rev.* (1916), p. 461.

73. *Washington* v. *Dawson*, 264 U.S. 219, 228, 236, 44 Sup. Ct. 302, 305, 308 (1923).

74. See Follett, *op. cit.*, *supra* note 68.

75. *Truax* v. *Corrigan*, *supra* note 33, p. 368, 42 Sup. Ct., p. 143.

76. For the view that the liberal minority is at present threatening to grow into a majority, see Pollard, "Four New Dissenters," 68 *New Republic* (1931), p. 61.

77. For Mr. Justice Brandeis' theory of *stare decisis* see *Washington* v. *Dawson*, *supra* note 73; *Jaybird Mining Co.* v. *Weir*, 271 U.S. 609, 619, 46 Sup. Ct. 592, 595 (1925); *Di Santo* v. *Pennsylvania*, *supra* note 28. "*Stare decisis* is ordinarily a wise rule of action. But it is not a universal, inexorable command." *Washington* v. *Dawson*, *supra*, p. 238, 44 Sup. Ct., p. 309.

III

1. "A great man represents a great ganglion in the nerves of society, or, to vary the figure, a strategic point in the campaign of history, and part of his greatness consists in his being *there*. I no more can separate John Marshall from the fortunate circumstance that the appointment of Chief Justice fell to John Adams, instead of to Jefferson a month later, and so gave it to a Federalist and loose constructionist to start the working of the Constitution, than I can separate the black line through which he sent his electric fire at Fort Wagner from Colonel Shaw." Holmes, "John Marshall," in *Speeches* (1913), p. 88; *Collected Legal Papers* (1920), p. 268.

2. Beveridge, *Life of John Marshall* (1916–20).

3. Story, *Life and Letters of Joseph Story* (1851).

4. Swisher, *Stephen J. Field: Craftsman of the Law* (1930), and see Walter Nelles' review of Swisher's *Field* in 40 *Y.L.J.* (1931), p. 998. The following books furnish additional serious biographical or autobiographical material concerning some of the Justices: Black and Smith, *Stephen J. Field as a Legislator, State Judge and Judge of the Supreme Court of the United States* (1881–95); Bradley, *Miscellaneous Writings* (1902); Brown, *The Life of Oliver Ellsworth* (1905); Clark, *The Constitutional Doctrines of Justice Harlan* (1915); Clifford, *Nathan Clifford, Democrat* (1922); Connor, *John Archibald Campbell* (1920); Curtis, *Memoir of Benjamin Robbins Curtis* (1879); Delaplaine, *Life of Thomas Johnson* (1927); Flanders, *Lives and Times of the Chief Justices* (rev. ed. 1897); Gregory, *Samuel Freeman Miller* (1907); Hart, *Salmon Portland Chase* (1909); Jay, *Life of John Jay* (1873); Kent, *Memoir of Henry Billings Brown* (1915); Lamar, *The Life of Joseph Rucker Lamar* (1926); Macree, *Life and Correspondence of James Iredell* (1857–58); Mayes, *Lucius Q. C. Lamar: His Life, Times and Speeches* (1896); Schuckers, *Life and Public Services of Salmon Portland Chase* (1874); Steiner, *Life of Roger Brooke Taney* (1922); Tyler, *Memorial of Roger B. Taney* (1872); Whitelock, *Life and Times of John Jay* (1887).

5. "On January 28, 1916, President Wilson nominated Louis D. Brandeis of Massachusetts to succeed Mr. Justice Lamar deceased: he was confirmed by the Senate on June 1, 1916; his commission was dated June 1, 1916, and he took his seat upon the bench June 5, 1916." 241 U.S. iii. The reporter thus veils one of the most stirring occurrences in the Court's history. This is not the occasion to explore the meaning of the contest that resulted in the confirmation of the nomination of Mr. Brandeis. See *Hearings and Report on Nomination of Louis D. Brandeis*, Sen. No. 409, 64th Cong. 1st Sess.

6. Selection of the dozen judges who have left the greatest mark upon the Court is largely a matter of personal choice. Of those no longer living, my twelve, with their respective years of service, follow: Marshall (34), William Johnson (30), Story (34), Taney (28), Curtis (6), Miller (28), Field (34), Chase (9), Bradley (22), Brewer (21), White (27), Moody (3). It will be noted that the minimum length of service of all but three was twenty-one terms. Chase had too dominant a share in constitutional and international issues following the Civil War to be omitted. I avouch for Curtis' claims, *inter alia*, *Cooley v. Board of Wardens of Philadelphia*, 12 How. 299 (1851) and *Murray's Lessee v. Hoboken Land and Improvement Co.*, 18 How. 272 (1885); for Moody's, *inter alia*, *Employers'*

Liability Cases, 207 U.S. 463, 504 (1908) (dissent) and *Twining* v. *New Jersey*, 211 U.S. 78 (1908).

7. Apparently, only Bradley (who merely headed the electoral ticket of Grant, in New Jersey, in 1868) and Miller had never held public office before their accession to the Supreme Court. For ascertaining these facts and for other help I am indebted to Mr. Paul A. Freund, Research Fellow, Harvard Law School.

Of the present Court, Mr. Justice Brandeis alone was without official experience, except as counsel for the Interstate Commerce Commission in the Rate Case and also as special counsel for the Government in the Riggs National Bank Case.

8. The Five Per Cent Case, 31 I.C.C. 351 (1914); s.c., 32 I.C.C. 325 (1914).

9. *Report of Subcommittee on Nomination of Louis D. Brandeis*, Sen. No. 409, 64th Cong. 1st Sess., p. 26.

10. See, for instance, the following published by the Justice while at the bar: *Financial Condition of the New York, New Haven and Hartford Railroad Company* (1907); Testimony before the Senate Committee on Interstate Commerce in considering Sen. No. 2941 "A Bill to Create an Interstate Trade Commission," *Hearings before the Interstate Commerce Commission pursuant to Sen. Res. 98*, 62d Cong., Dec. 14, 15 and 16, 1911, pp. 1146 *et seq.*; *Other People's Money* (1914); *Business—A Profession* (1914, 1925).

11. Shortly before his appointment to the Court, he delivered an address before the Chicago Bar Association in which he analyzed why law, particularly public law, was then finding itself in heavy waters. "The Living Law" (1916), 10 *Ill. L. Rev.*, p. 461; *Business—A Profession* (1925), p. 344. His "true remedy" for making law and courts adequate "to meet contemporary economic and social demands" is in striking contrast to the usual mechanical panaceas that, from time to time, are offered:

We are powerless to restore the general practitioner and general participation in public life. Intense specialization must continue. But we can correct its distorting effects by broader education—by study undertaken preparatory to practice—and continued by lawyer and judge throughout life: study of economics and sociology and politics which embody the facts and present the problems of today. *Ibid.*, p. 362.

12. 208 U.S. 412 (1908).

13. The unusual reference by Mr. Justice Brewer, for the Court, to the argument by Mr. Brandeis bears repetition:

In patent cases counsel are apt to open the argument with a discussion of the state of the art. It may not be amiss, in the present case, before examining the constitutional question, to notice the course of legislation as well as expressions of opinion from other than judicial sources. In the brief filed by Mr. Louis D. Brandeis, for the defendant in error, is a very copious collection of all these matters, an epitome of which is found in the margin. 208 U.S. 412, 419 (1908).

14. *McCulloch* v. *Maryland*, 4 Wheat. 315, 407 (1819).

15. *United States* v. *Moreland*, 258 U.S. 433, 451 (1922) (dissent).

16. *Olmstead* v. *United States*, 277 U.S. 438, 472 (1928) (dissent).

17. *Gilbert* v. *Minnesota*, 254 U.S. 325, 336–337 (1920) (dissent).

18. *Jacob Ruppert* v. *Caffey*, 251 U.S. 264, 299–300 (1920).

19. *Maul* v. *United States*, 274 U.S. 501, 524–525 (1927) (concurrence).

20. Mr. Justice Holmes, dissenting, in *Adkins* v. *Children's Hospital*, 261 U.S. 525, 568 (1923).

Judge Learned Hand has also put the matter in telling language. The provisions of the Fifth Amendment "represent a mood rather than a command, that sense of moderation, of fair play, of mutual forebearance, without which states become the prey of faction. They are not the rules of a game; their meaning is lost when they are treated as though they were." *Daniel Reeves, Inc.* v. *Anderson*, 43 F.(2d) 679, 682 (C.C.A. 2d, 1930).

21. *Untermeyer* v. *Anderson*, 276 U.S. 440, 447, 450–452 (1928) (dissent).

22. *National Life Ins. Co.* v. *United States*, 277 U.S. 508, 527–528, 533 (1928) (dissent).

23. *Adams* v. *Tanner*, 244 U.S. 590, 613–615 (1917) (dissent).

24. *Pennsylvania Coal Co.* v. *Mahon*, 260 U.S. 393, 416–417, 419, 422 (1922) (dissent). Dissenting opinions are apt to express in ampler form than views voiced for the Court the constitutional philosophy of the Justices. Mr. Justice Brandeis is not, quantitatively speaking, a dissenting Justice. As to the duty to utter dissents, see Mr. Justice Story in *Briscoe* v. *Bank of Kentucky*, 11 Pet. 257, 349–350 (1837); Mr. Chief Justice Taney in *Rhode Island* v. *Massachusetts*, 12 Pet. 657, 752 (1838); Mr. Justice Moody in Employers' Liability Cases, 207 U.S. 463, 505 (1908). And see (Mr. Justice) Brown, "The Dissenting Opinions of Mr. Justice Harlan," 46 *Am. L. Rev.* (1912), pp. 321, 350–352.

25. *Jay Burns Baking Co.* v. *Bryan*, 264 U.S. 504, 519–520, 533–534 (1924) (dissent).

26. *Missouri Pac. R.R.* v. *Western Crawford Road Improv. Dist.*, 266 U.S. 187, 190 (1924).

27. *Truax* v. *Corrigan*, 257 U.S. 312, 355–357 (1921) (dissent).

28. Mr. Justice Holmes, dissenting, in *Truax* v. *Corrigan*, 257 U.S. 312, 342 (1921).

29. *Royster Guano Co.* v. *Virginia*, 253 U.S. 412, 417–418 (1920) (dissent).

30. *Truax* v. *Corrigan*, 257 U.S. 312, 374–375 (1921) (dissent).

31. *Louisville Gas & Elec. Co.* v. *Coleman*, 277 U.S. 32, 50–52 (1928) (dissent).

32. *Quaker City Cab Co.* v. *Pennsylvania*, 277 U.S. 389, 403–404, 405–406, 410–411 (1928) (dissent).

33. *Frost* v. *Corporation Comm.*, 278 U.S. 515, 531, 535–538, 547–548 (1929) (dissent).

34. *Wis. Laws 1907*, c. 499.

35. *N.Y. Laws 1907*, c. 429; Hughes, *Addresses* (1908), p. 139.

36. See *Munn* v. *Illinois*, 94 U.S. 113, 134 (1876); *Railroad Commission Cases*, 116 U.S. 307, 331 (1886); *Chicago, etc. Ry.* v. *Minnesota*, 134 U.S. 418 (1890); *Ohio Valley Co.* v. *Ben Avon Borough*, 253 U.S. 287 (1920).

37. 169 U.S. 466 (1898). See Frankfurter, *The Public and Its Government* (1930).

38. 262 U.S. 276, 289 (1922).

39. *Ibid.*, pp. 290, 290–292, 308–310. See also *Groesbeck* v. *Duluth S. S. & A. Ry.*, 250 U.S. 607 (1919); *Georgia Ry.* v. *Railroad Comm.*, 262 U.S. 625 (1923); *McCardle* v. *Indianapolis Water Co.*, 272 U.S. 400, 421 (1926) (dissent).

40. *Pacific Gas & Elec. Co.* v. *San Francisco*, 265 U.S. 403, 422–425 (1924) (dissent).

41. *United Railways* v. *West*, 280 U.S. 234, 277–280 (1930) (dissent). See *St. Louis & O'Fallon Ry.* v. *United States*, 279 U.S. 461, 488 (1929) (dissent).

42. *Report of Commission on Revision of the Public Service Commissions Law* (N.Y. Legis. Doc. No. 75, 1930).

43. *Report of the Special Commission on Control and Conduct of Public Utilities* (House No. 1200, 1930).

44. See Frankfurter, *The Public and Its Government* (1930), pp. 95 *et seq.*, and the tortuous litigation in *Smith* v. *Illinois Bell Tel. Co.*, 282 U.S. 133 (1930), which is still in process before the District Court for the Northern District of Illinois.

45. See, e.g., testimony of Mr. Owen D. Young before the Senate Committee on Interstate Commerce, as quoted by Joseph B. Eastman on behalf of the Interstate Commerce Commission in a letter dated January

20, 1930, to Chairman Couzens of the Senate Committee on Interstate Commerce.

46. The decision of the majority in *Southwestern Bell Tel. Co.* v. *Public Service Comm.*, 262 U.S. 276 (1923), must surely have been influenced by the then common belief in the permanence of a "new plateau of prices." This assumption Mr. Justice Brandeis did not share; indeed he believed the contrary. It is characteristic of his prophetic insight into economic causes and their effects that in 1923 he should have been bold enough to prophesy, in one of his succulent footnotes, that "the present price level may fall to that of 1914 within a decade; and that, later, it may fall much lower." 262 U.S., at p. 303, note 16.

47. 169 U.S. 466 (1898).

48. *Di Santo* v. *Pennsylvania*, 273 U.S. 34, 37–39 (1927) (dissent).

49. *Public Utility Comm.* v. *Attleboro Co.*, 273 U.S. 83, 91–92 (1927) (dissent).

50. *Texas Transport & Terminal Co.* v. *New Orleans*, 264 U.S. 150, 155, 157 (1924) (dissent).

51. *Cudahy Packing Co.* v. *Hinkle*, 278 U.S. 460, 467–468, 470 (1929) (dissent).

52. *Jaybird Mining Co.* v. *Weir*, 271 U.S. 609, 615, 617–619 (1926) (dissent).

53. *N.Y. Cent. R.R.* v. *Winfield*, 244 U.S. 147, 168–170 (1917) (dissent).

54. *Napier* v. *Atlantic Coast Line R.R.*, 272 U.S. 605, 612–613 (1926).

55. *Davis* v. *Farmers' Co-operative Co.*, 262 U.S. 312, 315–316, 317 (1923).

56. *Buck* v. *Kuykendall*, 267 U.S. 307, 315–316 (1925).

57. *Lawrence* v. *St. Louis-San Francisco Ry.*, 278 U.S. 228, 233–234 (1929).

58. *Hammond* v. *Schappi Bus Line*, 275 U.S. 164, 170–172 (1927).

59. The following criteria have guided him:

It [the Court] has no jurisdiction to pronounce any statute, either of a State or of the United States, void, because irreconcilable with the Constitution, except as it is called upon to adjudge the legal rights of litigants in actual controversies. In the exercise of that jurisdiction, it is bound by two rules, to which it has rigidly adhered, one, never to anticipate a question of constitutional law in advance of the necessity of deciding it; the other never to formulate a rule of constitutional law broader than is required by the precise facts to which it is to be applied. These rules are safe guides to sound judgment. It is the dictate of wisdom to follow them closely and carefully. *Steamship Co.* v. *Emigration Commissioners*, 113 U.S. 33, 39 (1885).

Whenever, in pursuance of an honest and actual antagonistic assertion of rights by one individual against another, there is presented a question involving the validity of any act of any legislature, State or Federal, and the decision necessarily rests on the competency of the legislature to so enact, the court must, in the exercise of its solemn duties, determine whether the act be constitutional or not; but such an exercise of power is the ultimate and supreme function of courts. It is legitimate only in the last resort, and as a necessity in the determination of real, earnest and vital controversy between individuals. *Chicago, etc. Ry. v. Wellman*, 143 U.S. 339, 345 (1892).

60. *Arizona v. California*, 283 U.S. 423, 463–464 (1931). See also *Swift Co. v. Hocking Valley Ry.*, 243 U.S. 281 (1917); *Bilby v. Stewart*, 246 U.S. 255 (1918); *Sugarman v. United States*, 249 U.S. 182 (1919); *Barbour v. Georgia*, 249 U.S. 454 (1919); *Collins v. Miller*, 252 U.S. 364 (1920); *Terrace v. Thompson*, 263 U.S. 197 (1923); *Oliver Co. v. Mexico*, 264 U.S. 440 (1924); *Willing v. Chicago Auditorium*, 277 U.S. 274 (1928).

61. *Chastleton Corp. v. Sinclair*, 264 U.S. 543, 549 (1924) (concurring in part).

62. *International News Service v. Associated Press*, 248 U.S. 215, 263–264, 267 (1918) (dissent).

63. *Pennsylvania v. West Virginia*, 262 U.S. 553, 621–623 (1923) (dissent).

64. *Railroad Comm. v. Los Angeles*, 280 U.S. 145, 163–166 (1929) (dissent). As to his general desire to confine the volume of the Supreme Court's business to limits consonant with excellence of judicial output, see *King Mfg. Co. v. Augusta*, 277 U.S. 100, 115 (1928) (dissent).

65. *The Works of George Saville, First Marquess of Halifax* (ed. Raleigh, 1912), p. 211.

66. *Jaybird Mining Co. v. Weir*, 271 U.S. 609, 619 (1926) (dissent).

67. *Washington v. Dawson & Co.*, 264 U.S. 219, 235–239 (1924) (dissent).

68. *Di Santo v. Pennsylvania*, 273 U.S. 34, 42–43 (1927) (dissent).

69. Scrutton, L. J., in *Rex v. Secretary of State for Home Affairs* [1923], 2 K.B. 361, 382.

70. *Schaefer v. United States*, 251 U.S. 466, 482–483 (1920) (dissent).

71. *Pierce v. United States*, 252 U.S. 239, 272–273 (1920) (dissent).

72. *Gilbert v. Minnesota*, 254 U.S. 325, 343 (1920) (dissent).

73. *Whitney v. California*, 274 U.S. 357, 374–377 (1927) (concurrence).

74. *Pierce v. United States*, 252 U.S. 239, 266–267 (1920) (dissent).

75. *Milwaukee Pub. Co.* v. *Burleson,* 255 U.S. 407, 417, 436 (1921) (dissent).

76. "The judge may enlighten the understanding of the jury and thereby influence their judgment; but he may not use undue influence. He may advise; he may persuade; but he may not command or coerce. He does coerce when without convincing the judgment he overcomes the will by the weight of his authority. . . .

"It is said that if the defendant suffered any wrong it was purely formal. . . . Whether a defendant is found guilty by a jury or is declared to be so by a judge is not, under the Federal Constitution, a mere formality. . . . The offence here in question is punishable by imprisonment. Congress would have been powerless to provide for imposing the punishment except upon the verdict of the jury." *Horning* v. *District of Columbia,* 254 U.S. 135, 139–140 (1920).

77. See "Report on the Third Degree" by Chafee, Pollak and Stern in *Reports, National Commission on Law Observance and Enforcement* (1931), IV, p. 13.

78. See 220 *Hans. Deb.* (Commons), cols. 5, 805 *et seq.* (July 20, 1928); Inquiry in regard to the Interrogation by the Police of Miss Savidge (1928, Cmd. 3147).

79. *Wan* v. *United States,* 266 U.S. 1, 14–17 (1924).

80. *Burdeau* v. *McDowell,* 256 U.S. 465, 476–477 (1921) (dissent).

81. *Casey* v. *United States,* 276 U.S. 413, 423 (1928) (dissent).

82. *Olmstead* v. *United States,* 277 U.S. 438, 483–484, 485 (1928) (dissent).

83. *Myers* v. *United States,* 272 U.S. 52, 291–295 (1926) (dissent).

84. *Bedford Cut Stone Co.* v. *Stone Cutters Ass'n,* 274 U.S. 37, 64–65 (1927) (dissent).

85. *Duplex Printing Press Co.* v. *Deering,* 254 U.S. 443, 488 (1921) (dissent). See also *Dorchy* v. *Kansas,* 272 U.S. 306 (1926).

86. Brandeis, *Other People's Money* (1914), p. 162.

87. In an address delivered at Brown University Commencement Day, 1912; Brandeis, *Business—A Profession* (1914, 1925), p. 1.

88. *American Column Co.* v. *United States,* 257 U.S. 377, 415, 416, 417–418 (1921) (dissent).

89. *Hughes* v. *Gault,* 271 U.S. 142, 152 (1926) (dissent).

90. *Collins* v. *Loisel,* 262 U.S. 426, 429–430 (1923).

91. See, e.g., *Bilokumsky* v. *Tod,* 263 U.S. 149 (1923); *Tisi* v. *Tod,* 264 U.S. 131 (1924); *Williamsport Co.* v. *United States,* 277 U.S. 551 (1928); *Tagg Bros.* v. *United States,* 280 U.S. 420, 443–445 (1930); *Campbell* v. *Galeno Chemical Co.,* 281 U.S. 599 (1930).

92. *Douglas* v. *Noble,* 261 U.S. 165, 169–170 (1923).

93. *Northern Pacific Ry.* v. *Department of Public Works*, 268 U.S. 39, 42–45 (1925).

94. Exigencies of space have enforced omission of footnotes from the quoted opinions. See, among others, the following cases in which the heavily documented footnotes in the opinions of Mr. Justice Brandeis are largely the result of his independent research: *Truax* v. *Corrigan*, 257 U.S. 312 (1921) (dissent); *Southwestern Bell Tel. Co.* v. *Public Serv. Comm.*, 262 U.S. 276 (1923) (dissent); *Jay Burns Baking Co.* v. *Bryan*, 264 U.S. 504 (1924) (dissent); *Myers* v. *United States*, 272 U.S. 52 (1926) (dissent); *Frost* v. *Corp. Comm.*, 278 U.S. 515 (1929) (dissent); *St. Louis & O'Fallon Ry.* v. *United States*, 279 U.S. 461 (1929) (dissent); *United Rys.* v. *West*, 280 U.S. 234 (1939) (dissent).

95. *Wan* v. *United States*, 266 U.S. 1 (1924).

IV

1. (Brentano's, 1930).

2. Introduction to *The Social and Economic Views of Mr. Justice Brandeis* (Vanguard Press, 1930).

3. Dissenting opinion in *Olmstead* v. *United States*, 277 U.S. 438, 478, 48 Sup. Ct. 564, 572 (1928).

4. Address before National Congress on Charities and Correction, Boston, June 8, 1911.

5. Statement in a hearing before a committee of the United States Senate on anti-trust legislation, December 14, 1911.

6. Statements before United States Commission on Industrial Relations, made April 16, 1914, and January 23, 1915.

7. "Cutthroat Prices," 128 *Harper's Weekly* (November 15, 1913), p. 10.

8. Statements before United States Commission on Industrial Relations, *supra* note 6.

9. Brief and argument before Interstate Commerce Commission, January 3, 11, 1911.

10. Statement before House Committee on Interstate and Foreign Commerce, January 9, 1915.

11. Dissenting opinion in *American Column & Lumber Co.* v. *United States*, 257 U.S. 377, 418, 42 Sup. Ct. 114, 123 (1921).

12. Address to New England Dry Goods Association, Boston, February 11, 1908.

13. Letter to Robert W. Bruere, February 25, 1922.

14. *Lochner* v. *New York*, 198 U.S. 45, 76, 25 Sup. Ct. 539, 547 (1905).

15. *Olmstead* v. *United States, loc. cit. supra* note 3.

16. See note 6, *supra*.

17. See note 5, *supra*.

18. Statement in behalf of a minimum wage law before New York State Factory Investigating Commission, January 22, 1915.

19. See note 4, *supra*.

20. Dissenting opinion in *Duplex Printing Press Co.* v. *Deering*, 254 U.S. 443, 488, 41 Sup. Ct. 172, 184 (1921).

21. Concurring opinion in *Whitney* v. *California*, 274 U.S. 357, 375, 47 Sup. Ct. 641, 648 (1927).

V

1. 31 I.C.C. 351 (1914), 32 I.C.C. 325 (1914).

2. 17 A.B.A.J. 428 (1931).

3. *Interstate Commerce Acts Annotated* (1930), pp. 75–87; Sharfman, *The Interstate Commerce Commission* (1931), I.

4. In *Western Union Tel. Co.* v. *Esteve Bros. & Co.*, 256 U.S. 566, 573 (1921), Mr. Justice Brandeis said:

It is true that a railroad rate does not have the force of law unless it is filed with the Commission. But it is not true that out of the filing of the rate grows the rule of law by which the terms of this lawful rate conclude the passenger. The rule does not rest upon the fiction of constructive notice. It flows from the requirement of equality and uniformity of rates laid down in § 3 of the Act to Regulate Commerce. Since any deviation from the lawful rate would involve either an undue preference or an unjust discrimination, a rate lawfully established must apply equally to all, whether there is knowledge of it or not. Congress apparently concluded, in the light of discrimination theretofore practiced by railroads among shippers and localities, that in transportation by rail equality could be secured only by provisions involving the utmost definiteness and constant official supervision. Accordingly by § 6 it forbade a carrier of goods from engaging in transportation unless its rates had been filed with the Commission; and it prohibited, under heavy penalties, departure in any way from the terms of those rates when filed.

5. 202 U.S. 242 (1906); cf. *Gulf, Colorado, & Santa Fé Ry.* v. *Hefly*, 158 U.S. 98 (1895).

6. See *Chicago & Alton R.R.* v. *Kirby*, 225 U.S. 155, 166 (1912); *Adams Exp. Co.* v. *Croninger*, 226 U.S. 491, 509 (1913); *Kansas City So. Ry.* v. *Carl*, 227 U.S. 639, 652–653 (1913); *Boston & Maine R.R.* v. *Hooker*, 233 U.S. 97, 110–111 (1914); *Turner Lumber Co.* v. *Chicago, Milwaukee & St. Paul Ry.*, 271 U.S. 259, 263 (1926). But, as pointed out in the excerpt from Mr. Justice Brandeis' opinion in *Western Union Tel. Co.* v. *Esteve Bros. & Co.*, *supra* note 4, the rule requiring ad-

herence to tariffs does not rest upon the fiction of constructive notice. And posting, as distinguished from filing, is not essential to the binding effect of the tariff. *Texas & Pac. Ry.* v. *Cisco Oil Co.*, 204 U.S. 449 (1907); *United States* v. *Miller*, 223 U.S. 599 (1912); *Berwind-White Coal Mining Co.* v. *Chicago & Erie R.R.*, 235 U.S. 371 (1914).

7. Obviously, however, a provision incorporated in a tariff will not prescribe the terms on which the interstate transportation must be conducted if such provision is contrary to law. *Boston & Maine R.R.* v. *Piper*, 246 U.S. 439 (1918); *Adams Exp. Co.* v. *Darden*, 265 U.S. 265 (1924) (opinion by Brandeis, J.).

8. Cf. Biklé, "Jurisdiction of Certain Cases Arising Under the Interstate Commerce Act," 60 *U. of Pa. L. Rev.*, 1 (1911), pp. 13–14.

9. *Armour Packing Co.* v. *United States*, 209 U.S. 56 (1908); *Chicago & Alton R.R.* v. *Kirby*, 225 U.S. 155 (1912); see *Pennsylvania R.R.* v. *International Coal Mining Co.*, 230 U.S. 184, 197 (1913); *Georgia, Fla. & Ala. Ry.* v. *Blish Milling Co.*, 241 U.S. 190, 197 (1916); *Missouri, Kan. & Tex. Ry.* v. *Ward*, 244 U.S. 383 (1917) (opinion by Brandeis, J.).

10. 266 U.S. 92 (1924). Cf. *Davis* v. *Cornwell*, 264 U.S. 560 (1924), where it is held that a contract by a railroad to furnish cars on a certain day for interstate transportation as common carrier is void if not in accordance with tariff provisions (opinion by Brandeis, J.).

11. 266 U.S. 92, 93 (1924).

12. 254 U.S. 357, 360 (1920).

13. 250 U.S. 478, 481 (1919).

14. See opinion in *Hollister* v. *Nowlen*, 19 Wend. 234 (N.Y. 1838), for an excellent discussion of the old cases.

15. And some not required to be filed, as, for example, rules governing the distribution of cars to coal mines. *Baltimore & Ohio R.R.* v. *United States*, 215 U.S. 481 (1910); *Morrisdale Coal Co.* v. *Pennsylvania R.R.*, 230 U.S. 304 (1913); *Midland Valley R.R.* v. *Barkley*, 276 U.S. 482 (1928) (opinion by Brandeis, J.).

16. The same is true of such rules, regulations, and practices as are not required to be filed.

17. 204 U.S. 426 (1907).

18. It is Mr. Justice White, as he then was, speaking. 204 U.S., p. 446.

19. 247 U.S. 477 (1918).

20. *Ibid.*, pp. 482–483.

21. 259 U.S. 285, 291–292 (1922). This opinion includes a helpful note (at 295) listing the cases in which the jurisdiction of the Court was sustained without preliminary resort to the Commission, and those in which

the Court refused to take jurisdiction because there had been no preliminary resort to the Commission.

22. *Midland Valley R.R.* v. *Barkley*, 276 U.S. 482 (1928) (opinion by Brandeis, J.).

23. *Alabama & Vicksburg Ry.* v. *Jackson & Eastern Ry.*, 271 U.S. 244 (1926) (opinion by Brandeis, J.). An unusual application of the general principle is found in *Keogh* v. *Chicago & Northwestern Ry.*, 260 U.S. 156 (1922), in which an unsuccessful effort was made to establish a right to action against a railroad, available in the courts, on the ground that, while the rates established by it were not unreasonably high, they had been put in effect in contravention of the Anti-Trust Act. The opinion is by Mr. Justice Brandeis.

24. *Increased Rates*, 1920, 58 I.C.C. 220 (1920).

25. *Reduced Rates*, 1922, 68 I.C.C. 676 (1922).

26. Charges for Passengers in Sleeping and Parlor Cars, 95 I.C.C. 469 (1925).

27. 77 I.C.C. 200 (1923), 98 I.C.C. 298 (1925); *United States* v. *New York Cent. R.R., et al.*, 263 U.S. 603 (1924).

28. See, in general, *Interstate Commerce Comm.* v. *Chicago, Rock Island & Pac. Ry.*, 218 U.S. 88 (1910).

29. In the matter of *Import Rates*, 24 I.C.C. 78 (1912); *Chamber of Commerce of N.Y.* v. *New York Cent. & Hudson River R.R.*, 24 I.C.C. 55 (1912), 24 I.C.C. 674 (1912); *Maritime Ass'n* v. *Ann Arbor R.R.*, 95 I.C.C. 539 (1925), 126 I.C.C. 199 (1927); *Baltimore Chamber of Commerce* v. *Ann Arbor R.R.*, 159 I.C.C. 691 (1929); *State of New Jersey* v. *New York Cent. R.R.*, I.C.C. Docket No. 22,824, now in course of litigation.

30. *Banner Milling Co.* v. *New York Cent. & Hudson River R.R.*, 14 I.C.C. 398 (1908), 19 I.C.C. 128 (1910); *Grain Products Rates via Great Lakes*, 43 I.C.C. 550 (1917); *Board of Trade of Chicago* v. *Pere Marquette R.R.*, 44 I.C.C. 345 (1917).

31. *Florida R.R. Comm.* v. *Aberdeen & Rockfish R.R.*, 144 I.C.C. 603 (1928), and cases cited at 621; *North Carolina Pine Ass'n* v. *Atlantic Coast Line R.R.*, 85 I.C.C. 270, 280–284 (1923); *cf. Adams-Bank Lumber Co.* v. *Aberdeen & Rockfish R.R.*, 157 I.C.C. 280 (1929).

32. *Advances in Coal Rates by Chesapeake & Ohio Ry.*, 22 I.C.C. 604 (1912); *Boileau* v. *Pittsburgh & Lake Erie R.R.*, 22 I.C.C. 640 (1912), 24 I.C.C. 129 (1912) (in this case Mr. Brandeis, as he then was, represented the complainant); *Lake Cargo Coal Rates*, 46 I.C.C. 159 (1917); *Lake Cargo Coal Rates*, 1925, 101 I.C.C. 513 (1925); *Lake Cargo Coal from Kentucky, etc., to Lake Erie Ports*, 139 I.C.C. 367 (1928); *United*

States v. *Anchor Coal Co.*, 279 U.S. 812 (1929); *Western Pennsylvania Coal Traffic Bureau* v. *Baltimore & Ohio R.R.*, I.C.C. Docket No. 23,241, now in course of litigation.

33. See Dickinson, *Administrative Justice and the Supremacy of Law in the United States* (1927), where the matter is thoroughly explored, and the cases and articles dealing with the subject exhaustively cited.

34. 222 U.S. 541 (1912).

35. *Ibid.*, p. 547.

36. *Skinner & Eddy Corp.* v. *United States*, 249 U.S. 557, 562 (1919); *Tagg Bros.* v. *United States*, 280 U.S. 420, 442 (1930) (opinions by Brandeis, J.). The scope of court review of Commission action under the Clayton Act is not discussed.

37. There are also two important lines of cases holding either that certain action by the Commission is not reviewable in the courts, or that certain parties do not have a legal interest sufficient to justify such challenge. The leading case of the first class is *Procter & Gamble Co.* v. *United States*, 225 U.S. 282 (1912), which is popularly cited as establishing the principle that negative orders of the Commission are not reviewable. Perhaps a more accurate statement of the rule would be that, where the Commission, taking jurisdiction, finds no basis for exerting its authority, the courts are without jurisdiction to pass on the propriety of its decision. Several important decisions in which the opinions have been rendered by Mr. Justice Brandeis outline helpfully the significance of this proposition. *Chicago Junction Case*, 264 U.S. 258 (1924); *Great Northern Ry.* v. *United States*, 277 U.S. 172 (1928); *Piedmont & Northern Ry.* v. *United States*, 280 U.S. 469 (1930).

Furthermore, it is an opinion of Mr. Justice Brandeis that established the necessity for a *legal* interest in order to contest the validity of Commission action. *Edward Hines Trustees* v. *United States*, 263 U.S. 143 (1923). And this rule has been applied and the character of interest necessary to constitute a legal interest indicated in several of his opinions. *Chicago Junction Case*, 264 U.S. 258, 266–268 (1924); *Sprunt & Son, Inc.* v. *United States*, 281 U.S. 249 (1930); *Pittsburgh & West Virginia Ry.* v. *United States*, 281 U.S. 479 (1930).

38. *United States* v. *Merchants etc. Ass'n*, 242 U.S. 178 (1916); *St. Louis S. W. Ry.* v. *United States*, 245 U.S. 136 (1917); *Louisville & Nashville R.R.* v. *United States*, 245 U.S. 463 (1918); *Louisiana & Pine Bluff Ry.* v. *United States*, 257 U.S. 114 (1921); *Central R.R. of N.J.* v. *United States*, 257 U.S. 247 (1921); *New England Divisions Case*, 261 U.S. 184 (1923); *United States* v. *Illinois Cent. R.R.*, 263 U.S. 515 (1924); *Peoria & Pekin Union Ry.* v. *United States*, 263 U.S. 528

(1924); *Chicago Junction Case*, 264 U.S. 258 (1924) (the opinion in this case involves important and interesting discussion as to whether the order was reviewable at all; whether it was essentially negative in character, and whether the appellants had a legal interest sufficient to give them a standing to challenge the order); *United States* v. *Abilene & So. Ry.*, 265 U.S. 274 (1924) (this case involves, among other things, the formalities required in making certain that information is properly before the Commission: see especially 286–290, and cf. *Chicago Junction Case, supra,* p. 263); *United States* v. *Pennsylvania R.R.*, 266 U.S. 191 (1924); *United States* v. *Village of Hubbard*, 266 U.S. 474 (1925); *Chicago, Indianapolis & Louisville Ry.* v. *United States,* 270 U.S. 287 (1926); *Western Chemical Co.* v. *United States,* 271 U.S. 268 (1926); *Virginian Ry.* v. *United States,* 272 U.S. 658 (1926) (this case involves, among other things, an expression of the Court's views as to when, in cases of this kind, stays pending appeal may be allowed); *United States* v. *Los Angeles & Salt Lake R.R.*, 273 U.S. 299 (1927) (in this case it is decided that an order of the Commission fixing the final value of a railroad is not reviewable by injunction); *Assigned Car Cases,* 274 U.S. 564 (1927); *Atchison, Topeka & Santa Fé Ry.* v. *United States,* 279 U.S. 768 (1929); *United States* v. *Erie R.R.*, 280 U.S. 98 (1929) (involving the question whether certain traffic transported by railroad from Hoboken, N.J., to Garfield, N.J., was import or intrastate traffic); *Sprunt & Son, Inc.* v. *United States,* 281 U.S. 249 (1930) (another important opinion involving the question of the necessary legal interest to justify the maintenance of a bill to enjoin an order of the Commission); *Pittsburgh & West Virginia Ry.* v. *United States,* 281 U.S. 479 (1930); cf. *Skinner & Eddy Corp.* v. *United States,* 249 U.S. 557 (1919); *Lambert Co.* v. *Baltimore & Ohio R.R.*, 258 U.S. 377 (1922); *Interstate Commerce Comm.* v. *Waste Merchants Ass'n,* 260 U.S. 32 (1922); *Edward Hines Trustees* v. *United States,* 263 U.S. 143 (1923); *Arkansas R.R. Comm.* v. *Chicago, Rock Island & Pac. R.R.*, 274 U.S. 597 (1927).

39. 261 U.S. 184 (1923).

40. *Supra* note 24.

41. 261 U.S. 184, 195 (1923).

42. *Ibid.*, p. 204. In connection with this case see *United States* v. *Abilene & Southern Ry.*, 265 U.S. 274 (1924), in which the Court, speaking through Mr. Justice Brandeis, sets aside another order of the Commission regarding divisions because the Commission had refused to exclude from consideration matter not properly brought into the record and because it had acted with respect to the divisions without having before it adequate evidence of what they were. The first of these grounds is espe-

cially important in view of the fact that the Commission, in various instances, has indicated a disinclination to confine itself to the record in deciding cases brought before it.

43. 261 U.S. 184, 196–199 (1923), and cf. *United States* v. *Abilene & Southern Ry.*, 265 U.S. 274, 290–291 (1924).

44. 274 U.S. 564 (1927).

45. *Ibid.*, pp. 582–583.

46. 264 U.S. 258 (1924).

47. *Ibid.*, p. 263.

48. Cf. *Baer Bros.* v. *Denver & Rio Grande R.R.*, 233 U.S. 479, 486–487 (1914).

49. Supplemented by the provisions of Sec. 13 incorporated in the Interstate Commerce Act by Transportation Act, 1920.

50. *Houston, East & West Texas Ry.* v. *United States*, 234 U.S. 342 (1914). This decision was forecast in the *Minnesota Rate Cases*, 230 U.S. 352, 419–420 (1913).

51. *Railroad Comm. of Wis.* v. *Chicago, Burlington & Quincy R.R.*, 257 U.S. 563 (1922). See also *New York* v. *United States*, 257 U.S. 591 (1922).

52. 257 U.S. 563, 591 (1922).

53. 283 U.S. 765 (1931). See also *Alabama* v. *United States*, 283 U.S. 776 (1931); *American Exp. Co.* v. *Caldwell*, 244 U.S. 617 (1917); *Nashville, Chattanooga & St. Louis Ry.* v. *Tennessee*, 262 U.S. 318 (1923); *United States* v. *Village of Hubbard*, 266 U.S. 474 (1925); *Arkansas R.R. Comm.* v. *Chicago Rock Island & Pac. R.R.*, 274 U.S. 597 (1927) (all opinions by Brandeis, J.).

54. 283 U.S. 765, 772–774 (1931).

55. 256 U.S. 554 (1921).

56. *Ibid.*, p. 557.

57. 260 U.S. 16, 17 (1922).

58. *Davis* v. *Donovan*, 265 U.S. 257 (1924) (opinion by McReynolds, J.).

59. *Davis* v. *Alexander*, 269 U.S. 114 (1925) (opinion by Brandeis, J.).

60. *Marion & Rye Valley Ry.* v. *United States*, 270 U.S. 280 (1926) (opinion by Brandeis, J.).

61. *Missouri Pac. R.R.* v. *Boone*, 270 U.S. 466 (1926) (opinion by Brandeis, J.).

62. *Mellon* v. *Weiss*, 270 U.S. 565 (1926) (opinion by Brandeis, J.).

63. See, e.g., *Davis* v. *Slocomb*, 263 U.S. 158 (1923); *St. Louis, Kennett & S.E. R.R.* v. *United States*, 267 U.S. 346 (1925); *Cairo, Truman & So. R.R.* v. *United States*, 267 U.S. 350 (1925); *Great Northern Ry.* v. *United States*, 277 U.S. 172 (1928) (all opinions by Brandeis, J.).

64. Aen. II. 6, 8. Railroad counsel were heartened during this trying period by the famous lines in Aen. I. 198–199, 202–203:

> O socii (neque enim ignari sumus ante malorum),
> O passi graviora, dabit deus his quoque finem.
>
> . . . .
> . . . revocate animos . . .
> . . . forsan et haec olim meminisse juvabit.

But with respect to this last sentiment they feel constrained to record in succinct modernistic fashion: Nondum.

65. 261 U.S. 184, 189–190 (1923).

66. 270 U.S. 266 (1926).

67. Ibid., p. 277.

68. Ibid., pp. 278–279. Mr. Justice Brandeis' opinion in Colorado v. United States, 271 U.S. 153 (1926), deals with the matter of abandonments. It is a clear exposition of the extent to which authority over this matter has been confided to the Interstate Commerce Commission and the reasons which underlie the grant of the power.

69. St. Louis & O'Fallon Ry. v. United States, 279 U.S. 461, 488 (1929).

70. 262 U.S. 276, 289 (1923). See also his opinion in Ohio Valley Water Co. v. Ben Avon Borough, 253 U.S. 287, 292 (1920).

71. 280 U.S. 234 (1930).

72. Ibid., pp. 280–285.

73. Ibid., p. 285.

74. The Commission's report on further hearing has since been issued. 177 I.C.C. 351 (1931).

75. 257 U.S. 247, 259 (1921).

76. 263 U.S. 515, 524 (1924).

77. This opinion was also by Mr. Justice Brandeis. Cf. his opinion in Chicago, Indianapolis & Louisville Ry. v. United States, 270 U.S. 287, 292–293 (1926).

78. 249 U.S. 557 (1919). See also Patterson v. Louisville & Nashville R.R., 269 U.S. 1 (1925) (opinion by Brandeis, J.).

79. 260 U.S. 166 (1922).

80. 10 Wall. 557 (U.S. 1870).

81. In Sprout v. South Bend, 277 U.S. 163, 168 (1928), Mr. Justice Brandeis says: "For this purpose, the destination intended by the passenger when he begins his journey and known to the carrier, determines the character of the commerce." (Italics supplied.) But such knowledge on the part of the carrier does not seem to have been a factor in the Settle case

nor in *United States* v. *Erie R.R.*, 280 U.S. 98 (1929), in which last named case Mr. Justice Brandeis also wrote the opinion.

82. 265 U.S. 59 (1924).

83. *Ibid.*, pp. 65–67.

84. *Patterson* v. *Louisville & Nashville R.R.*, 269 U.S. 1 (1925); *Louisville & Nashville R.R.* v. *Sloss-Sheffield Steel & Iron Co.*, 269 U.S. 217 (1925); *St. Louis & San Francisco R.R.* v. *Spiller*, 274 U.S. 304 (1927).

85. *Di Santo* v. *Pennsylvania*, 273 U.S. 34, 37 (1927).

86. *Boileau* v. *Pittsburgh & Lake Erie R.R.*, 22 I.C.C. 640 (1912), 24 I.C.C. 129 (1912); *The Five Per Cent Case*, 31 I.C.C. 351 (1914), 32 I.C.C. 325 (1914).

87. See his dissenting opinion in *Federal Trade Comm.* v. *Gratz*, 253 U.S. 421, 430 (1920).

88. See, e.g., *St. Louis S. W. Ry.* v. *United States*, 245 U.S. 136, 139–140 (1917); *Atchison, Topeka & Santa Fé Ry.* v. *United States*, 279 U.S. 768 (1929).

89. *Pennsylvania R.R.* v. *Kittanning Iron & Steel Co.*, 253 U.S. 319 (1920); *Edward Hines Trustees* v. *United States*, 263 U.S. 143 (1923); *Turner, Dennis & Lowry Lumber Co.* v. *Chicago, Milwaukee & St. Paul Ry.*, 271 U.S. 259 (1926).

90. *Skinner & Eddy Corp.* v. *United States*, 249 U.S. 557, 568 (1919).

91. As the writer found, to his sorrow, in *United States* v. *Pennsylvania R.R.*, 266 U.S. 191 (1924).

92. Dissenting opinion in *Adams* v. *Tanner*, 244 U.S. 590, 600 (1917). In this connection it is interesting to note the following sentences from Judge Cardozo's "Introduction" to the recently published *Selected Readings on the Law of Contracts* (1931), p. x:

> The new habit of citation is symptomatic of something more, however, than a developing recognition of the authority of the modern law school; it is symptomatic also of a new conception of the function of citations, of the meaning of authorities. . . . The modern outlook . . . is bringing us to recognition of the truth that an opinion derives its authority, just as law derives its existence, from all the facts of life. The judge is free to draw upon these facts wherever he can find them, if only they are helpful. No longer is his material confined to precedents in sheepskin.

93. Mr. Justice Holmes in *Hyde and Schneider* v. *United States*, 225 U.S. 347, 391 (1912).

94. *The Common Law* (1881), p. 1.

95. "The Path of the Law," *Collected Legal Papers* (1920), p. 187.

VI

1. Dissenting, in *Adams* v. *Tanner*, 244 U.S. 590, 600, 37 Sup. Ct. 662, 666 (1916).

2. *O'Gorman and Young* v. *Hartford Insurance Co.*, 282 U.S. 251, 51 Sup. Ct. 130 (1931).

3. 105 N.J. Law 642, 146 Atl. 370 (1929).

4. At the time of the original argument, April 30, 1930, the vacancy caused by the death of Mr. Justice Sanford on March 8, had not yet been filled.

5. The usual practice is for the dissenting Justice to read his own opinion and to announce the names of the justices who concur. The unusual resort of the four dissenting Justices to a joint opinion attests the keen appreciation of the importance of the constitutional principle at stake. It is of note that although Mr. Justice Van Devanter's name appears first, it was Mr. Justice McReynolds who in court announced the opinion of the dissenters.

6. See especially *Tyson* v. *Banton*, 273 U.S. 418, 47 Sup. Ct. 426 (1927); *Ribnik* v. *McBride*, 277 U.S. 350, 48 Sup. Ct. 545 (1928); *Williams* v. *Standard Oil Co.*, 278 U.S. 235, 49 Sup. Ct. 115 (1929).

7. *Adkins* v. *Children's Hospital*, 261 U.S. 525, 546, 43 Sup. Ct. 394, 397 (1923).

8. Brandeis has, to serve judicial necessity, remade an old device. His presumption, rebuttable only by a recitation of fact, is a compound of the older presumption of constitutionality and Holmes's formula "It is not unconstitutional." The use of the double negative may logically add nothing; but it has a high rhetorical value, and has come to furnish a basis for an ingenious procedural device.

9. Of late there has been much debate over how the Court, if it were minded to declare a minimum wage act valid, could distinguish the *Adkins* case. The device employed here by Brandeis would make such distinction unnecessary. Whether it was intention or accident, the Court in *Abie State Bank* v. *Bryan*, 282 U.S. 765, 51 Sup. Ct. 252 (1931), and *Missouri Pacific Railroad Co.* v. *Norwood*, 283 U.S. 249, 51 Sup. Ct. 458 (1931), has established an adequate legal foundation for such a decision. See pp. 176 *et seq.* below, and compare 40 *Y.L.J.* (1931), p. 1101.

10. In view of the evidence of the importance which the Court attached to it, it is surprising that the case has provoked very little comment.

11. The headnote, number 2, in the official report, *O'Gorman and Young* v. *Hartford Insurance Co.*, *supra* 'note 2, p. 252, 51 Sup. Ct. 130 is an interesting side light: "A state statute, dealing with a subject clearly within the police power, cannot be declared void upon the ground that

the specific method of regulation prescribed by it is unreasonable, in the absence of any factual foundation in the record to overcome the presumption of constitutionality." The whole matter, of course, has to do with the technique by which the Court determines what lies within, and what without, the police power. In this case five Justices found the subject "clearly within the police power," and four discovered it to be as clearly without. The headnotes are submitted to the Justices before publication; how much scrutiny this paragraph had it is impossible to say.

12 An engaging discussion of the rhetoric of judicial opinion is to be found in the essay which gives title to Chief Judge Cardozo's book, *Law and Literature* (1931).

13. *The Legal Tender Cases*, 12 Wallace 457 (1871), p. 634.

14. *Northern Securities Co. v. United States*, 193 U.S. 197, 24 Sup. Ct. 436 (1904); *Southern Pacific R.R. Co. v. United States*, 168 U.S. 1, 18 Sup. Ct. 18 (1897).

15. *United States v. Delaware and Hudson R.R. Co.*, 213 U.S. 366, 29 Sup. Ct. 527 (1909); *Clark Distilling Co. v. Western Maryland Ry. Co.*, 242 U.S. 311, 37 Sup. Ct. 180 (1917).

16. *The Employers' Liability Cases*, 207 U.S. 463, 520–522, 28 Sup. Ct. 141, 154 (1908).

17. For example see the discussion of the concept of "public interest" in *Tyson v. Banton, supra* note 6, pp. 451–452, 47 Sup. Ct. p. 435.

18. See especially *New York Central Railroad Co. v. Winfield*, 244 U.S. 147, 154, 37 Sup. Ct. 546, 549 (1917).

19. *Ziang Sung Wan v. United States*, 266 U.S. 1, 45 Sup. Ct. 1 (1924).

20. *St. Louis and O'Fallon Railroad Co. v. United States*, 279 U.S. 461, 488, 49 Sup. Ct. 384, 389 (1929).

21. A striking contrast exists in manner of writing between Mr. Justice Holmes and Mr. Justice Brandeis. The opinions of Holmes, lifted from the reports, live; *The Dissenting Opinions of Mr. Justice Holmes* (1929), ed. Alfred Lief, have been read with enjoyment and profit by many persons who could have had but the vaguest ideas of the controversies which prompted them and the judicial issues which are their subject-matter. The opinions of Brandeis, taken from their habitat, lose much of their vitality; *The Social and Economic Views of Mr. Justice Brandeis* (1930), ed. Alfred Lief, fails, because of the lack of setting, to reveal the strength and variety of his workmanship.

22. "The tricks of the trade" is used, for want of a less colorful expression, to describe the devices and procedures which make up the technology of legal judgment. It is impossible for cases to be decided without

impersonal formulas of decision. For that reason the reader will understand that no invidious meaning lies in the words.

23. *Pennsylvania v. West Virginia*, 262 U.S. 553, 43 Sup. Ct. 658 (1923).

24. *Ibid.*, p. 605, 43 Sup. Ct. p. 668.

25. *Tagg Brothers and Morehead v. United States*, 280 U.S. 420, 50 Sup. Ct. 220 (1930).

26. See *Wolff Packing Co. v. Industrial Court*, 262 U.S. 522, 43 Sup. Ct. 630 (1923), and cases cited in note 6, *supra*.

27. In *Bunting v. Oregon*, 243 U.S. 426, 37 Sup. Ct. 435 (1917), Mr. Justice McKenna employed the same device to avoid the holding in *Lochner v. New York*, 198 U.S. 45, 25 Sup. Ct. 539 (1905). The attorney for the plaintiff-in-error had argued that the statute, by the provision of time-and-a-half for overtime, was a regulation of wages. McKenna answered that it was only a regulation of hours, hence there was no error, hence the decision of the Oregon court was to be affirmed. His strategy made it unnecessary to refer to the *Lochner* case and the one citation employed, to a case which has nothing to do with hours of labor, is a work of judicial supererogation.

28. In *Williams v. Standard Oil Co.*, *supra* note 6, Mr. Justice Brandeis technically "concurred in the result."

29. In a footnote it is perhaps permissible to set down the problem with which Brandeis was confronted in writing this opinion. He had really to meet three conditions: (1) to distinguish recent holdings adverse to price-fixing; (2) to write an argument acceptable to the majority of the Court; and (3) to make the opinion as useful as possible in future cases concerned with the same issue. The conflicting demands of these values deny to the argument logical symmetry, but they give occasion for a superb display of the jurist's art. It would be interesting to know the number of drafts out of which the finished product emerged.

30. *Duplex Printing Press Co. v. Deering*, 254 U.S. 443, 41 Sup. Ct. 172 (1921).

31. *Ibid.*, p. 479, 41 Sup. Ct. p. 181.

32. *International News Service v. The Associated Press*, 248 U.S. 215, 39 Sup. Ct. 68 (1918).

33. *Ibid.*, p. 248, 39 Sup. Ct. p. 75.

34. A rather different, but equally realistic, example is Brandeis' distinction of *Bedford Cut Stone Co. v. Journeymen Stone Cutters' Association*, 274 U.S. 37, 56, 47 Sup. Ct. 522, 528 (1927), from *Duplex Printing Press Co. v. Deering*, *supra* note 30.

35. *Jay Burns Baking Co.* v. *Bryan*, 264 U.S. 504, 44 Sup. Ct. 412 (1924).

36. *Ibid.*, p. 517, 44 Sup. Ct. p. 415.

37. *Adams* v. *Tanner*, *supra* note 1.

38. *Ibid.*, p. 597, 37 Sup. Ct. p. 665.

39. *Ibid.*, p. 594, 37 Sup. Ct. p. 664.

40. *Myers* v. *United States*, 272 U.S. 52, 240, 47 Sup. Ct. 21, 66 (1926).

41. *Quaker City Cab Co.* v. *Pennsylvania*, 277 U.S. 389, 403, 48 Sup. Ct. 553, 555 (1928).

42. *United Railways and Electric Co. of Baltimore* v. *West*, 280 U.S. 234, 255, 50 Sup. Ct. 123, 127 (1930).

43. The text must be reserved for matters which may be documented; but surely one may employ a footnote to set down the personal conclusion that often neat bits of Brandeis' work are to be discovered in the opinions of others. In the last of the leading cases concerned with workmen's compensation, *Arizona Employers' Liability Cases*, 250 U.S. 400, 39 Sup. Ct. 553 (1919), it was argued that, under the operation of competitive forces, a workman could be induced to go into a dangerous trade only by the payment of a differential in wages, and hence that an authoritative provision of work accident benefits imposed upon the employer a double payment for the risks the employee had to run. The Court answered that if compensation had its separate provision, the operation of the same competitive forces could be depended upon to remove the differential for risk from the rate of wages. In the case of *Wilson* v. *New*, 243 U.S. 332, 37 Sup. Ct. 298 (1917), it was argued that in the matter of wages and hours Congress had, through the Adamson Act, substituted its will for a contract between the parties. The Court answered that since authority had not been invoked until after the process of bargaining had failed to lead to an agreement, there had been no replacement of private consent by public action. One of these answers-in-kind appears in an opinion by Pitney, the other in an opinion by White; yet both bear on their face the marks of a Brandeisian authorship.

44. *American Column and Lumber Co.* v. *United States*, 257 U.S. 377, 413, 42 Sup. Ct. 114, 121 (1921).

45. An interesting contrast between the factual method of Brandeis and the philosophic approach of Holmes is afforded by their dissents in this case. As against Brandeis' detailed presentation of the practical operation of the "Open Competitive Plan," is to be set Holmes's presumption, "I should have supposed that the Sherman Act did not set itself against knowledge. . . . I should have thought that the ideal of commerce was an in-

telligent interchange made with full knowledge of the facts as a basis for a forecast of the future on both sides." *Ibid.*, p. 412, 42 Sup. Ct. p. 121.

46. *Di Santo* v. *Pennsylvania*, 273 U.S. 34, 37, 47 Sup. Ct. 267, 268 (1927).

47. *Hitchman Coal and Coke Co.* v. *Mitchell*, 245 U.S. 229, 38 Sup. Ct. 65 (1917).

48. *Ibid.*, p. 263, 38 Sup. Ct. p. 76.

49. *Frost* v. *Corporation Commission of Oklahoma*, 278 U.S. 515, 528, 49 Sup. Ct. 235, 240 (1929).

50. *Olmstead* v. *United States*, 277 U.S. 438, 478, 48 Sup. Ct. 564, 572 (1928).

51. *Gilbert* v. *Minnesota*, 254 U.S. 325, 338, 41 Sup. Ct. 125, 129 (1920).

52. *Pierce* v. *United States*, 252 U.S. 239, 273, 40 Sup. Ct. 205, 217 (1920).

53. *Olmstead* v. *United States*, *supra* note 50, p. 479, 48 Sup. Ct. p. 572.

54. *Gilbert* v. *Minnesota*, *supra* note 51, p. 343, 41 Sup. Ct. p. 131.

55. *Near* v. *Minnesota*, 283 U.S. 697, 51 Sup. Ct. 625 (1931). The case may become a landmark in constitutional law. The use of the concept "liberty," rather than "property," seems deliberate; it enables the Court to read the guarantees of the First Amendment into the Fourteenth. In a previous case, *Gitlow* v. *New York*, 268 U.S. 652, 45 Sup. Ct. 625 (1925), it was assumed, for purposes of jurisdiction, that freedom of speech and of the press were comprehended within the word "liberty" of the Fourteenth Amendment; in their dissent, Holmes and Brandeis, JJ., were "of opinion" that "the general principle of free speech" must "be taken to be included" within the words. In the case of *Meyer* v. *Nebraska*, 262 U.S. 390, 43 Sup. Ct. 625 (1923), "the right to teach" was found to be included in the word "liberty." See also *Pierce* v. *Society of Sisters*, 268 U.S. 510, 45 Sup. Ct. 571 (1925). For a full discussion see "The Bill of Rights and the Fourteenth Amendment," 31 *Columbia Law Rev.* (1931), p. 468.

56. It is of interest, in passing, to note the neat contrast between the *O'Gorman*, *supra* note 2, and the *Near*, *supra* note 55, cases. The former abridging freedom of contract is found constitutional, and the latter abridging freedom of the press unconstitutional by the same vote, five to four. The off-hand conclusion would be that one member of the Court is more willing to indulge the presumption of the constitutionality of a state statute in cases involving freedom of contract than in cases involving freedom of speech. The fact is that nine Justices make presumption count for

more in the one case than in the other. Every vote cast for constitutionality in the *O'Gorman* case was cast against constitutionality in the *Near* case, and *vice versa*. The two cases throw the conflict within the Court between personal and property rights into sharp relief.

57. *Schaefer* v. *United States*, 251 U.S. 466, 482, 483, 40 Sup. Ct. 259, 264, 265 (1920).

58. *Truax* v. *Corrigan*, 257 U.S. 312, 355, 42 Sup. Ct. 124, 138 (1921).

59. *Quaker City Cab Co.* v. *Pennsylvania*, *supra* note 41, p. 403, 48 Sup. Ct. p. 555.

60. *State Board of Tax Commissioners of Indiana* v. *Jackson*, 283 U.S. 527, 51 Sup. Ct. 540 (1931). Brandeis, J., concurs in the opinion of the court.

61. *Frost* v. *Corporation Commission of Oklahoma*, *supra* note 49, p. 528, 49 Sup. Ct. p. 240.

62. *American Column and Lumber Co.* v. *United States*, *supra* note 44, p. 418, 42 Sup. Ct. p. 123.

63. *Hitchman Coal and Coke Co.* v. *Mitchell*, *supra* note 47, p. 263, 38 Sup. Ct. p. 76; *Duplex Printing Co.* v. *Deering*, *supra* note 30, p. 448, 41 Sup. Ct. p. 184; *Truax* v. *Corrigan*, *supra* note 58, p. 354, 42 Sup. Ct. p. 137; *Bedford Cut Stone Co.* v. *Stone Cutters' Assn.*, *supra* note 34, p. 56, 47 Sup. Ct. p. 528.

64. See especially *American Column and Lumber Co.* v. *United States*, *supra* note 44, p. 418, 42 Sup. Ct. p. 123, and *Duplex Printing Co.* v. *Deering*, *supra* note 30, p. 488, 41 Sup. Ct. p. 184.

65. *American Column and Lumber Co.* v. *United States*, *supra* note 44 p. 419, 42 Sup. Ct. p.123, and *Bedford Cut Stone Co.* v. *Journeymen Stone Cutters' Assn.*, *supra* note 34, p. 65 Sup. Ct. 523, 531.

66. *United States* v. *United States Steel Corporation*, 251 U.S. 417, 40 Sup. Ct. 293 (1920). In this case "the opinion of the Court" did not represent the prevailing views of a majority of its members. The decision came by a vote of four to three, and McReynolds and Brandeis, JJ., who regarded themselves as technically disqualified to sit, would have voted with the minority.

67. *United States* v. *United Shoe Machinery Co.*, 247 U.S. 32, 38 Sup. Ct. 473 (1918). In this case, likewise, McReynolds and Brandeis, JJ., did not sit, and the decision was announced by a vote of four to three.

68. *Truax* v. *Corrigan*, *supra* note 58, p. 376, 42 Sup. Ct. p. 146.

69. *Washington* v. *W. C. Dawson and Co.*, 264 U.S. 219, 238, 44 Sup. Ct. 302, 309.

70. *Di Santo* v. *Pennsylvania*, *supra* note 46, p. 42, 47 Sup. Ct. p. 270.

71. *International News Service* v. *Associated Press, supra* note 32, p. 267, 39 Sup. Ct. p. 82.

72. *Duplex Printing Press Co.* v. *Deering, supra* note 30, p. 488, 41 Sup. Ct. p. 184.

73. *Great Northern Railway Co.* v. *Merchants Elevated Co.*, 259 U.S. 285, 291, 42 Sup. Ct. 477, 479 (1922).

74. Compare the statement of Mr. Justice Stone, speaking for the Court, in *United States* v. *Trenton Potteries Co.*, 273 U.S. 392, 398, 47 Sup. Ct. 377, 379 (1927):

Moreover, in the absence of express legislation requiring it, we should hesitate to adopt a construction making a difference between legal and illegal conduct in the field of business relations depend upon so uncertain a test as whether prices are reasonable—a determination which can be satisfactorily made only after a complete survey of our economic organization and a choice between rival philosophies.

75. *Jay Burns Baking Co.* v. *Bryan, supra* note 35, p. 534, 41 Sup. Ct. p. 421.

76. Excellent examples of recent date are his opinions in *Buck* v. *Jewell LaSalle Realty Co.*, 283 U.S. 191, 51 Sup. Ct. 410 (1931) and *Arizona* v. *California*, 283 U.S. 423, 51 Sup. Ct. 522 (1931).

77. "More truly characteristic of dissent is a dignity, an elevation, of mood and thought and phrase. Deep conviction and warm feeling are saying their last say with knowledge that the cause is lost. The voice of the majority may be that of force triumphant, content with the plaudits of the hour, and recking little of the morrow. The dissenter speaks to the future, and his voice is pitched in a key that will carry through the years." [Cardozo, *Law and Literature* (1931), p. 36.]

78. *St. Louis and O'Fallon Ry. Co.* v. *United States, supra* note 20, p. 488, 49 Sup. Ct. p. 409.

79. Goldmark, *Pilgrims of '48* (1931).

80. Woodrow Wilson to Charles A. Culbertson, *Cong. Rec.* 64th Cong. 1st Sess. Vol. 53, p. 9048 (1916).

81. "Now and then an extraordinary case may turn up, but constitutional law like other mortal contrivances has to take some chances, and in the great majority of instances no doubt justice will be done." Mr. Justice Holmes, in *Blimm* v. *Nelson*, 22 U.S. 1, 7, 32 Sup. Ct. 1, 2 (1911).

82. *American Column and Lumber Co.* v. *United States, supra* note 44, p. 413, 42 Sup. Ct. p. 121.

83. *Maple Flooring Manufacturers Assn.* v. *United States*, 268 U.S. 563, 45 Sup. Ct. 578 (1925); *Cement Manufacturers Protective Assn.* v. *United States*, 268 U.S. 588, 45 Sup. Ct. 586 (1925). On technical points these cases may possibly be distinguished from *American Column*

and Lumber Co. v. *United States, supra* note 82. But it seems the more significant that of the five Justices who sat in the earlier case and the later cases only one, Mr. Justice Van Devanter, was able to make the distinction.

84. *Frost* v. *Corporation Commission, supra* note 49, p. 528, 49 Sup. Ct. p. 240.

85. *Corporation Commission of Oklahoma* v. *Lowe,* 281 U.S. 431, 50 Sup. Ct. 159 (1930).

86. *Quaker City Cab Co.* v. *Pennsylvania, supra* note 41, p. 403, 48 Sup. Ct. p. 555.

87. *State Board of Tax Commissioners of Indiana* v. *Jackson, supra* note 60.

88. *Washington* v. *W. C. Dawson and Co., supra* note 69, p. 228, 44 Sup. Ct. p. 305.

89. Longshoremen's and Harbor Workers' Compensation Act, 33 U.S. C. A. §§901–950 (1927).

90. *Toledo Newspaper Co.* v. *United States,* 247 U.S. 402, 426, 38 Sup. Ct. 560, 566 (1918); *Abrams* v. *United States,* 250 U.S. 616, 631, 40 Sup. Ct. 17, 22 (1919); *Schaefer* v. *United States, supra* note 57, p. 482, 40 Sup. Ct. p. 264; *Pierce* v. *United States, supra* note 52, p. 253, 40 Sup. Ct. p. 211; *Gilbert* v. *Minnesota, supra* note 51, p. 334, 41 Sup. Ct. p. 128; *Milwaukee Social Democratic Publishing Co.* v. *Burleson,* 255 U.S. 407, 417, 41 Sup. Ct. 352, 356 (1921); *Gitlow* v. *New York, supra* note 55, p. 672, 45 Sup. Ct. p. 632; *Whitney* v. *California,* 274 U.S. 357, 372, 47 Sup. Ct. 641, 647 (1927). In the last case Brandeis, J., writes a concurring opinion.

91. These cases, of course, involve a number of rather distinct legal questions. But a careful reading of them leaves the impression that the attitudes of the Justices were determined by the values which they placed upon freedom of speech.

92. *Near* v. *Minnesota, supra* note 55. See also the discussion in note 55, *supra.*

93. *Hitchman Coal and Coke Co.* v. *Mitchell, supra* note 47, p. 263, 38 Sup. Ct. p. 76.

94. *Texas and New Orleans Railroad Co.* v. *Brotherhood of Railway and Steamship Clerks,* 281 U.S. 548, 50 Sup. Ct. 427 (1930).

95. During the last term Brandeis, J., has dissented six times, as compared with twice for the Justice most, and twelve times for the Justice least, in accord with the Court. In *Beidler* v. *South Carolina Tax Commission,* 282 U.S. 1, 10, 51 Sup. Ct. 54, 55 (1930), Holmes, J., announced his own and Brandeis' dissent, "without repeating reasons which did not prevail with the Court"; in *United States* v. *Chicago, Milwaukee, St. Paul*

and Pacific Ry. Co., 282 U.S. 311, 344, 51 Sup. Ct. 159, 161 (1931), and in *Coolidge* v. *Long*, 282 U.S. 582, 638, 51 Sup. Ct. 306, 324 (1931), Brandeis, J., concurred in the dissents of Stone, J., and Roberts, J., respectively; in *United States* v. *Macintosh*, 283 U.S. 605, 635, 51 Sup. Ct. 570, 579 (1931), and in *United States* v. *Bland*, 283 U.S. 636, 637, 51 Sup. Ct. 569, 570 (1931), in dissents expressed by Hughes, C.J.; and in *Indian Motorcycle Co.* v. *United States*, 283 U.S. 570, 583, 51 Sup. Ct. 601, 606 (1931), in the dissenting opinion of Stone, J.

96. *Di Santo* v. *Pennsylvania, supra* note 46, p. 42, 47 Sup. Ct. p. 270; *Washington* v. *W. C. Dawson and Co., supra* note 69, p. 238, 44 Sup. Ct. p. 309.

97. *Abie State Bank* v. *Bryan, supra* note 9, p. 772, 51 Sup. Ct. p. 255.

98. *Abie State Bank* v. *Bryan,* and *Missouri Pacific R. Co.* v. *Norwood,* both *supra* note 9.

Appendix to Mr. Frankfurter's Essay

List of Opinions

FOLLOWING is a topical list of cases involving constitutional questions and other issues of public law, in which opinions were written by Mr. Justice Brandeis, beginning with his first opinion, on December 4, 1916 (*Hutchinson Ice Cream Co. v. Iowa*, 242 U.S. 153) through June 1, 1931 (283 U.S.).

DUE PROCESS AND EQUAL PROTECTION OF THE LAW

Hutchinson Ice Cream Co. v. Iowa, 242 U.S. 153 (1916); *Chaloner v. Sherman*, 242 U.S. 455 (1917); *Van Dyke v. Geary*, 244 U.S. 39 (1917); *Sutton v. New Jersey*, 244 U.S. 258 (1917); *Adams v. Tanner*, 244 U.S. 590, 597 (1917) (dissent); *Jones v. Buffalo Creek Coal & Coke Co.*, 245 U.S. 328 (1917); *Omaechevarria v. Idaho*, 246 U.S. 343 (1918); *New York Life Ins. Co. v. Dodge*, 246 U.S. 357, 377 (1918) (dissent); *Stadelman v. Miner*, 246 U.S. 544 (1918); *Union Pac. R.R. v. Laughlin*, 247 U.S. 204 (1918); *Standard Scale Co. v. Farrell*, 249 U.S. 571 (1919); *Groesbeck v. Duluth, S. S. & A. Ry.*, 250 U.S. 607 (1919); *McCloskey v. Tobin*, 252 U.S. 107 (1920); *Oklahoma Operating Co. v. Love*, 252 U.S. 331 (1920); *Oklahoma Gin Co. v. Oklahoma*, 252 U.S. 339 (1920); *Hiawassee River Power Co. v. Carolina-Tenn. Power Co.*, 252 U.S. 341 (1920); *Calhoun v. Massie*, 253 U.S. 170 (1920); *Ohio Valley Co. v. Ben Avon Borough*, 253 U.S. 287, 292 (1920) (dissent); *Truax v. Corrigan*, 257 U.S. 312, 354 (1921) (dissent); *Galveston Elec. Co. v. Galveston*, 258 U.S. 388 (1922); *Pennsylvania Coal Co. v. Mahon*, 260 U.S. 393, 416 (1922) (dissent); *Southwestern Bell Tel. Co. v. Public Serv. Comm.*, 262 U.S. 276, 289 (1923) (dissent); *Kentucky Finance Corp. v. Paramount Auto Exchange Corp.*, 262 U.S. 544, 551 (1923) (dissent); *Georgia Ry. v. Railroad Comm.*, 262 U.S. 625 (1923); *Security Bank v. California*, 263 U.S. 282 (1923); *Dorchy v. Kansas*, 264 U.S. 286 (1924); *Burns Baking Co. v. Bryan*, 264 U.S. 504, 517 (1924) (dissent); *Pacific Gas Co. v. San Francisco*, 265 U.S. 403, 416 (1924) (dissent); *Fort Smith Traction Co. v. Bourland*, 267 U.S. 330 (1925); *Northern Pac. v. Department Public Works*, 268 U.S. 39 (1925); *Dorchy v. Kansas*, 272 U.S. 306 (1926); *McCardle v. Indianapolis Co.*, 272 U.S. 400, 421 (1926) (dissent); *James-Dickinson Co. v. Harry*, 273 U.S. 119 (1927); *Bothwell v. Buckbee, Mears Co.*, 275 U.S. 274 (1927); *Wuchter v. Pizzutti*, 276 U.S. 13, 25 (1928) (dissent); *Richardson Mach. Co. v. Scott*, 276 U.S. 128

(1928); *Delaware, L. & W. R.R.* v. *Morristown*, 276 U.S. 182, 195 (1928) (concurring in part); *Liggett* v. *Baldridge*, 278 U.S. 105 (1928); *Frost* v. *Corporation Comm.*, 278 U.S. 515, 528 (1929) (dissent); *Railroad Comm.* v. *Los Angeles Ry.*, 280 U.S. 145, 158 (1929) (dissent); *United Railways* v. *West*, 280 U.S. 234, 255 (1930) (dissent); *Miller* v. *McLaughlin*, 281 U.S. 261 (1930); *Home Ins. Co.* v. *Dick*, 281 U.S. 397 (1930); *Brinkerhoff-Faris Co.* v. *Hill*, 281 U.S. 673 (1930); *Wampler* v. *Lecompte*, 282 U.S. 172 (1930); *O'Gorman & Young, Inc.* v. *Hartford Fire Ins. Co.*, 282 U.S. 251 (1931).

TAXATION

(National and State, including Amendments V, XIV, and XVI)

McCurdy v. *United States*, 246 U.S. 263 (1918); *Eisner* v. *Macomber*, 252 U.S. 189, 220 (1920) (dissent); *Penn Mutual Co.* v. *Lederer*, 252 U.S. 523 (1920); *Cream of Wheat Co.* v. *Grand Forks*, 253 U.S. 325 (1920); *Royster Guano Co.* v. *Virginia*, 253 U.S. 412, 417 (1920) (dissent); *Underwood Typewriter Co.* v. *Chamberlain*, 254 U.S. 113 (1920); *Watson* v. *State Comptroller*, 254 U.S. 122 (1920); *Dawson* v. *Kentucky Distilleries Co.*, 255 U.S. 288 (1921); *Choctaw, O. & G. R.R.* v. *Mackey*, 256 U.S. 531 (1921); *Keokuk Bridge Co.* v. *Salm*, 258 U.S. 122 (1922); *Greiner* v. *Lewellyn*, 258 U.S. 384 (1922); *Heald* v. *District of Columbia*, 259 U.S. 114 (1922); *Fidelity & Deposit Co.* v. *United States*, 259 U.S. 296 (1922); *Fidelity Title Co.* v. *United States*, 259 U.S. 304 (1922); *Lipke* v. *Lederer*, 259 U.S. 557, 563 (1922) (dissent); *Greenport Co.* v. *United States*, 260 U.S. 512 (1923); *Southern Ry.* v. *Watts*, 260 U.S. 519 (1923); *Thomas* v. *Kansas City So. Ry.*, 261 U.S. 481 (1923); *Cullinan* v. *Walker*, 262 U.S. 134 (1923); *Atlantic Coast Line* v. *Daughton*, 262 U.S. 413 (1923); *Baker* v. *Druesedow*, 263 U.S. 137 (1923); *Pierce Oil Corp.* v. *Hopkins*, 264 U.S. 137 (1924); *Missouri Pac. R.R.* v. *Road District*, 266 U.S. 187 (1924); *Ozark Pipe Line* v. *Monier*, 266 U.S. 555, 567 (1925) (dissent); *Ray Copper Co.* v. *United States*, 268 U.S. 373 (1925); *Marr* v. *United States*, 268 U.S. 536 (1925); *Burk-Waggoner Ass'n* v. *Hopkins*, 269 U.S. 110 (1925); *Edwards* v. *Douglas*, 269 U.S. 204 (1925); *Iselin* v. *United States*, 270 U.S. 245 (1926); *Jaybird Mining Co.* v. *Weir*, 271 U.S. 609, 615 (1926) (dissent); *United States* v. *One Ford Coupe*, 272 U.S. 321 (1926); *Miller* v. *Milwaukee*, 272 U.S. 713, 716 (1927) (concurring); *United States* v. *Ludey*, 274 U.S. 295 (1927); *Clark* v. *Poor*, 274 U.S. 554 (1927); *Mason* v. *Routzahn*, 275 U.S. 175 (1927); *Gulf Fisheries Co.* v. *MacInerney*, 276 U.S. 124 (1928); *Untermyer* v. *Anderson*, 276 U.S. 440, 446 (1928); *Humes* v. *United States*, 276 U.S. 487 (1928);

Louisville Gas & Electric Co. v. *Coleman,* 277 U.S. 32, 42 (1928) (dissent); *Quaker City Cab Co.* v. *Pennsylvania,* 277 U.S. 389, 403 (1928) (dissent); *National Life Ins. Co.* v. *United States,* 277 U.S. 508, 522 (1928) (dissent); *Williamsport Wire Rope Co.* v. *United States,* 277 U.S. 551 (1928); *Cudahy Packing Co.* v. *Hinkle,* 278 U.S. 460, 467 (1929) (dissent); *Salomon* v. *State Tax Comm.,* 278 U.S. 484 (1929); *Pampanga Sugar Mills* v. *Trinidad,* 279 U.S. 211 (1929); *Lucas* v. *American Code Co.,* 280 U.S. 445 (1930); *Florsheim Bros. Co.* v. *United States,* 280 U.S. 453 (1930); *Lucas* v. *Structural Steel Co.,* 281 U.S. 264 (1930); *Strange* v. *United States,* 282 U.S. 270 (1931); *Aiken* v. *Burnet,* 282 U.S. 277 (1931); *Brown & Sons* v. *Burnet,* 282 U.S. 283 (1931); *Burnet* v. *Railway Equipment Co.,* 282 U.S. 295 (1931); *Phillips* v. *Commissioner of Int. Rev.,* 283 U.S. 589 (1931).

FREEDOM OF SPEECH

(Arising under Amendments I and XIV)

Schaefer v. *United States,* 251 U.S. 466, 482 (1920) (dissent); *Pierce* v. *United States,* 252 U.S. 239, 253 (1920) (dissent); *Gilbert* v. *Minnesota,* 254 U.S. 325, 334 (1920) (dissent); *Milwaukee Pub. Co.* v. *Burleson,* 255 U.S. 407, 417 (1921) (dissent); *Whitney* v. *California,* 274 U.S. 357, 372 (1927) (concurring).

BILL OF RIGHTS

(Not otherwise classified)

Pease v. *Rathbun-Jones Engineering Co.,* 243 U.S. 273 (1917); *Horning* v. *District of Columbia,* 254 U.S. 135, 139 (1920) (dissent); *United States* v. *Moreland,* 258 U.S. 433, 441 (1922) (concurring); *Ng Fung Ho* v. *White,* 259 U.S. 276 (1922); *Wan* v. *United States,* 266 U.S. 1 (1924); *McCarthy* v. *Arndstein,* 266 U.S. 34 (1924); *Sherwin* v. *United States,* 268 U.S. 369 (1925); *Hughes* v. *Gault,* 271 U.S. 142, 152 (1926) (dissent); *Albrecht* v. *United States,* 273 U.S. 1 (1927); *United States* v. *Lee,* 274 U.S. 559 (1927); *Gambino* v. *United States,* 275 U.S. 310 (1927); *Olmstead* v. *United States,* 277 U.S. 438, 471 (1928) (dissent).

IMPAIRMENT OF OBLIGATION OF CONTRACT

Kryger v. *Wilson,* 242 U.S. 171 (1916); *Sears* v. *City of Akron,* 246 U.S. 242 (1918); *Milwaukee Elec. Ry.* v. *Milwaukee,* 252 U.S. 100 (1920).

COMMERCE CLAUSE

(Including Interstate Commerce and Anti-Trust Acts)

Kane v. *New Jersey,* 242 U.S. 160 (1916); *United States* v. *Merchants Ass'n,* 242 U.S. 178 (1916); *Western Transit Co.* v. *Leslie & Co.,* 242 U.S. 448 (1917); *Philadelphia & Reading Ry.* v. *McKibbin,* 243 U.S. 264 (1917); *Pennington* v. *Fourth Natl. Bank,* 243 U.S. 269 (1917); *Swift & Co.* v. *Hocking Valley Ry.,* 243 U.S. 281 (1917); *New York Cent. R.R.* v. *Winfield,* 244 U.S. 147, 154 (1917) (dissent); *Missouri, Kans. & Tex. Ry.* v. *Ward,* 244 U. S. 383 (1917); *American Express Co.* v. *Caldwell,* 244 U.S. 617 (1917); *St. Louis S. W. Ry.* v. *United States,* 245 U.S. 136 (1917); *Hitchman Coal & Coke Co.* v. *Mitchell,* 245 U.S. 229, 263 (1917) (dissent); *Eagle Glass & Mfg. Co.* v. *Rowe,* 245 U.S. 275, 284 (1917) (dissent); *Louisville & Nashville R.R.* v. *United States,* 245 U.S. 463 (1918); *Chicago Board of Trade* v. *United States,* 246 U.S. 231 (1918); *Northern Pac. Ry.* v. *Solum,* 247 U.S. 477 (1918); *Chicago, R. I. & Pac. Ry.* v. *Maucher,* 248 U.S. 359 (1919); *Merchants Exchange* v. *Missouri,* 248 U.S. 365 (1919); *United States* v. *Brooklyn Terminal,* 249 U.S. 296 (1919); *Yazoo & Mississippi Valley R.R.* v. *Mullins,* 249 U.S. 531 (1919); *Skinner & Eddy Corp.* v. *United States,* 249 U.S. 557 (1919); *Carey* v. *South Dakota,* 250 U.S. 118 (1919); *Texas & Pac. Ry.* v. *Leatherwood,* 250 U.S. 478 (1919); *Pennsylvania R.R.* v. *Kittanning Co.,* 253 U.S. 319 (1920); *Federal Trade Comm.* v. *Gratz,* 253 U.S. 421, 429 (1920) (dissent); *Galveston, Harrisburg & San Antonio Ry.* v. *Woodbury,* 254 U.S. 357 (1920); *Duplex Co.* v. *Deering,* 254 U.S. 443, 479 (1921) (dissent); *Pere Marquette Ry.* v. *French & Co.,* 254 U.S. 538 (1921); *Missouri Pac. Ry.* v. *McGrew Coal Co.,* 256 U.S. 134 (1921); *Yazoo & M. V. R.R.* v. *Nichols & Co.,* 256 U.S. 540 (1921); *Western Union Tel. Co.* v. *Esteve Bros. & Co.,* 256 U.S. 566 (1921); *Louisiana & Pine Bluff Ry.* v. *United States,* 257 U.S. 114 (1921); *Central R.R.* v. *United States,* 257 U.S. 247 (1921); *American Column & Lumber Co.* v. *United States,* 257 U.S. 377, 413 (1921) (dissent); *Lemke* v. *Farmers Grain Co.,* 258 U.S. 50, 61 (1922) (dissent); *Lambert Run Coal Co.* v. *Baltimore & Ohio R.R.,* 258 U.S. 377 (1922); *Federal Trade Comm.* v. *Winsted Hosiery Co.,* 258 U.S. 483 (1922); *Hill* v. *Wallace,* 259 U.S. 44, 72 (1922) (concurring); *Great Northern Ry.* v. *Merchants Elev. Co.,* 259 U.S. 285 (1922); *Keogh* v. *Chicago & N. W. Ry.,* 260 U.S. 156 (1922); *Baltimore & Ohio S. W. R.R.* v. *Seattle,* 260 U.S. 166 (1922); *New England Divisions Case,* 261 U.S. 184 (1923); *Davis* v. *Farmers' Coöperative Co.,* 262 U.S. 312 (1923); *Nashville Ry.* v. *Tennessee,* 262 U.S. 318 (1923); *Edward Hines Trustees* v. *United States,* 263 U.S. 143 (1923); *United States* v. *Illinois Cent. R.R.,* 263

U.S. 515 (1924); *Peoria & Pekin Union Ry.* v. *United States*, 263 U.S. 528 (1924); *Texas Transport Co.* v. *New Orleans*, 264 U.S. 150, 155 (1924) (dissent); *Chicago Junction Case*, 264 U.S. 258 (1924); *Davis* v. *Cornwell*, 264 U.S. 560 (1924); *Louisville & Nashville R.R.* v. *Central Iron Co.*, 265 U.S. 59 (1924); *Atchison Ry.* v. *Wells*, 265 U.S. 101 (1924); *Adams Express Co.* v. *Dardeen*, 265 U.S. 265 (1924); *United States* v. *Abilene & So. Ry.*, 265 U.S. 274 (1924); *United States* v. *American Ry. Express Co.*, 265 U.S. 425 (1924); *Davis* v. *Henderson*, 266 U.S. 92 (1924); *United States* v. *Pennsylvania R.R.*, 266 U.S. 191 (1924); *St. Louis, B. & M. Ry.* v. *Taylor*, 266 U.S. 200 (1924); *United States* v. *Village of Hubbard*, 266 U.S. 474 (1925); *Buck* v. *Kuykendall*, 267 U.S. 307 (1925); *Bush Co.* v. *Maloy*, 267 U.S. 317 (1925); *Missouri Pac. R.R.* v. *Reynolds-Davis Grocery Co.*, 268 U.S. 366 (1925); *Patterson* v. *Louisville & Nashville R.R.*, 269 U.S. 1 (1925); *Louisville & Nashville R.R.* v. *Sloss-Sheffield Co.*, 269 U.S. 217 (1925); *Chesapeake & Ohio Ry.* v. *Westinghouse Co.*, 270 U.S. 260 (1926); *Texas & Pac. Ry.* v. *Gulf, Colorado & Santa Fe Ry.*, 270 U.S. 266 (1926); *Chicago, I. & L. Ry.* v. *United States*, 270 U.S. 287 (1926); *Missouri Pac. R.R.* v. *Boone*, 270 U.S. 466 (1926); *Minneapolis & St. Louis R.R.* v. *Peoria & Pekin Union Ry.*, 270 U.S. 580 (1926); *Colorado* v. *United States*, 271 U.S. 153 (1926); *Alabama & Vicksburg Ry.* v. *Jackson & Eastern Ry.*, 271 U.S. 244 (1926); *Chicago & N. W. Ry.* v. *Durham Co.*, 271 U.S. 251 (1926); *Turner, Dennis & Lowry Lumber Co.* v. *Chicago, Milwaukee & St. Paul Ry.*, 271 U.S. 259 (1926); *Western Chemical Co.* v. *United States*, 271 U.S. 268 (1926); *Federal Trade Comm.* v. *Western Meat Co.*, 272 U.S. 554, 563 (1926) (dissent); *Napier* v. *Atlantic Coast Line R.R.*, 272 U.S. 605 (1926); *Virginian Ry.* v. *United States*, 272 U.S. 658 (1926); *Di Santo* v. *Pennsylvania*, 273 U.S. 34, 37 (1927) (dissent); *Public Util. Comm.* v. *Attleboro Steam & Elec. Co.*, 273 U.S. 83, 91 (1927) (dissent); *United States* v. *Los Angeles & Salt Lake R.R.*, 273 U.S. 299 (1927); *Bedford Cut Stone Co.* v. *Stone Cutters Ass'n*, 274 U.S. 37, 56 (1927) (dissent); *Maul* v. *United States*, 274 U.S. 501, 512 (1927) (concurring); *Assigned Car Cases*, 274 U.S. 564 (1927); *Lawrence* v. *St. Louis-San Francisco Ry.*, 274 U.S. 588 (1927); *Arkansas R.R. Comm.* v. *Chicago, R. I. & Pac. R.R.*, 274 U.S. 597 (1927); *Hammond* v. *Schappi Bus Line*, 275 U.S. 164 (1927); *Hammond* v. *Farina Bus Line*, 275 U.S. 173 (1927); *Cleveland, Cincinnati, Chicago & St. Louis Ry.* v. *United States*, 275 U.S. 404 (1928); *Swift & Co.* v. *United States*, 276 U.S. 311 (1928); *Texas & New Orleans R.R.* v. *Northside Belt Ry.*, 276 U.S. 475 (1928); *Midland Valley R.R.* v. *Barkley*, 276 U.S. 482 (1928); *Sprout* v. *South Bend*, 277 U.S.

163 (1928); *Lawrence v. St. Louis-San Francisco Ry.*, 278 U.S. 228 (1929); *St. Louis & O'Fallon Ry. v. United States*, 279 U.S. 461, 488 (1929) (dissent); *St. Louis-San Francisco Ry. v. Pub. Serv. Comm'n*, 279 U.S. 560 (1929); *Atchison, Topeka & Santa Fe Ry. v. United States*, 279 U.S. 768 (1929); *Federal Trade Comm. v. Klesner*, 280 U.S. 19 (1929); *United States v. Erie R.R.*, 280 U.S. 98 (1929); *Tagg Bros. & Moorhead v. United States*, 280 U.S. 420 (1930); *Piedmont & No. Ry. v. United States*, 280 U.S. 469 (1930); *United States v. Guaranty Trust Co.*, 280 U.S. 478 (1930); *Sprunt & Son, Inc. v. United States*, 281 U.S. 249 (1930); *Pittsburgh & W. Va. Ry. v. United States*, 281 U.S. 479 (1930); *United States v. Atlanta, B. & C. R.R.*, 282 U.S. 522 (1931); *Standard Oil Co. v. United States*, 283 U.S. 163 (1931); *Interstate Transit, Inc. v. Lindsey*, 283 U.S. 183 (1931); *Georgia Comm. v. United States*, 283 U.S. 765 (1931); *Alabama v. United States*, 283 U.S. 776 (1931).

NATIONAL VERSUS STATE POWERS

(*Not otherwise classified*)

Burton v. New York Cent. & Hudson River R.R., 245 U.S. 315 (1917); *Barbour v. Georgia*, 249 U.S. 454 (1919); *Vigliotti v. Pennsylvania*, 258 U.S. 403 (1922); *Farmers & Merchants Bank v. Federal Reserve Bank*, 262 U.S. 649 (1923); *Red Cross Line v. Atlantic Fruit Co.*, 264 U.S. 109 (1924); *Lambert v. Yellowley*, 272 U.S. 581 (1926).

SUITS BY AND BETWEEN STATES

Iowa v. Slimmer, 248 U.S. 115 (1918); *Pennsylvania v. West Virginia*, 262 U.S. 553, 605 (1923) (dissent); s.c., 263 U.S. 350, 351 (1923) (dissent); *Arizona v. California*, 283 U.S. 423 (1931).

CLAIMS BY AND AGAINST GOVERNMENT

Duncan Townsite Co. v. Lane, 245 U.S. 308 (1917); *Egan v. McDonald*, 246 U.S. 227 (1918); *Brogan v. National Surety Co.*, 246 U.S. 257 (1918); *United States v. Soldana*, 246 U.S. 530 (1918); *Tempel v. United States*, 248 U.S. 121 (1918); *Turner v. United States*, 248 U.S. 354 (1919); *Gilcrease v. McCullough*, 249 U.S. 178 (1919); *United States v. Babcock*, 250 U.S. 328 (1919); *United States v. North American Transportation & Trading Co.*, 253 U.S. 330 (1920); *Pierce v. United States*, 255 U.S. 398 (1921); *United States v. Pfitsch*, 256 U.S. 547 (1921); *Missouri Pac. R.R. v. Ault*, 256 U.S. 554 (1921); *Sutton v. United States*, 256 U.S. 575 (1921); *Western Union Tel. Co. v. Poston,*

256 U.S. 662 (1921); *Louisville & Nashville R.R. v. United States*, 258 U.S. 374 (1922); *United States v. Oregon Lumber Co.*, 260 U.S. 290, 302 (1922) (dissent); *Portsmouth Harbor Land & Hotel Co. v. United States*, 260 U.S. 327, 330 (1922) (dissent); *Morrison v. Work*, 266 U.S. 481 (1925).

ADMINISTRATIVE LAW

(Excluding Taxation and Commerce Clause)

United States v. Morehead, 243 U.S. 607 (1917); *Burnap v. United States*, 252 U.S. 512 (1920) (executive power); *International Ry. v. Davidson*, 257 U.S. 506 (1922); *Zucht v. King*, 260 U.S. 174 (1922); *Douglas v. Noble*, 261 U.S. 165 (1923); *Bilokumsky v. Tod*, 263 U.S. 149 (1923); *Tisi v. Tod*, 264 U.S. 131 (1924); *Chastleton Corp. v. Sinclair*, 264 U.S. 543, 549 (1924) (concurring in part); *Tutun v. United States*, 270 U.S. 568 (1926) (naturalization); *Myers v. United States*, 272 U.S. 52, 240 (1926) (dissent—power of removal); *West v. Standard Oil Co.*, 278 U.S. 200 (1929); *Campbell v. Galeno Chemical Co.*, 281 U.S. 599 (1930); *Campbell v. Long & Co., Inc.*, 281 U.S. 610 (1930).

PATENTS AND COPYRIGHTS

Boston Store of Chicago v. American Graphophone Co., 246 U.S. 8, 27 (1918) (concurring); *Union Tool Co. v. Wilson*, 259 U.S. 107 (1922); *Carbice Corp. v. American Patents Corp.*, 283 U.S. 27 (1931); *Buck v. Jewell-LaSalle Realty Co.*, 283 U.S. 191 (1931); *Jewell-LaSalle Realty Co. v. Buck*, 283 U.S. 202 (1931); *Carbice Corp. v. American Patents Development Co.*, 283 U.S. 420 (1931).

MISCELLANEOUS CASES

United States v. Ness, 245 U.S. 319 (1917) (naturalization); *United States v. Weitzel*, 246 U.S. 533 (1918) (penal legislation); *International News Serv. v. Associated Press*, 248 U.S. 215, 248 (1918) (dissent—judicial power); *Hamilton v. Kentucky Distilleries & Warehouse Co.*, 251 U.S. 146 (1919) (war powers); *Jacob Ruppert v. Caffey*, 251 U.S. 264 (1920) (same); *Grand Trunk Western Ry. v. United States*, 252 U.S. 112 (1920) (federal aid); *Collins v. Miller*, 252 U.S. 364 (1920) (extradition); *Ex parte Peterson*, 253 U.S. 300 (1920) (judicial power); *Stallings v. Splain*, 253 U.S. 339 (1920) (removal proceedings); *Marshall v. New York*, 254 U.S. 380 (1920) (sovereign prerogative); *Port of Seattle v. Oregon & Washington R.R.*, 255 U.S. 56 (1921) (navigable waters); *Burdeau v. McDowell*, 256 U.S. 465, 476 (1921) (dissent—

official misbehavior); *Fairchild* v. *Hughes,* 258 U.S. 126 (1922) (amending power of Constitution); *Leser* v. *Garnett,* 258 U.S. 130 (1922) (same); *Collins* v. *Loisel,* 259 U.S. 309 (1922) (extradition); *Collins* v. *Loisel,* 262 U.S. 426 (1923) (extradition); *Washington* v. *Dawson & Co.,* 264 U.S. 219, 228 (1924) (dissent—admiralty); *Skinner & Eddy Corp.* v. *McCarl,* 275 U.S. 1 (1927) (government-owned corporation); *Emergency Fleet Corp.* v. *Western Union Co.,* 275 U.S. 415 (1928) (government-owned corporation); *Casey* v. *United States,* 276 U.S. 413, 421 (1928) (dissent—government instigation of crime); *Willing* v. *Chicago Auditorium Ass'n,* 277 U.S. 274 (1928) (judicial power).